TISSOT
SWISS WATCHES SINCE 1853
INNOVATORS BY TRADITION

TISSOT T-RACE MOTOGP
LIMITED EDITION 2010
Become part of racing history with a robust
316L stainless steel watch. Scratch-resistant
sapphire crystal, quartz chronograph and water
resistance up to 100m/330ft.

IN TOUCH WITH YOUR TIME

OFFICIAL TIMEKEEPER

motoGP

Get in touch at www.tissot.ch

MotoGP
Season Review 2010
Julian Ryder

Published in November 2010

A catalogue record for this book is available from the British Library

ISBN 978 0 85722 000 0

Library of Congress catalog card no 2010927387

Haynes Publishing, Sparkford, Yeovil,
Somerset BA22 7JJ, UK
Tel: +44 (0) 1963 442030
Fax: +44 (0) 1963 440001
E-mail: sales@haynes.co.uk
Website: www.haynes.co.uk

Haynes North America, Inc.,
861 Lawrence Drive, Newbury Park,
California 91320, USA

Printed and bound in the UK by JF Print

Managing Editor Mark Hughes
Design Lee Parsons
Sub-editor Kay Edge
Special Sales & Advertising Manager
David Dew (david@motocom.co.uk)
Photography Front cover, race action, bike side views and portraits by Andrew Northcott/AJRN Sports Photography, except: Neil Spalding pp22-29, pp188-194

Author's acknowledgements

Thanks to:

Andrew Northcott for his wonderful images, Neil Spalding and Toby Moody for commentary box comedy, Tom Jojic, Bradley Smith, Scott Redding, Danny Webb, Marc Martin, Mike & Irene Trimby and the staff of IRTA, Martin Raines, Nick Harris, Dave Dew, and the team at Haynes Publishing

CONTENTS
MotoGP 2010

A dazzling record of pole positions, race victories and podium places delivered Jorge Lorenzo the 2010 MotoGP World Championship title in fine style. His skills and determination, combined with the state-of-the-art technology of our Yamaha M1 helped realise the goal of sealing the third

MotoGP world title in a row and the fifth in the past seven years.

Those very qualities help us deliver you the best range of motorcycles and scooters, the best back up and the best support, so that you really can enjoy your motorcycling experience. Get out there!

RIDER
99
Jorge Lorenzo
2010 MOTOGP WORLD CHAMPION
YAMAHA
FACTORY RACING

YAMALUBE

GET OUT THERE
www.yamaha-motor.co.uk

Get on
Life's better on two wheels
www.geton.co.uk

YAMAHA

FOREWORD
CARMELO EZPELETA

The 2010 season has been a landmark year for the FIM MotoGP World Championships, with the big change coming in the intermediate class and the introduction of the four-stroke Moto2 bikes. The new class has proved to be a success beyond everybody's expectations; there is a queue of teams wanting to form part of this exciting new Grand Prix World Championship and it has provided us with fantastic racing throughout the season.

In the Grand Prix Commission we have also been working hard on finalising the new regulations for the MotoGP category in 2012, which is an ongoing process, and the rules for the new four-stroke 250cc single-cylinder Moto3 category, which will replace the 125cc class at the end of next season.

These changes to the rules are necessary due to the harsh economic climate that is affecting everyone involved in the world-class sporting arena. Our sport is not alone in being forced to adapt and evolve because of this challenging situation, and changes to the regulations such as the decision to limit engine numbers in MotoGP is just one of the many measures taken to try and find a way to endure the financial crisis.

Most importantly, however, everybody in the sport is working together to improve the quality of racing and the competitiveness of all the bikes out on track, and the future rule changes should go some way to improving that situation.

At Dorna we have invested heavily this season in the television production quality, by broadcasting the entire season in crystal-clear High Definition (HD), and the introduction of innovations such as the gyroscopic effect on-board camera that brings the racing to life on viewers' screens at home.

From an event point of view, we made a successful return to Silverstone in the UK after a 24-year hiatus, and the work done on the racetrack made it a truly exciting event. Similarly, the brand new track at Aragón impressed everyone as it stepped up from being a reserve track to seal itself a place on the 2011 calendar after a memorable weekend of action.

On-track safety is of course a priority for us, but we must not forget that MotoGP is still an inherently dangerous sport and this became only too apparent after the tragic loss of Shoya Tomizawa at Misano. The MotoGP family will always remember the talented Japanese youngster with affection. He is sadly missed.

In this *Official MotoGP Season Review* we will see how Jorge Lorenzo's consistency in the face of the adversity of his rivals Pedrosa, Rossi and Stoner brought the Mallorcan his first premier-class championship in some style, whilst Toni Elías and Marc Márquez sealed the championships in Moto2 and 125cc with their stand-out performances.

I hope you enjoy reading about the thrilling battles between the MotoGP rivals at Jerez and Motegi, or the drama of the 125cc race at Estoril – these are the reasons that we continue to support, watch and admire the racers as they give their all in their quest for glory at the highest level.

CARMELO EZPELETA
DORNA SPORTS CEO
NOVEMBER 2010

STRANGE DAYS

MotoGP was enthralling in all kinds of different ways in 2010, and yet already we were looking forward to 2011 and 2012

It was a strange year for MotoGP, with the action happening in four different dimensions. On track, Jorge Lorenzo left his rivals trailing with a devastating campaign. He pretty much made sure of winning the title by finishing the first ten races either first or second. Only two other premier-class riders have managed that – Giacomo Agostini and Mick Doohan – which gives a heady perspective to the Spaniard's achievement. Some of the racing action may have been somewhat processional, but if tension was sometimes lacking on track, it was never lacking off it.

The second and third dimensions of the 2010 MotoGP season were the medical centre and the negotiating table. This was a horrible year for injuries, with half the grid suffering broken bones, keeping the Clinica Mobile busier than ever. It was a frantic year, too, for MotoGP's management types, hunkering down in the paddock's mirror-windowed VIP units to thrash out new deals for the MotoGP elite. For the first time in many decades the world's four fastest riders were all up for new contracts, so the game of musical chairs played out loudly for much of the season.

The fourth dimension was thus the future. While fans watched Lorenzo's relentless march to the title, they were already looking forward to 2011, with Casey Stoner defecting from Ducati to Honda and, in the deal of the century, Valentino Rossi switching from Yamaha to Ducati.

Lorenzo certainly deserved the crown, especially since he was one of the year's walking wounded. The Mallorcan crashed and broke his right hand just weeks before the season opener at Qatar. He kept the real cause of the injury secret for some while, and who could blame him? Lorenzo didn't get bitten by a 230 horsepower MotoGP bike, but by a teeny-weeny minimoto. He crashed while trying to outdo

Above Casey Stoner contemplates moving from Ducati to Honda

Upper right Dani Pedrosa's body took a battering in 2010; here he's carried away from one of his Silverstone crashes

Lower right Would he, wouldn't he? There was much speculation over whether Jerry Burgess and his mainly Aussie crew would follow Rossi to Ducati. They will

friend and fellow-racer Carlos Checa at a Barcelona kid's track. A racer's ego can be a dangerous thing...

Perhaps chastened by that experience, Lorenzo didn't put a wheel wrong for the rest of the year. The cocky young upstart who had been king crasher during 2008 and 2009 had matured into a cool, calculating winning machine in time for the 2010 campaign.

'At the beginning of my career in MotoGP I was fast: my first race I made pole and finished second, so I had the speed, but I didn't have control of the motorcycle at 100 per cent,' said Lorenzo, who crashed 15 times in his first two MotoGP seasons, but only twice during 2010.

'In 2008 I think I had control of the motorcycle at 60 per cent. Now I don't have 100 per cent control, but I am close. This is the difference between 2008 and 2010 – the speed is more or less the same but the control I have in all situations is bigger.

'But when you get confident you must be cautious, because if you overtake your confidence it's dangerous because you can crash. That has happened a lot in my career. Now I understand when I overtake my confidence before it happens. Experience makes you understand that you may crash in the next corner, so it's better to slow down a little, to not turn into the corner at the maximum.'

Second at Qatar, in spite of the injury, Lorenzo then won five of the next six races, often running away at the front, no-one else able to get close. In a year when so many riders were crashing heavily, he made it look easy. But of course winning in bike racing's most challenging category is never easy.

'It feels great to open a gap and win all alone, but in some ways maybe it is easier when you know a rider is just

behind you because you have less to lose than when you are leading with a big gap,' he added. 'When you have a big gap you can crash and you are an idiot; if you crash when you are fighting with other riders, it is normal. Also, when you are leading with a big gap, your confidence is high, but also you start to feel the fear of crashing. To play with that is not easy.'

Lorenzo's strength on the motorcycle is smoothness and he knows it – his front brake lever is etched with the word *mantequilla* (Spanish for butter), telling fans that his riding style is buttery smooth. It is the perfect technique for the 800s and for Bridgestone's super-stiff MotoGP slicks, which require smooth, arcing cornering lines that deliver consistent load throughout the corner. Without that load, the tyres don't grip. Lorenzo is the arch exponent of segueing the three phases of cornering – entry, mid-turn and exit – into one. No doubt, Mike Hailwood is perched on a fluffy white cloud somewhere, nodding his head in approval.

'Jorge's is a very, very 250 style, and the way the 800s are, he's not had to change his style,' said 1990s legend Wayne Rainey, who used a very different technique to win his three 500 crowns. 'The 800 and the tyres, it all looks like it was designed for him. It's so easy for him to get on the pace – everything's right there – it's all about corner speed.'

Lorenzo had so much speed during 2010 that even his team-mate couldn't keep up. Rossi may have won at Qatar but Lorenzo beat him fair and square at the next two races, causing the reigning champion to mutter: 'These guys are younger – they are more fresh.' Perhaps it was his right shoulder injury (sustained during a charity motocross event) that was to blame, or perhaps the pressure really was getting to him – Am I too old? Am I over the hill? – because at the very next race Rossi made the biggest mistake of his career. In a rare moment of carelessness he allowed his tyres to reach a critically low temperature during a chilly morning practice session. When he got back on the gas he was highsided halfway to the moon. His right leg was broken and the crown was lost.

Lorenzo pours scorn on anyone who dares suggest that the 2010 crown has a hollow ring to it because Rossi wasn't around to defend the title: 'It was his fault that he crashed. No-one put a gun to his head and told him to crash.'

The new World Champion makes no secret of the fact that he doesn't just want to beat Rossi on the racetrack, he also wants to overtake his global profile. But even as Lorenzo rode towards his coronation, Rossi continued to grab the headlines – first by breaking that leg at Mugello, then by commencing talks with the Bolognese. The Rossi/Ducati romance is a long story – it has been running since August 2003, when the possibility of the Italian dream team was first mooted.

At a time when MotoGP is several bikes short of a full grid, the marriage is manna from heaven for Dorna. It will guarantee packed grandstands and sky-high TV audience figures, no matter what else is going on in the sport. No-one knows how much Marlboro are paying Rossi. The paddock guesstimate sits at 15 million euros for two years, but whatever the deal, there's no doubt it's worth it for MotoGP as a whole.

HRC's newest recruit, Casey Stoner, will be earning much less at Repsol Honda, but the Aussie insists his deal wasn't about the money; it was factory resources that made up his mind. 'Filippo [Preziosi, Ducati's engineering genius] hasn't got the budget to work with to develop things,' said the 2007 champ. 'He has got to do the best job he can once, he hasn't got the chance to throw five different answers at a problem and see if one works. I believe that Honda is a company that can give you what you ask for.'

So will Ducati be able to give Rossi what he asks for? Company president Gabriele Del Torchio insists they will, even in these tough financial times, because the company's controllers – the super-rich Bonomi family – are raising extra cash through their private equity empire.

Once Stoner and Rossi had finalised their contract negotiations, the other two so-called 'Aliens' had little room for manoeuvre. And yet it took Pedrosa and Lorenzo months finally to announce deals with their current employers. Lorenzo held out until October, his manager Marcus Hirsch driving a hard bargain with Lin Jarvis, even though his rider effectively had nowhere else to go.

Rossi had to leave Yamaha because he had backed himself into a corner. At the end of 2009 he'd announced that the factory must choose between its two stars because the team wasn't big enough for both of them. So when 23-year-old Lorenzo started to run away with the 2010 championship while 31-year-old Rossi lay in hospital, up to his eyeballs on morphine, the direction of Yamaha's future allegiance seemed obvious.

Rossi wasn't the only one knocking back the painkillers in 2010. MotoGP's list of walking wounded grew and grew: Lorenzo, Rossi, Randy de Puniet, Mika Kallio, Loris Capirossi, Dani Pedrosa, Hiroshi Aoyama and keen young rookie Alvaro Bautista all suffered serious injuries during the year. Many of the accidents happened in similar circumstances to Rossi's: cold morning practice, cold tyres, whammo!

The real reasons behind this orgy of pain and suffering

were the single-tyre rule and the global economic crisis. These two factors combined to create a perfect storm of a tyre regulation that offered riders a choice of just two compounds. This was too few to cover a full range of track temperatures because riders had asked Bridgestone to offer them two compounds that would both do race distance. Thus both tyres were at the harder end of the spectrum, which is why they sometimes provided iffy grip in cooler conditions. Not surprisingly, riders changed their minds mid-season, requesting one soft choice (for cool conditions and for qualifying) and one hard choice (for the race). In other words, from now on, all riders will run the same race tyres.

Inevitably there were those who predicted that the first serious injury of Valentino Rossi's career would nudge the nine-times World Champion into retirement. After all, he'd got a lot of toys and he had nothing else to prove. But that's not Rossi. Then were those who suggested that several lacklustre results – sixth at Aragon, fifth at Brno and a distant fourth at Indy after three crashes – proved he had lost the will to exercise his god-like talent. Ducati must have been getting worried.

Motegi proved otherwise. Rossi unleashed a full-frontal attack on Lorenzo reminiscent of his 2008 Laguna assault on Stoner. This was the outgoing champ up against a wall and unwilling to accept defeat. Their battle wasn't for the four-point difference between second and third places, or for the satisfaction of joining the podium champagne party; this was Rossi proving that he wasn't drifting into the twilight of his career, that he was still a contender.

A win at Sepang – his first since Qatar – and another successful last-lap duel for third place at Phillip Island, this time with past and future team-mate Nicky Hayden, proved

Above How would the Mugello accident affect Valentino Rossi? Would he retire? Would he switch to four wheels? No, he came back and won. But he did need help with walking

beyond doubt that Rossi retained his killer instinct. More than that, it proved that he was still king of the last-lap assassins. Lorenzo didn't approve of Rossi's riding tactics at Motegi and neither did Stoner. The Aussie promised that if Rossi ever tried anything like that with him again 'It'll come back tenfold.'

Stoner had another weird season in 2010. His 2009 championship attempt had been derailed by lactose intolerance; this time it was the bike that was out of sorts. Ducati had supposedly revitalised the Desmosedici, giving it a rider-friendly big-bang engine designed to turn the GP10 into an everyman motorcycle. The bike was certainly more rideable for men like Hayden, but Stoner could no longer magic race-winning speed out of the thing. Only late in the year did Ducati find a set-up that allowed him to win again, but by then it was too late. Stoner had already signed to join Honda.

How will Stoner get on with the RC212V in 2011? The bike certainly got a lot better during 2010, but the improvements had been a long time coming. The RCV started the year in horrible shape – throwing frightening tank-slappers down Qatar's main straight, factory men Pedrosa and Andrea Dovizioso hanging on for grim life.

The bike was some way behind both the Yamaha and the Ducati in all aspects of performance apart from top speed, so HRC spent most of their 2010 R&D efforts on chassis and electronics. And yet Pedrosa believed it was the V4 engine that was still the root of the bike's problems. 'The 800 engines we've had are all so peaky and aggressive, with nothing at the bottom and lots of power at the top, so the power delivery isn't smooth, so the chassis is unstable,' he said. Nevertheless, by mid-season the RCV

was good enough to get Pedrosa on a roll. The tough little Spaniard won three races – more victories than he had managed during each of his previous four seasons in MotoGP – and started closing down Lorenzo's points advantage. It seemed unlikely that he would overhaul his compatriot, and yet...

MotoGP's big technical shift in 2010 was its first ever engine-rationing rule – riders had to go the whole season with only six engines. When one considers that teams had been in the habit of using anything between a dozen and 25 engines per season, it's easy to understand just how much of a challenge the new regulations were going to be.

Honda came out of it best; which is probably as it should be for a company founded by a metallurgist. Their engines were both the fastest and the longest lasting, so much so that as Pedrosa's speed increased, Lorenzo's withered. By Brno he was already using his fifth M1 engine, so the theory went that Yamaha were turning down the horsepower to help their engines last the season. Pedrosa's charge ended when his throttle stuck open during Japanese GP practice, the resulting tumble smashing his collarbone into four pieces.

Sadly, Pedrosa's nasty Motegi fall wasn't the worst accident of the season. During September, GP racing suffered its worst week in decades when 13-year-old Peter Lenz was killed in a support race at Indy and then grinning Moto2 hero Shoya Tomizawa lost his life during the Misano race. Both Lenz and Tomizawa died in similar circumstances – they crashed and were hit by following motorcycles. Advances in riding gear, track safety and machinery have dramatically improved in recent years, but in motorcycle racing there will always be other motorcycles.

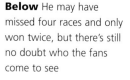

Below He may have missed four races and only won twice, but there's still no doubt who the fans come to see

The tragic deaths certainly stirred up a debate about racetrack safety, a subject Stoner had been keen to discuss earlier in the year. His theory goes that tracks are getting too safe – largely due to the introduction of tarmac run-offs (nicknamed 'get-out-of-jail-free cards') – which encourage some riders to take huge risks. In other words, excessive safety is making racing more dangerous.

'I've been saying this for ages, but no-one listens: the tarmac run-offs push people to be more on the ragged edge,' said Stoner. 'Riders have got so much confidence that they're not scared. All they see on the other side of the kerb is more tarmac, so there's no fear.' It's easy to see his point.

There were several great new names in MotoGP in 2010. Ben Spies was the stand-out rookie, impressing with his sheer speed and his remorseless ability to improve from the very first round. He was a deserving winner of the Rookie of the Year prize. Nicknamed 'The Machine', Spies has that laid-back intensity of a Rainey or a Lawson.

Marco Simoncelli and Alvaro Bautista were the other newcomers who showed serious promise. Former 250 champion Simoncelli struggled until he got comfortable on his Gresini RCV, his wild, all-attack style a welcome addition to the MotoGP grid. Once he had recovered from injury (another motocross accident) Bautista had some great rides, usually at hot races, where Suzuki's GSV-R could find the grip that it usually lacked. Simoncelli, Bautista and Spies – promoted to Yamaha's factory team – should come nicely to the boil in 2011 when there will be only two rookies: World Superbike star Cal Crutchlow and Czech Moto2 rider Karel Abraham.

With Rossi at Ducati and Stoner at Honda, there is much to look forward to in 2011, although there is also cause for concern. Suzuki are downsizing to a single-rider team, Interwetten are calling it a day after just one year in the big class and other teams are still struggling to raise the necessary finance. Maybe that will all change in 2012 when the class returns to a 1,000cc limit (in fact the original MotoGP capacity was 990cc) and tuned street-bike engines are welcomed on to the grid.

In that sense, next season will be a bit like last season – throughout the last year of the unloved 800s we will be looking forward to the return of the mighty litre bikes. But don't expect the new 1000s to provide the super-sideways entertainment that made the 990s so thrilling to watch.

'If they don't limit the electronics, the 1000s will be no different to the 800s,' explained Nicky Hayden. 'I don't want the fans to get their hopes up because it's going to be really difficult to do something about the electronics.'

Electronics continued to be a matter of debate in 2010. Many paddock people blamed the frequently processional races on high-tech rider aids, though in fact it's not as simple as that. It is a combination of extraordinarily good technologies that has created a follow-my-leader style of racing (or 'parade racing', according to Rossi's crew chief Jeremy Burgess). The tyres, chassis and electronics are so good that riders can do the same lap times from start to finish, so there's no juggling of positions as bikes enter and exit their own sweet spots.

Rossi was the most vociferous cheerleader for a return to the good old days when the rider worked the throttle, not a little black box. 'If you want more funny races and more fighting, then the organisation needs to remove traction control and wheelie control,' he said. Hopefully, the extra torque of the 1000s will at least allow a return to a variety of MotoGP riding styles. Currently there's only one fast way

around a corner because high corner speed is the only way with the lower-torque 800s. The 1000s should allow riders to choose their own styles, perhaps squaring off corners to great effect. Rossi, Stoner, Spies and Hayden all believe that the 1000s will better suit their more animated riding techniques, which may mean the machines will be worse for ultra-smooth riders like Lorenzo and Pedrosa.

In the long term it might not be the change of capacity that will be most significant to MotoGP. The introduction of street-engined machines – like the BMW S1000RR-powered Suter which was on track in late 2010 – may turn out to be a real landmark event. From 2012 onwards Dorna will no longer be totally reliant on the manufacturers to fill the grid, and that may entirely change the MotoGP landscape in the coming years.

Above Spain didn't just have the three World Champions: Toni Elias (Moto2), Jorge Lorenzo (MotoGP and Marc Marquez (125). The runners-up in each championship were Spanish too

Below Rookie of the Year Ben Spies impressed everyone with his methodical approach

RIDERS' RIDER OF THE YEAR 2010

VOTED FOR BY Kousuke Akiyoshi, Alex de Angelis, Hiroshi Aoyama, Hector Barbera, Alvaro Bautista, Loris Capirossi, Carlos Checa, Andrea Dovizioso, Colin Edwards, Aleix Espargaro, Nicky Hayden, Mika Kallio, Jorge Lorenzo, Marco Melandri, Dani Pedrosa, Randy de Puniet, Ben Spies, Valentino Rossi, Marco Simoncelli and Casey Stoner

Now in its seventh year, the Riders' Rider of the Year poll asks every rider who has ridden in more than one MotoGP race to name their six toughest rivals. The scrutineers then count up the votes and award six points for a first place down to one for sixth. Here are the results

Just like in real life, Jorge Lorenzo came out on top of our poll by a significant margin, with his fellow 'Aliens' – Dani Pedrosa, Valentino Rossi and Casey Stoner – at a very respectful distance. The votes of the riders put the second, third and fourth place men in the same order as the championship, but with very small margins between them.

Of the 19 racers eligible to vote for him, 14 of them rated Jorge as the best, three of them put him second and two of them third. The only other racers to receive a first-place nomination were Pedrosa with three, Rossi with two and Loris Capirossi with one. That vote for Loris could be regarded either as some sort of lifetime achievement award or simply taking the mickey.

While every voter put Lorenzo in his top three, Pedrosa's postions, by contrast, were spread from first to fifth, and two voters didn't mention him at all. The only men who were listed on every ballot paper were

2nd
DANI
PEDROSA
73 POINTS

3rd
VALENTINO
ROSSI
67 POINTS

4th
CASEY
STONER
64 POINTS

5th
BEN
SPIES
59 POINTS

6th
ANDREA
DOVIZIOSO
36 POINTS

7th
NICKY
HAYDEN
13 POINTS

8th
MARCO SIMONCELLI
7 POINTS

9th
LORIS CAPIROSSI
6 POINTS

10th
COLIN EDWARDS
2 POINTS

Lorenzo and Stoner. Last year the riders voted Casey third in front of Dani, a reversal of their championship positions. This year, there is clearly some serious respect for Dani's handling of a wayward motorcycle at the start of the year and his blazing form in the run-up to his injurious crash in Japan. As well as his first places, Dani was placed second by eight voters and third by one.

The major deviation from the championship order is that the riders voted Ben Spies fifth and first 'Non-Alien' at the expense of Andrea Dovizioso, who was ranked a distant sixth. Only one voter missed Ben out altogether. Third place is the lowest Valentino Rossi has ever been in this poll, and he too was ignored by one voter. Not only was Valentino pushed down the table, but he was also nominated in every position from first to sixth, another indication of what he refers to as 'the sharks scenting blood'.

There was not a single vote for Randy de Puniet despite his heroic first half of the season, nor of fellow top-ten championship man Marco Melandri. The riders preferred Loris Capirossi and Colin Edwards in their top ten. Compared to last year's top ten, we have lost Melandri and Aleix Espargaro and impressive rookies Spies and Marco Simoncelli have taken their places.

Fewer riders than ever before were named in our secret ballot, as the small number of points for our eighth, ninth and tenth place men illustrate. Aleix Espargaro and Alvaro Bautista were the only other two to get a vote.

The seventh Riders' Rider of the Year poll confirms the domination of the top four, but also says that Ben Spies will be the next to attain 'Alien' status.

RIDERS' RIDER
PREVIOUS RESULTS

	2004	2005	2006	2007	2008	2009
1	Rossi	Rossi	Capirossi	Stoner	Rossi	Rossi
2	Gibernau	Capirossi	Rossi	Rossi	Stoner	Lorenzo
3	Biaggi	Melandri	Pedrosa	Pedrosa	Lorenzo	Stoner
4	Edwards	Hayden	Hayden	Hopkins	Pedrosa	Pedrosa
5	Nakano	Edwards	Melandri	Vermeulen	Dovizioso	Edwards
6	Capirossi	Gibernau	Stoner	Hayden	Hayden	Dovizioso
7	Tamada	Nakano	Roberts	Melandri	Capirossi	Melandri
8	Hopkins	Hopkins	Hopkins	Guintoli	Hopkins	Capirossi
9	Barros	Biaggi	Checa	Capirossi	Edwards	Hayden
10	Hayden	Barros	Vermeulen	De Puniet	Vermeulen	Espargaro

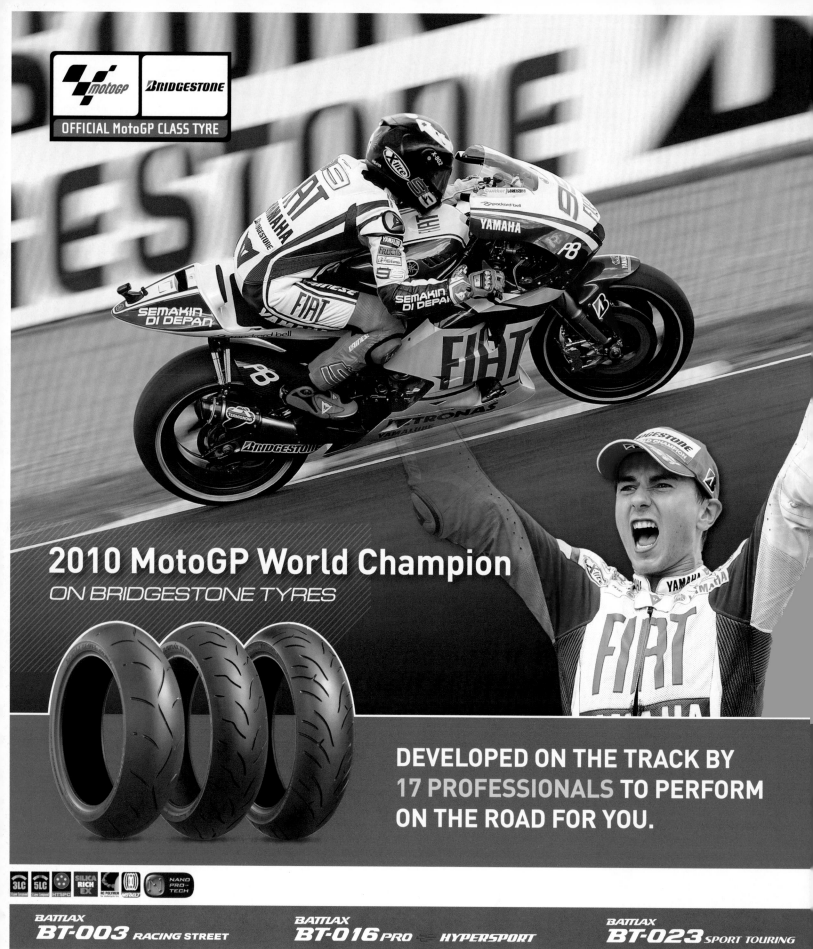

THE BIKES
2010 MotoGP MACHINERY

YAMAHA
M-1 800 2010

1 The works Fiat Yamahas were a clear evolution of the 2009 bikes. Improved oil and water cooling and revised chassis rigidity were the main changes

2 Yamaha revised the engine mounts and the section of the main frame, thinning it down for more flex, and improved grip at high lean angles

3 Lowering engine revs was one of the keys to increasing engine life to over 1,500km; Yamaha's longer secondary pipes were probably designed to work best 2,000rpm lower than in 2009

4 Spies and Edwards used 2009 frames and swingarms, but the difference on track wasn't very big

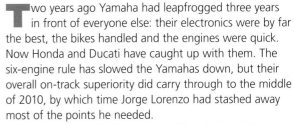

Two years ago Yamaha had leapfrogged three years in front of everyone else: their electronics were by far the best, the bikes handled and the engines were quick. Now Honda and Ducati have caught up with them. The six-engine rule has slowed the Yamahas down, but their overall on-track superiority did carry through to the middle of 2010, by which time Jorge Lorenzo had stashed away most of the points he needed.

This year's Yamaha is another mild evolution (a few frame flex upgrades and some work on the engine) of the bike brought in to respond to the first-year 800 Ducati. That M-1 took motorcycle electronic controls up to a whole new level, and the bike's ability to calculate grip levels front and rear – irrespective of lean angle – and modulate power appropriately revolutionised the game. Using a pair of gyroscopes (in the nose fairing), accelerometers and GPS, the Yamaha can tell where it is on track, what angle of lean it is at, and what attitude it is holding, and on the basis of that it can accurately deliver the correct amount of power to the rear tyre.

Yamaha's racing motors are built to enhance handling as much as they are to make power. This has meant that Yamaha riders may not have the most power available but they have always had acceleration out of slow corners and agile bikes. The addition of this throttle system gave them the best possible drive out of corners, their cross-plane reverse-rotating crank was already giving the best possible mechanical grip, and their understanding of chassis design was making sure that they had edge grip. Now they had the ability to use maximum power as early as possible. Honda, in particular, have started to get their own system working, aided by the same engineers who built Yamaha's system.

The arrival of the six-engine rule has made life difficult for Yamaha, who have always regarded the engine as virtually disposable – as many as 25 engines (a combination of rebuilds and new) were required to win Rossi's championships. The new rule required Yamaha to reduce peak power, maximise their mid-range acceleration (and therefore discourage high-rpm abuse) and change their combustion chamber design, ignition advance and fuel settings to reduce piston temperatures. Yamaha will not be drawn on the precise internal engine modifications needed, but clearly a wholesale upgrade of materials, plating and coating technologies has taken place.

HONDA
RC212V 2010

1 Honda's high-risk strategy led to fraught faces at the start of the year; by mid-season things were much better

2 It took many different designs but by Sachsenring Dovizioso had the 'final' version of the swingarm on both of his bikes

3 As the works bikes got new parts the old ones were passed down, Aoyama finally getting ex-Repsol carbon reinforced frames and swingarms on his return from injury

4 Pedrosa steadfastly followed a different frame concept to the other Honda riders, reintroducing the cross-member that holds the top of the shock absorber

Honda have been on the back foot ever since Rossi left, and that's now a long time. The 800cc MotoGP formula has been a barren period for them, with no championships and, until the middle of this year, very few wins, but then things began to change. Two years ago Honda shut down their F1 operation. The man who ran that was Shuhei Nakamoto, the same guy who had previously organised Colin Edwards' successful World Superbike assault. Since Nakamoto's arrival in MotoGP he's changed the make-up and organisation of the Honda team and started hiring, with two of Yamaha's electronics engineers and Ducati's team manager, Livio Suppo, accepting the challenge.

As the team structure changed, so did the bike. This year's RC212V has taken on most of the chassis design aspects that Yamaha have made their own, including the through-rod Ohlins forks. Honda have been working to understand them, but it hasn't been easy. Their V4 engine is a masterpiece of power and reliability, but it isn't built to enhance the handling, like the Yamaha engine. This year's frame was nearly 5kg lighter, open-backed like the Yamaha, with no top rear cross-strut, and it wobbled and weaved from the start. Honda brought five new frames to Qatar, but Pedrosa chose the one with the cross-strut back in place. Honda's strategy was to increase the frame and swinging arm's rigidity incrementally, first with a new aluminium piece, then with at least two stages of added carbon. The target was to finally pin down how much 'frame flex' was needed to obtain the best grip at the very high angles of lean the Bridgestones allow.

Pedrosa managed a few good results in the first part of the year, thanks to his riding skill, and by mid-season Honda had a bike he could cope with. To their frustration he would still criticise it, but Ohlins managed to make their suspension work for him. Honda, though, still wanted him to use the 'open rear frame' concept as raced by all their other riders. They brought a new one for Dani to try in Brno, but he didn't want to use it.

In a series where only six engines are allowed for 18 races, reliability and power are essential, and in this Honda have been clear winners. They are alone on the grid in not having been forced to reduce their maximum rpm limits this year, and that has shown on the straights. Honda's new 'Torducter' (a torque sensor mounted on to the output shaft) controlled throttle system has finally given Pedrosa some of the throttle accuracy he has always craved, an impressive feat considering just how fast Honda was getting this motorcycle to go on a very lean mixture.

DUCATI
DESMOSEDICI D16-10

1 When the 'longer life' engine changes began, Ducati introduced a new CNC-machined sidecover. Besides looking extremely cool, it also allows access to the crank end seal, an item that has to be changed regularly for reliability

2 Ducati's new winglets were about improving cooling as much as reducing lift

3 Ducati fitted grilles to the exhaust to keep rocks out of the engine in crashes

4 Stoner's handling renaissance started with a pair of tungsten rods

The second year of Ducati's carbon-framed Desmosedici started as one of great hope. New parts tested pre-season seemed to work: a new irregular-firing-order engine smoothed the power delivery and improved grip exiting corners, along with new 48mm 'through-rod' forks and a more flexible swinging arm. More grip and more drive plus a happy and relaxed Casey Stoner on a roll: what could go wrong?

Front grip was what went wrong. Stoner lost the front while leading in Qatar, then went down again at Le Mans. By Mugello the old 42mm forks were back in the search for the small additional amount of grip that can come from slight deflections of the forks at full lean, where the conventional suspension is no longer effective. They made something of a difference, but not enough. At Brno new 48mm 2011 Ohlins forks were tried, a mix of the through-rod and Stoner's preferred TTX designs. They were prototypes, but Casey raced them at Indy – and he went down again. By Misano flexy top triple clamps were on the agenda, and weight distribution experiments were under way. Two tungsten bars were attached to the radiator sides, just to see what changed. By Aragon the new weight distribution was in place, with the engine back 20mm, courtesy of a revised headstock position and a shorter swingarm – and the rest is history.

During the year new fairings were also tried, featuring small winglets that helped control lift and also improved cooling through the small radiator sections each side of the front cylinder head. Nicky Hayden initially used an old fairing that had better high-speed aerodynamics, but he relented when Ducati made him a special taller version.

SUZUKI
GSV-R XRG-2

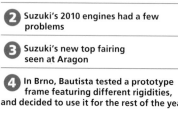

1 Suzuki tried out new swingarms – look at the welds

2 Suzuki's 2010 engines had a few problems

3 Suzuki's new top fairing seen at Aragon

4 In Brno, Bautista tested a prototype frame featuring different rigidities, and decided to use it for the rest of the year

Suzuki haven't had a lot of luck recently and, since the introduction of the control tyres, they have struggled to get their bike to work well in long corners. It became apparent that the modifications being made to get the centre of gravity correct, raising the front of the engine and therefore shortening the front engine mounts, were causing an increase in the rigidity of the main frame and that was causing front-end grip problems. Modifications made a difference, including a deliberate weakening of the headstock and the beams behind the steering head, but it wasn't until July that really new frames arrived. Loris Capirossi got the first one, now with main beams CNC-machined out of solid. The actual construction looked similar, but replacing the pressings with machined beams allowed Suzuki to vary the wall thicknesses and the way in which they flexed at full lean.

Alvaro Bautista tested a further development of the main frame after Brno, with a main beam of completely different section and a changed design for the swinging arm supports, and he immediately asked to use it for the rest of the year.

Suzuki continued to lag behind in the electronics battle. Their choice of Mitsubishi electronics might seem unusual, but it provided them with a direct development path for their road bikes. Their engines aren't short of power and seem to be quite economical, but they're plagued by inconsistent quality control from one or more of their aftermarket suppliers. Problems with lubrication led to the withdrawal of two engines from each of their rider allocations. At its meeting in Brno the MSMA, the manufacturers' body, decided to allow 'manufacturers that had not won a MotoGP race in the dry in the last two years' to be allowed an additional three engines for the 2010 season.

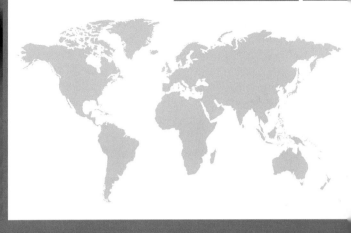

THE SEASON IN FOCUS

Every MotoGP rider's season analysed, from the World Champion to the wild-card entry whose race lasted less than a lap

1	Jorge Lorenzo	383
2	Dani Pedrosa	245
3	Valentino Rossi	233
4	Casey Stoner	225
5	Andrea Dovizioso	206
6	Ben Spies	176
7	Nicky Hayden	163
8	Marco Simoncelli	125
9	Randy de Puniet	116
10	Marco Melandri	103
11	Colin Edwards	103
12	Hector Barbera	90
13	Alvaro Bautista	85
14	Aleix Espargaro	65
15	Hiroshi Aoyama	53
16	Loris Capirossi	44
17	Mika Kallio	43
18	Alex de Angelis	11
19	Roger Lee Hayden	5
20	Kousuke Akiyoshi	4
21	Carlos Checa	1
22	Wataru Yoshikawa	1

1 JORGE LORENZO
FIAT YAMAHA TEAM

NATIONALITY Spanish
DATE OF BIRTH 4 May 1987
2010 SEASON 9 wins, 16 rostrums,
7 pole positions, 4 fastest laps
TOTAL POINTS 383

If ever you wanted proof that consistency wins titles, here it is. Jorge started on the front row for every race except Japan and only finished off the rostrum twice. His first non-rostrum finish was at the 13th race of the year. He simply didn't make mistakes and his pace forced the rest into mistakes, a fact acknowledged by all of his close rivals.

In 2009 he showed that he was quite capable of withstanding Valentino Rossi's mind games and in 2010 Rossi only got to him once – in Japan. And even then Jorge could claim to be thinking of the championship rather than the race.

It's easy to forget that Jorge started the year with the legacy of a nasty hand injury. At Qatar he couldn't shake hands yet managed a late charge to second place. His home win next time out, his first victory at Jerez, put him to the top of the table and he was never deposed. Every time it looked as if the pressure was getting to him – on the grid at Brno, after the race in Motegi – Jorge swiftly regained control. His best race, he thought, was the demolition job at Silverstone, but only from a technical aspect. The last-lap fairing-bashing showdown for that win at Jerez was the most satisfying emotionally – at least until Valencia.

There was also a growing maturity about his public pronouncements. Lorenzo grew up in the paddock, in public, and has changed from – frankly – a bit of a brat into a very impressive champion who copes effortlessly with the responsibility of speaking for the sport.

2 DANI PEDROSA
REPSOL HONDA TEAM

NATIONALITY Spanish
DATE OF BIRTH 29 September 1985
2010 SEASON 4 wins, 9 rostrums,
4 pole positions, 8 fastest laps
TOTAL POINTS 245

For once Dani started the year fully fit; unfortunately he didn't end it that way. His handicap in the first few races was a Honda that was unstable going into corners and even managed to shake its head on straights.

Once a massive effort from HRC had given him a bike he could use, Dani was as fast as anyone and usually faster. He is, as ever, the best starter on the gird but he was also willing to take risks in the early stages of a race; his round-the-outside move at Laguna's fearsome first corner was a candidate for the bravest pass of the year. Anyone who still clung to the notion that Dani could only win by disappearing off from the start had that idea firmly dispelled this year.

But just when Dani looked to be capable of putting late pressure on Lorenzo's title aspirations, he was the victim of a sticking throttle. After a run of four races in which he didn't finish lower than second, Dani smashed his left collarbone and missed three GPs. Worse, there appeared to be some nerve and vascular damage that led to numbness in the arm and hand after just a few laps. Surgery may prove to be necessary.

From Assen right through to that crash in Japan, Pedrosa looked to be a genuine threat to Lorenzo. However, he too was a victim of the Yamaha man's remorseless pressure. Dani fell while leading the US GP and being closed down by Jorge. However, though far from fit he managed to hang on to second place in the championship. If he stays fit and if Honda keep working as they did at the end of 2010, Dani will be a serious contender in 2011.

IVECO AND FIAT YAMAHA TEAM.
FIRST TO LEAVE, FIRST TO ARRIVE.

IVECO. OFFICIAL SPONSOR OF THE WORLD CHAMPION FIAT YAMAHA TEAM
AND TRUCKS & COMMERCIAL VEHICLES SUPPLIER OF THE MotoGP.

Our partners' victories make us proud. And even more proud to know that without
the timely, efficient and accurate work of the 19 STRALIS and of the 5 ECODAILY which
have accompanied the Fiat Yamaha Team and the entire "circus" of the MotoGP worldwide,
the show wouldn't even have started. To be world champion is a double satisfaction for us
today. A special thank you to Jorge, the new champion, to Valentino, to the Fiat Yamaha Team
and to Dorna Sports for this unforgettable season together.

IVECO
TRANSPORT IS ENERGY

www.iveco.com

3 VALENTINO ROSSI
FIAT YAMAHA TEAM

NATIONALITY Italian
DATE OF BIRTH 16 February 1979
2010 SEASON 2 wins, 10 rostrums,
1 pole position, 2 fastest laps
TOTAL POINTS 233

There were a lot of firsts for Valentino this season. He had a team-mate who was as fast as him and also immune to pressure, and he suffered the first really serious injury of his career.

It is tempting to assume that the accident that broke his leg at Mugello was the pivotal moment in his year, but with hindsight it was the seemingly trivial tweaked shoulder he suffered in a motocross spill before Jerez that really made life difficult. Crucially, it also cracked the aura of invincibility that has built up around the Doctor; he was no longer insensitive to attacks from what he referred to as 'the young sharks'.

It all started so well with the unexpected victory in Qatar but the other Fiat Yamaha rider soon took command. When they came to Mugello, Vale had been beaten by Jorge twice and was 11 points down in the championship. And, in another first, he was the one under pressure.

His return from injury was rapid and spectacular, and accompanied by a resumption of the mind games. Stoner was the target after Sachsenring, Lorenzo after Motegi – and there couldn't have been a more theatrical gesture than throwing his crutches to the crowd below the podium at Laguna. However, he only won one more race, a stormer at Sepang that reminded everyone just what we'd been missing, but he did end the season with a run of five rostrums.

Now Valentino moves on to the challenge of Ducati intent on once again rewriting the record books.

4 CASEY STONER
DUCATI TEAM

NATIONALITY Australian
DATE OF BIRTH 16 October 1985
2010 SEASON 3 wins, 9 rostrums,
4 pole positions, 3 fastest laps
TOTAL POINTS 225

What to make of Casey's last season with Ducati? It started with an unforced error, progressed through complete confusion from which the old, unbeatable Casey suddenly emerged, only to lapse back into old habits and crash out of two of the last four races.

Right up until Aragon, Casey had a serious problem with front-end feel. The team couldn't tell whether the front needed more weight on it or less, and when the Desmosedici did push there was no way Casey could persuade it back up on to its wheels. Then the team tried reverting to the 2009-spec forks and Casey put together a run of rostrum finishes, but he still said that the front would betray him if he pressed hard. Then at Aragon the team found a solution.

Casey had realised that his wrist, repaired the previous winter, wasn't letting him get where he wanted to be on the bike in corners. Ducati moved him forward, pushed the engine back to compensate, and had to run a shorter swinging arm. Casey promptly won the next two races and blew the new world champion into the weeds at home in Phillip island.

In typical Casey fashion, the resurgence came just after he was at his most pessimistic and the whispers about him losing his motivation had started. When all was well, Casey was undoubtedly the fastest man out there; when it wasn't, he crashed or finished a disgruntled third or lower.

In 2011 the fastest guy on the gird gets on the fastest bike; Casey on a Honda will be something to watch.

5 ANDREA DOVIZIOSO
REPSOL HONDA TEAM

While his team-mate was complaining about the Honda's handling early in the season, Andrea was more worried about the power delivery. No amount of electronic control, he said, could regulate the way the RC212V made power. Nevertheless, he started the year with four rostrums in the first five races and after Silverstone he lay second in the table.

However, his next rostrum finish came nine races later in Japan, but at least he qualified on the front row for the first time ever at Laguna and got his first pole at Motegi.

Qualifying has never really been one of Andrea's strong points, but he often made up for lowly grid positions with starts nearly as good as his team-mate's. Comparisons between the performance of the two Repsol Hondas is difficult as the riders set up their bikes at almost opposite ends of the spectrum, Dovi going for a 'long' bike with his weight well back.

Andrea was also distracted by arguments over his future. He hit with ease the performance requirement in his contract that guaranteed him a factory bike for 2011, but by this stage HRC had already signed Stoner. Unless they were going to sack Pedrosa (very unlikely) that meant either a three-bike team or Andrea riding for Team Gresini in 2011. In the end, circumstances forced Honda into a three-bike line-up for the Repsol team in 2011 with Andrea alongside Dani and Casey – not a comfortable prospect for the man who this year was only beaten by the four 'Aliens'.

NATIONALITY Italian
DATE OF BIRTH 23 March 1986
2010 SEASON 7 rostrums, 1 pole position, 1 fastest lap
TOTAL POINTS 206

6 BEN SPIES
MONSTER YAMAHA TECH 3

The Texan continued where he broke off last season, with some astounding performances in his first year as a full-time MotoGP rider. The Rookie of the Year title was his with races to spare, as was the distinction of being top satellite team rider.

Ben continued with his now familiar but frighteningly methodical approach: once he made progress he never took a step back. First it was coping with cold tyres at the start of a race, then it was getting the best out of the bike in qualifying – he qualified on the front row for the first time at Brno and took pole next time out at Indianapolis.

When he did have a problem, he was still able to recover and his ability to ride past people when tyres were sliding late in the race was phenomenal. His first rostrum finish came with a last-lap pass on Nicky Hayden at Silverstone. In Japan he ran off the track on the second lap and rejoined last, yet he still managed to finish eighth. In Valencia he rode past all three factory Hondas in the final laps. And all this despite injuring his left ankle in France and aggravating it at Silverstone.

The only blots on his copybook were a rather mysterious retirement at Jerez and falling off on the sighting lap in Portugal – where he banged the ankle again and couldn't make the start. Apart from those two incidents, it was implacable progress all the way.

Ben Spies looks the man most likely to join the four 'Aliens' and in 2011 he will take Rossi's place in the Yamaha factory team.

NATIONALITY American
DATE OF BIRTH 11 July 1984
2010 SEASON 2 rostrums, 1 pole position
TOTAL POINTS 176

7 NICKY HAYDEN
DUCATI TEAM

NATIONALITY
American

DATE OF BIRTH
30 July 1981

2010 SEASON
1 rostrum

TOTAL POINTS
163

So near and yet so far. Nicky finished fourth five times, missing out on the rostrum by tiny margins four times in the first five races. Apart from Japan, where he ran off track, his lowest finish was eighth place. At Indianapolis he qualifed on the front row for the first time as a Ducati rider, repeating the feat in Malaysia and Portugal. In an uncomfortable echo of his race results, each time he looked to have secured pole it was snatched from him in the final moments of qualifying. In 2011 he will have Valentino Rossi as a team-mate but what he really wants is more power. He'll get that in 2012 when the 1,000cc bikes return.

8 MARCO SIMONCELLI
SAN CARLO HONDA GRESINI

NATIONALITY
Italian

DATE OF BIRTH
20 January 1987

TOTAL POINTS
125

If you want to know how difficult life is for a rookie, take a close look at Marco's season. After two big crashes in the limited pre-season testing, his 'daily crash' at the races meant he only just got in the top ten in the first half of the year. A new electronics package arrived at Laguna and he had to start learning all over again – 'from 90 per cent understanding to 40 per cent'. His style also tended to wear his rear tyre very quickly. In the final few races of the year it all came together. Marco ran with the leaders in Malaysia and only just missed out on third place in Portugal. He'll be dangerous in 2011; as Rossi has noted, 'He's *** aggressive and he's *** big.'

9 RANDY DE PUNIET
LCR HONDA MotoGP

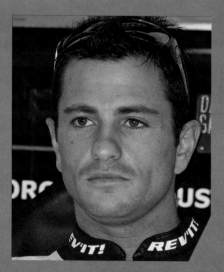

NATIONALITY
French

DATE OF BIRTH
14 February 1981

TOTAL POINTS
116

Before the crash in Germany that broke his leg, Randy looked like an odds-on favourite to be top satellite rider of the year. Not only did he qualify on the front row three consecutive times, he scared the living daylights out of the factory riders in both qualifying and the race. Even if his opponents didn't always appreciate his riding style, the fans loved it. Fourth at Catalunya was his best result and a rostrum looked on the cards before very long. Then he crashed at the Sachsenring and broke his leg. He came back amazingly quickly at Brno but never regained his form.

10 MARCO MELANDRI
SAN CARLO HONDA GRESINI

NATIONALITY
Italian

DATE OF BIRTH
7 August 1982

TOTAL POINTS
103

After the purgatory of his year at Ducati and struggling against the odds with the Hayate Kawasaki last season, Marco's third stint with Fausto Gresini's team should have been his redemption. Unfortunately, history repeated itself and Marco just couldn't get the Honda to do what he wanted. By the end of the season it was painful to watch and to hear Marco, always a demon on the brakes, say he hadn't been able to outbrake anyone all year. He said he had received no help; the team said it had done everything it could. He will be in World Superbike in 2011 on a factory Yamaha.

11 COLIN EDWARDS
MONSTER YAMAHA TECH 3

NATIONALITY
American

DATE OF BIRTH
27 February 1974

TOTAL POINTS
103

From being by far the best of the rest after the four 'Aliens' in 2009, Colin had a perplexing year with his fifth place in Motegi standing out as his best result. Fifth was also his best qualifying performance, although he managed that three times. There were signs of the old Edwards later in the season, but finishing precisely half the races in the top ten is not the sort of form expected of him. However, the Tech 3 team and Yamaha were keen to retain his services for 2011, although the man himself has intimated that it will be his last year before he retires to spend more time with his golf clubs.

12 HECTOR BARBERA
PAGINAS AMARILLAS ASPAR

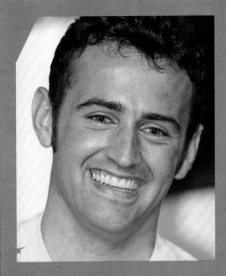

NATIONALITY
Spanish

DATE OF BIRTH
2 November 1986

TOTAL POINTS
90

For a rider with a reputation as a bit of a wild man, Hector had a very measured rookie season. He only failed to finish one race, and that was when his chain jumped the sprocket at Laguna Seca. Otherwise he always finished in the points, including eight top-ten results. Hector usually found himself involved in the midfield fight with his fellow rookies – the other two satellite Ducati riders, Edwards and, sometimes, de Puniet. He didn't back down. His biggest problem was finding a set-up that generated confidence, the usual rookie issue. He got completely lost during the 'flyaway' races but back in Europe he recovered and the last race of the year was his best.

13 ALVARO BAUTISTA
RIZLA SUZUKI MotoGP

NATIONALITY
Spanish

DATE OF BIRTH
21 November 1984

TOTAL POINTS
85

Of all the rookies, Alvaro had the most difficult job. The Suzuki just doesn't like cold tracks and getting heat in the tyres is difficult at the best of times. Add in a broken collarbone thanks to a motocross accident before Le Mans and broken ribs from a crash in France, and it's no surprise he didn't show well early on. When he was almost fit (and the track was hot) he finished fifth in Catalunya. When he was really fit (and stopped crashing while chasing Simoncelli) he put together a run of five top-ten finishes, and his ninth place in Valencia from last on the grid was brilliant.

14 ALEIX ESPARGARO
PRAMAC RACING TEAM

NATIONALITY
Spanish

DATE OF BIRTH
30 July 1989

TOTAL POINTS
65

His first full season in MotoGP was a reward for promising rides as a replacement rider in 2009. However, Aleix Espargaro didn't have an easy time and crashed a lot; five crashes in 18 races is too many. A best finish of eighth and a best qualifying position of ninth (both achieved twice) meant he wasn't retained by the Pramac Ducati team, who will instead go for experience in 2011. However, Aleix is young and the experience will stand him in good stead when he moves to a good ride in Moto2 (with Sito Pons' team) where we will be able to see him race his younger brother Pol for the first time.

15 HIROSHI AOYAMA
INTERWETTEN HONDA MotoGP

NATIONALITY
Japanese

DATE OF BIRTH
25 October 1981

TOTAL POINTS
53

Hiro was desperately unlucky to have the middle taken out of his season by a cold-tyre crash in warm-up for the Silverstone race. It broke a vertebra in his back and put him out for six races and on his back for a month. Missing the first six or last six races of the season would have been preferable and would have given him a decent run at learning a MotoGP bike. Not surprisingly, Hiro didn't have too much confidence on cold tyres when he came back, although a seventh place in the heat of Malaysia cheered him up. The Interwetten team will not run a MotoGP bike in 2011 so Hiroshi will move to the Gresini team.

16 LORIS CAPIROSSI
RIZLA SUZUKI MotoGP

NATIONALITY
Italian

DATE OF BIRTH
4 April 1973

TOTAL POINTS
44

This was undoubtedly the most disappointing season of Loris's career. The Suzuki has always had its problems, chief among whch is getting heat in the tyres. Loris crashed three times in the first five races and twice more in mid-season. The incident at Misano with Hayden required an operation on his little finger and when he came back a practice crash damaged his ankle. That was followed by a practice crash in Australia that tore a thigh muscle. When things did go right, as in Catalunya, he found he was on the wrong tyre and was beaten by his rookie team-mate. Loris's season is summed up by the fact that he only finished two races after the summer break.

17 MIKA KALLIO
PRAMAC RACING TEAM

NATIONALITY
Finnish

DATE OF BIRTH
8 November 1982

TOTAL POINTS
43

The 2009 Rookie of the Year had an awful season. He was one of a trio of cold-tyre fallers in Saturday morning free practice at Le Mans and he received the same sort of lingering shoulder injury that afflicted Rossi's season. Add in some serious personal problems off-track and an early-season injury and you have the recipe for a horrible year. Mika came nowhere near his form of 2009 and decided not to compete in the last two races of the year. The team handed the bike to Carlos Checa and for 2011 will employ the experienced Capirossi and de Puniet while Mika moves to Moto2 with the Marc VDS team.

18 ALEX DE ANGELIS
INTERWETTEN HONDA MotoGP

NATIONALITY
San Marinese

DATE OF BIRTH
26 February 1984

TOTAL POINTS
11

REPLACEMENT RIDER

When Hiro Aoyama was injured at Silverstone the Interwetten Honda team first put Honda test rider Akiyoshi on the bike while they looked for a long-term replacement. Alex de Angelis, who was available as he had just seen his Moto2 team run out of money, took over for Germany, the USA and the Czech Republic, improving on his qualifying position by five, four and two places respectively in the races. When Aoyama returned, Alex found a berth with the JIR Moto2 team, who had fallen out with Mattia Pasini. He won in Australia and will stay with the team in 2011.

19 ROGER LEE HAYDEN
LCR HONDA MotoGP

REPLACEMENT RIDER

NATIONALITY
American

DATE OF BIRTH
30 May 1983

TOTAL POINTS
5

The youngest Hayden brother has become the go-to guy for replacement rides at Laguna Seca. Three years ago he impressed by finishing tenth as a wild card on a Kawasaki, and this time he got to ride Randy de Puniet's LCR Honda. He also rode in Moto2 this year, at Indianapolis as a wild card on a Moriwaki entered by Honda USA and managed by Kevin Schwantz. At Laguna, Roger did a solid job finishing 11th after qualifying on the back of the grid. Indianapolis wasn't so much fun: he was at the bottom of the pile of riders on the outside of turn two on the first lap.

20 KOUSUKE AKIYOSHI
INTERWETTEN HONDA MotoGP

REPLACEMENT RIDER

NATIONALITY
Japanese

DATE OF BIRTH
12 January 1975

TOTAL POINTS
4

When Hiro Aoyama crashed at Silverstone and put himself out of racing for a third of the season, HRC test rider Akiyoshi-san got the call. The 35-year-old rides in the All-Japan Superbike Championship and is a Suzuka 8 Hours regular – he won the 2008 event with Yukio Kagayama on a Suzuki. Previously, he had only ridden in four GPs with a best finish of 13th. He rode at Assen and Catalunya before the team handed the bike to Alex de Angelis for the next three races. Akiyoshi got off on the wrong foot by destroying the bike in free practice for the Dutch race but he managed to get the bike to the flag for points in both races.

21 CARLOS CHECA
PRAMAC RACING TEAM

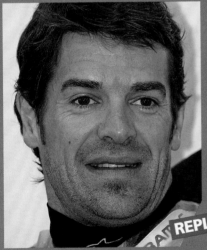

REPLACEMENT RIDER

NATIONALITY
Spanish

DATE OF BIRTH
15 October 1972

TOTAL POINTS
1

After a three-year break, the Spanish veteran and winner of two GPs returned to the GP paddock to replace Mika Kallio on the Pramac Ducati for the last two races of the year. He had ridden a few laps of Mugello on a MotoGP Ducati as a reward for his third place in the World Superbike Championship on a private Ducati, but didn't get any dry-weather practice for the race in Portugal. Not surprisingly, the riding position was all wrong and Carlos suffered severe arm pump and had to retire. In Valencia he at least got to finish the race and score a world championship point.

22 WATARU YOSHIKAWA
FIAT YAMAHA TEAM

REPLACEMENT RIDER

NATIONALITY
Japanese

DATE OF BIRTH
26 September 1968

TOTAL POINTS
1

Yamaha held out for as long as possible before replacing Valentino Rossi. His bikes didn't turn a wheel at Silverstone or Assen, but for Catalunya veteran test rider and ex-factory Superbike racer Yoshikawa was sent over from Japan. Now 41 years old, the double All-Japan Superbike Champion's task was simple. Don't wear out any of Valentino's six engines. He duly circulated at the back of the field and came home with a single point before Rossi returned in Germany. The immensely likeable Yoshikawa then went back to his day job of developing the Yamaha M1.

THE RACES
MotoGP 2010

QATARI GP
LOSAIL INTERNATIONAL CIRCUIT
ROUND 1
April 11

GREAT EXPECTATIONS

Rossi opened his title defence with a win, Stoner crashed, and Lorenzo's late charge made it a Yamaha one–two

It didn't take long for the formbook to be torn up; just over five laps in fact. Casey Stoner, the man who had never been beaten on a MotoGP 800 at the Losail track, crashed out of the race while leading by over two seconds. He lost the front going into the first corner. Immediately after the race Casey said it was a simple case of pilot error, that he'd had a couple of warnings from the front end and altered his approach to take a bit of weight off the tyre. 'I should have carried on riding the way I'd been doing all weekend.' He thought the warnings were telling him that he was overloading the front Bridgestone, but in fact he'd not been loading it enough. Data analysis later showed he was hard on the brakes when he went down, but he was adamant that the bike was 'a huge step forward from last year'.

Ducati's new big-bang motor was much easier to use, especially at the lower end of the rev range. It helped the rear tyre to perform better, and consequently made the riders' lives simpler at the end of the race. Nicky Hayden's form seemed to back up these assertions, although he was keen to emphasise that a year of working with the factory and his team meant that communication was now much improved. His combative race, especially a high-speed round-the-outside move on Dovizioso in the battle for third, as well as a noticeably tougher attitude off the track, reminded the paddock why he'd been World Champion in 2006. However, Casey's worries about the front end, and similar crashes from both satellite Ducati teams, were a taste of troubles to come.

The team with serious machinery problems looked to be Repsol Honda. Randy de Puniet on the satellite LCR bike was top Honda qualifier in fourth place, well

Above Valentino Rossi leads Hayden and Dovizioso – and Lorenzo prepares his late charge

Below Randy de Puniet gave notice that he would be a force to be reckoned with in 2010

'WE KNOW WE SHOULD HAVE WON THAT RACE'
CASEY STONER

ahead of the factory Repsol men in sixth and seventh. One TV picture from Saturday showed Pedrosa's bike weaving alarmingly at high speed down the front straight. Dovizioso, on the other side of the garage, seemed more concerned with the engine's characteristics. Despite the bewildering amount of new chassis hardware pouring though the back door of the Repsol pit garage, and Dani's lacklustre qualifying, the Spanish rider made it to the first corner in the lead, but it wasn't long before his problems made themselves felt and he started slipping backwards. However, in the early stages Pedrosa was able to tough it out with a charging Rossi, blasting back into the lead down the straight at the start of the second lap.

Whatever Honda's problems were, they were not top end. The Repsol bikes pulled away from the Yamahas and the Ducatis on the straight, and both Pedrosa and Dovizioso were able to pass Rossi in a straight line. Andrea's move five laps from the flag may have been a tactical error, for Rossi immediately retook the lead and put the hammer down. That left the Honda man in a dice with the rejuvenated Hayden, until an astonishing late charge from Jorge Lorenzo. In another premonition of one of the issues of the early races, Jorge had injured himself in a training accident on a minibike, breaking and dislocating his thumb. The repair work left him with a right hand that looked as though it had recently been assembled by Dr Frankenstein – and a disinclination to shake hands.

Lorenzo claimed not to know how hard he'd be able to race and 'was thinking about being quiet and not taking many risks'. That frame of mind didn't last long, plus he wasn't comfortable with the bike fully fuelled. When he

Above Casey Stoner looked to be charging to victory, until he crashed at the start of lap six

saw the rostrum within range, Jorge started riding 'with the heart not the head'. He went past Hayden with a lap and a half to go, and a few corners later put a tough pass on Dovizioso before hugging the right side of the track down the straight to make a repass difficult. That, plus Dovi's wheelie coming out the last turn, ensured a Fiat Yamaha one–two finish. Nicky Hayden's weekend-long problem with the final corner ensured that Dovizioso was able to turn inside him and outdrag the Ducati to the line. Ben Spies was convincingly the best of the rookies, only losing touch with Lorenzo in the last three laps, while Hiro Aoyama was the most successful of the ex-250 quartet, despite making a complete hash of the start.

Once Stoner was out, Rossi expected to have an easy race. He knew he wouldn't have been able to catch Casey, but the early scrap with Pedrosa stopped him pulling away. Then his tyre started to 'slide too much' and, despite the Yamaha being the slowest bike through the speed trap, Valentino ran out petrol three corners into the slow-down lap – a possible cause for worry about his M1 engine's efficiency compared to the opposition, notwithstanding the unexpected victory. The machine suffered from a lot of wheelspin, which would undoubtedly have hurt fuel consumption, but using a tall top gear also had an effect. Rossi's team had geared the M1 to take advantage of the slipstream of the Ducati, so after Stoner's shock early exit Vale was left with an over-geared bike. Did the wheelspin and the gearing explain the strange combination of a slow yet thirsty engine, or was this the first manifestation of the new rule that limited riders to just six engines for the season? Rossi was unsure, but he did know one thing: '25 points are like gold, especially at this track.'

Above Qatar 2010 was Loris Capirossi's 300th GP. He celebrated by ditching his usual number 65

Below Fifth place made Ben Spies top rookie and top satellite team rider on his debut as a full-time MotoGP rider

Opposite Lorenzo's late charge took him past Dovizioso and Hayden on consecutive laps

WHAT'S GOING ON AT HONDA?

Over winter, HRC had modified the RC212V significantly in an attempt to improve performance on the brakes and corner entry. This, of course, involved a slight reduction in stability as the inevitable trade-off.

The area in which this instability made itself felt seemed to overlap with the way Dani Pedrosa and Marco Melandri like to set up their bikes, although every Honda rider had a stability problem to a greater or lesser degree. Pedrosa said: 'The bike is shaking all the time, even in a straight line.' As for the engine: 'It's the engine I had for the last two years, not an engine I really like but now I can't find a feeling.' Dovizioso was less pessimistic: 'Last year our situation was too far, now we are closer our situation is much better.' He was more concerned with the engine's characteristics, only mentioning the chassis modifications as an afterthought.

Honda responded to Pedrosa's predicament with a barrage of new parts. He used three completely different chassis over the weekend, and there were two sets of serious modifications involving sheets of carbon fibre bonded to various chassis members – so, in effect, five different chassis. This was either a factory working flat-out to help its lead rider (the party line), or a sign that HRC didn't know where the problem was, let alone what to do about it (Jerry Burgess). At least Pedrosa's bike didn't try to shake him off down the straight during the race, as it had on Saturday.

And Dovizioso's bike? 'We changed nothing,' he said after the race.

QATARI GP
LOSAIL INTERNATIONAL CIRCUIT

ROUND 1
April 11

RACE RESULTS

CIRCUIT LENGTH 3.343 miles
NO. OF LAPS 22
RACE DISTANCE 73.546 miles
WEATHER Dry, 24°C
TRACK TEMPERATURE 26°C
WINNER Valentino Rossi
FASTEST LAP 1m 55.537s, 102.173mph, Casey Stoner
LAP RECORD 1m 55.153s, 104.510mph, Casey Stoner, 2008

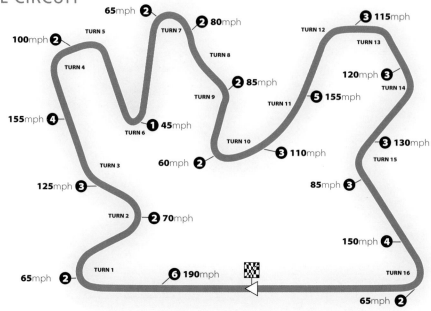

QUALIFYING

	Rider	Nationality	Team	Qualifying	Pole +	Gap
1	Stoner	AUS	Ducati Marlboro Team	1m 55.007s		
2	Rossi	ITA	Fiat Yamaha Team	1m 55.362s	0.355s	0.355s
3	Lorenzo	SPA	Fiat Yamaha Team	1m 55.520s	0.513s	0.158s
4	De Puniet	FRA	LCR Honda MotoGP	1m 55.831s	0.824s	0.311s
5	Capirossi	ITA	Rizla Suzuki MotoGP	1m 55.899s	0.892s	0.068s
6	Dovizioso	ITA	Repsol Honda Team	1m 55.963s	0.956s	0.064s
7	Pedrosa	SPA	Repsol Honda Team	1m 55.990s	0.983s	0.027s
8	Edwards	USA	Monster Yamaha Tech 3	1m 56.005s	0.998s	0.015s
9	Hayden	USA	Ducati Marlboro Team	1m 56.163s	1.156s	0.158s
10	Aoyama	JPN	Interwetten Honda MotoGP	1m 56.227s	1.220s	0.064s
11	Spies	USA	Monster Yamaha Tech 3	1m 56.271s	1.264s	0.044s
12	Kallio	FIN	Pramac Racing Team	1m 56.283s	1.276s	0.012s
13	Bautista	SPA	Rizla Suzuki MotoGP	1m 56.450s	1.443s	0.167s
14	Espargaro	SPA	Pramac Racing Team	1m 56.652s	1.645s	0.202s
15	Simoncelli	ITA	San Carlo Honda Gresini	1m 56.957s	1.950s	0.305s
16	Barbera	SPA	Paginas Amarillas Aspar	1m 57.130s	2.123s	0.173s
17	Melandri	ITA	San Carlo Honda Gresini	1m 57.325s	2.318s	0.195s

FINISHERS

1 VALENTINO ROSSI Never expected to win and his set-up was far from perfect, but took advantage of Stoner's misfortune, though significantly slower on the straight than both the Ducati and the Honda. First win at the first race of the year since 2005 and that infamous incident with Gibernau at Jerez. 'These 25 points are like gold.'

2 JORGE LORENZO Despite the recent operation on his broken right hand and a sub-standard start, Jorge charged through from sixth, passing Dovizioso and Hayden in the final laps. Later admitted that his plans for a risk-free race were abandoned early on, but was in pain for two days afterwards.

3 ANDREA DOVIZIOSO Saved a potentially disastrous weekend for the factory Honda team with a fine ride. Used the acceleration of what is still not a very user-friendly engine to blast past Hayden on the run to the flag. Much happier with the bike than at the end of last season, despite the problems.

4 NICKY HAYDEN A transformed racer thanks to Ducati's new motor and, he says, the understanding that comes from a year's work with his team. His round-the-outside passes on Dovi were the bravest moves of the race, and he was only kept off the rostrum by the Honda's straight-line speed.

5 BEN SPIES By far the best of the rookies. Might have challenged for the podium if he hadn't made mistakes on the softer tyres in qualifying. A brutal first lap put him in touch with the leaders, and he set the fourth-best lap of the race despite being slowest through the speed trap.

6 RANDY DE PUNIET Best Honda in qualifying, in fourth, but his usual average start robbed him of a chance to go with the leaders. A missed gear meant he lost touch with Spies, but more than happy to finish less than 10s behind the winner. One of his best races in MotoGP.

7 DANI PEDROSA Afflicted by stability problems so serious the bike was wobbling like a jelly down the front straight on Saturday. HRC threw three different chassis at the bike over the weekend. Still took the

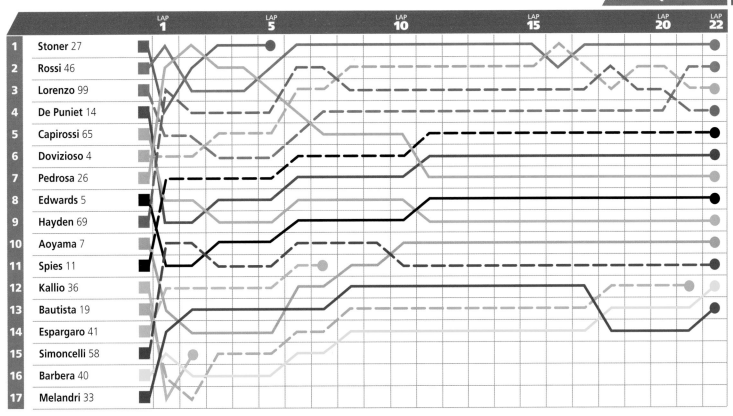

			LAP 1	LAP 5	LAP 10	LAP 15	LAP 20	LAP 22
1	Stoner 27							
2	Rossi 46							
3	Lorenzo 99							
4	De Puniet 14							
5	Capirossi 65							
6	Dovizioso 4							
7	Pedrosa 26							
8	Edwards 5							
9	Hayden 69							
10	Aoyama 7							
11	Spies 11							
12	Kallio 36							
13	Bautista 19							
14	Espargaro 41							
15	Simoncelli 58							
16	Barbera 40							
17	Melandri 33							

RACE

	Rider	Motorcycle	Race Time	Time +	Fastest Lap	Av Speed	🅱
1	Rossi	Yamaha	42m 50.099s		1m 56.043s	103.021mph	XH/H
2	Lorenzo	Yamaha	42m 51.121s	1.022s	1m 56.042s	102.980mph	XH/H
3	Dovizioso	Honda	42m 51.964s	1.865s	1m 56.157s	102.946mph	XH/H
4	Hayden	Ducati	42m 51.975s	1.876s	1m 56.162s	102.946mph	XH/H
5	Spies	Yamaha	42m 54.002s	3.903s	1m 56.087s	102.865mph	XH/H
6	De Puniet	Honda	42m 59.421s	9.322s	1m 56.221s	102.649mph	XH/H
7	Pedrosa	Honda	43m 06.607s	16.508s	1m 56.398s	102.363mph	XH/H
8	Edwards	Yamaha	43m 09.966s	19.867s	1m 56.756s	102.230mph	XH/H
9	Capirossi	Suzuki	43m 10.992s	20.893s	1m 56.794s	102.190mph	XH/H
10	Aoyama	Honda	43m 11.199s	21.100s	1m 56.677s	102.182mph	XH/H
11	Simoncelli	Honda	43m 21.737s	31.638s	1m 57.119s	101.768mph	XH/H
12	Barbera	Ducati	43m 22.672s	32.573s	1m 57.229s	101.731mph	XH/H
13	Melandri	Honda	43m 30.879s	40.780s	1m 57.359s	101.412mph	XH/H
14	Bautista	Suzuki	41m 25.290s	1 lap	1m 57.104s	101.694mph	XH/H
15	Espargaro	Ducati	13m 53.062s	15 laps	1m 57.272s	101.129mph	XH/H
16	Stoner	Ducati	9m 48.964s	17 laps	1m 55.537s	102.173mph	XH/H
17	Kallio	Ducati	4m 08.133s	20 laps	1m 57.931s	97.006mph	XH/M

CHAMPIONSHIP

	Rider	Team	Points
1	Rossi	Fiat Yamaha Team	25
2	Lorenzo	Fiat Yamaha Team	20
3	Dovizioso	Repsol Honda Team	16
4	Hayden	Ducati Marlboro Team	13
5	Spies	Monster Yamaha Tech 3	11
6	De Puniet	LCR Honda MotoGP	10
7	Pedrosa	Repsol Honda Team	9
8	Edwards	Monster Yamaha Tech 3	8
9	Capirossi	Rizla Suzuki MotoGP	7
10	Aoyama	Interwetten Honda MotoGP	6
11	Simoncelli	San Carlo Honda Gresini	5
12	Barbera	Paginas Amarillas Aspar	4
13	Melandri	San Carlo Honda Gresini	3

lead on the second lap, despite starting on the third row, but his problems came back and he slipped downfield.

8 COLIN EDWARDS A surprisingly low-key start for the man who was by far the best of the rest in 2009. Never found a good set-up and reverted to his 2009 settings, reporting problems with both front and rear grip.

9 LORIS CAPIROSSI Disappointed not to be more competitive in his 300th GP start, for which Loris sported the number 300 rather than his customary 65. Things looked promising in practice and qualifying but the sensitive Suzuki reacted badly to the significantly different conditions on race day.

10 HIROSHI AOYAMA Despite a terrible start that saw him last into the first corner, Hiro rode an impressive race to finish in front of the three other 250 graduates. Frustrated by the lack of testing now allowed and felt it was slowing his progress towards competitiveness.

11 MARCO SIMONCELLI After a crash-strewn pre-season and looking lost in practice this had to count as an encouraging MotoGP debut, but couldn't stay with Edwards and Capirossi when the tyres started to go off and failed to find a rhythm on his own.

12 HECTOR BARBERA A good start to his MotoGP career, though made a mistake early on when tailing Capirossi and Edwards

which forced him back into a dice with Bautista. The two closed on Simoncelli in the closing stages.

13 MARCO MELANDRI The worst weekend of his illustrious career – and that includes his traumatic season with Ducati. Suffered from the same handling problems as Pedrosa, only more so. Qualified last and was the final finisher. 'It was impossible for me to ride.'

NON-FINISHERS

ALVARO BAUTISTA Qualified well and looked as competitive as the other ex-250 men, but a bad start and a push from Barbera put him out of touch with the group. Used the race as a rather lonely test, then crashed on the final corner with old enemy Simoncelli in his sights.

ALEIX ESPARGARO Crashed out of 11th place on lap seven when he lost the front. Attempted to carry on but was forced to retire, completing a miserable weekend for Pramac Ducati. His first MotoGP DNF in his fifth race.

CASEY STONER The man who has owned the Losail track since 2007 set pole, as

expected, but then crashed out on lap six while leading by over 2s. Blamed himself for altering his riding style to take the load off the front, but later analysis showed he'd lost it on the brakes.

MIKA KALLIO Made what he said was the worst start of his life, then got shuffled back five places by one of Spies's hard moves. Crashed out when he lost the front on lap three trying to pass Barbera.

IN THE DEEP END

Lorenzo defeated Pedrosa in hand-to-hand combat, then jumped in the lake to celebrate, while Rossi and Ducati suffered

The Icelandic ash cloud did the Fiat Yamaha team a major favour because it caused the postponement of the Japanese Grand Prix and gave Jorge Lorenzo an extra week to recuperate fully from his hand injury. Rossi also had cause to be grateful. He'd fallen off a motocross bike and tried very hard to dislocate his right shoulder. The extent of the injury was played down, but lack of strength under hard braking and the set-up problems that always seemed to trouble him at Jerez demoted Vale to a supporting role all weekend. Kevin Schwantz described Rossi as 'a little bit under the weather and not willing to push as hard as normal'. The World Champion later admitted that if the Japanese GP had taken place on its scheduled date he wouldn't have been able to race.

For once, it looked as if Casey Stoner would be a threat at the Andalucian track, a place he's never enjoyed, but he too ended the weekend frustrated. Although the bike was 'so much better than previous years', Casey crashed in practice, and during the race had some trouble with the front end early on, including three or four near-crashes in one lap that he described as 'big time'. Nicky Hayden also crashed in practice, at over 130mph, an experience he laconically said 'wasn't exactly like falling in the pool'.

Honda had extra time to try to sort out their chassis problems, and when Dani Pedrosa claimed pole one could have been forgiven for thinking they'd been successful. Not judging by the Spanish rider's demeanour after qualifying, however, for he looked and sounded as if the family dog had just made a one-way trip to the vet. He did concede that there had been an improvement in direction changes, but

stability remained a problem. As in Qatar? 'I don't know.' So when Dani got away first on race day no-one was surprised, but everyone was waiting for the Qatar effect to kick in and the Repsol Honda to start slipping back into the clutches of Rossi and the pursuing Ducatis. It didn't happen, and it seemed as if the usual Pedrosa pattern was being followed, for whenever he has been allowed to escape and run his own race he has been untouchable. Although Rossi kept the gap at under two seconds for most of the second half of the race, it was obvious he wasn't in a position to go for the lead. The threat, when it arrived, came from the other Fiat Yamaha.

Jorge Lorenzo again had a relatively slow start, but he was past the troubled Stoner by lap five and overtook Hayden five laps later. The pattern seemed to be set, the gaps between the top three staying almost constant until lap 22 of 27 when Lorenzo

closed on Rossi who, as he'd predicted, looked to be having trouble under hard braking. Jorge passed his team-mate cleanly on the brakes at the end of the back straight, putting himself just fractionally over two seconds adrift of Pedrosa; he was within a second of his compatriot in two laps, and then, with two laps remaining, the pair were together. Half-way round the penultimate lap and Jorge tried the same pass that had worked on Rossi, only to have the door firmly slammed in his face not once but twice. He was squeezed so hard the second time that he had to use the kerb on the inside of the corner – this was like the old days of the pair's bitter rivalry in 250s – but Lorenzo was going to win or crash in the attempt. Standing on the rostrum on a lower step than Pedrosa simply wasn't an option.

Some people are of the opinion that Dani has never had the stomach for a fight; the last laps of this Grand

'THIS WAS LIKE A MOVIE. EVERYTHING THAT COULD POSSIBLY HAPPEN DID'
JORGE LORENZO

Prix showed them otherwise. Lorenzo's next move was an improbable and outrageous round-the-outside attack at the final corner of the penultimate lap. Jorge took his 'X-Fuera' motto, Spanish for 'around the outside', from a pass he put on Pedrosa back in 250s. This time Dani refused to be intimidated and held his ground, the two touching hard as the Honda man held the lead going into the final lap. He knew there'd be another Lorenzo attack on the brakes at the Pons corner and chose not

Above Lorenzo leans on Pedrosa on the last corner of the penultimate lap

Opposite As usual, Pedrosa got the holeshot

Above The fight for seventh kept the crowd entertained as they waited for Lorenzo to close in on Pedrosa

Below The factory Ducatis finished fourth and fifth, with Hayden beating his team-mate for the first time

to run a tight defensive line that would slow up his exit, instead going deep on the brakes, but running wide and leaving Jorge an easy pass.

Lorenzo then set a new level of lunacy for post-victory celebrations by jumping in a lake in his leathers, a decision he regretted very quickly. Back on dry land, Jorge struck some poses in front of the fans, reminiscent of a winning boxer after a tough fight. Dani was much, much happier than he'd been after setting pole, despite having lost the win on the last lap. He hadn't known before the race whether the Honda would work for race distance but now,

for the first time, he had some measure of confidence in the 2010 RC212V. 'It was always difficult to ride but I gave everything in front of my public.' He and Jorge managed a cordial handshake on the rostrum and a bit of banter in the press conference that followed. The relationship between the pair has mellowed from a couple of years ago when King Juan Carlos had to force them to shake hands on the podium.

And Valentino? He tried to laugh off losing the championship lead with a weak quip about not wanting to spoil the Spanish party. It wasn't his most convincing joke.

SHOULDER CHARGE

At first, it didn't seem like an important story. Valentino Rossi had crashed a motocrosser and tweaked his shoulder. It took weeks and months for the full story to emerge and for the implications to be understood. There was damage to the cartilage that was considered a minor issue; some gym work would compensate. The real problem was a ligament that had been pinched between the shoulder blade and the upper arm bone. Valentino warned that it would handicap him under hard braking.

The full story started to come out at Mugello, but was obviously overshadowed by Rossi's leg-breaking crash. It transpired that the Clinica Mobile hadn't revealed the full extent of the injury or its implications until shortly before Mugello. Now Valentino understood that while the injury wouldn't get any worse, he would need an operation if it didn't get any better. Hopefully that could wait until the end of the season as the recovery time would be two months.

The double whammy of this type of injury is that a rider is handicapped in the race and cannot train to improve the situation. Valentino now knew he would have to go through the season carrying the injury. Predominantly right-handed tracks were worse, although he had an easier time if the braking was in a straight line rather than with the bike heeled over. His team also had to find a way of making the bike more comfortable for the rider rather than finding the ideal setting. The net result was usually competitive but not quite on a par with the other 'Aliens'; just occasionally, as at Aragon,

Valentino was almost invisible. However, the operation was now inevitable, not probable. The question was this: when would he have it?

By the end of the season, surprised by his competitiveness in the back-to-back races in Japan, Malaysia and Australia, Valentino had decided to complete the season. He had also realised that a comparatively small injury to a ligament had a bigger impact on his season than the compound fracture he suffered in Mugello.

SPANISH GP
CIRCUITO DE JEREZ

ROUND 2
May 2

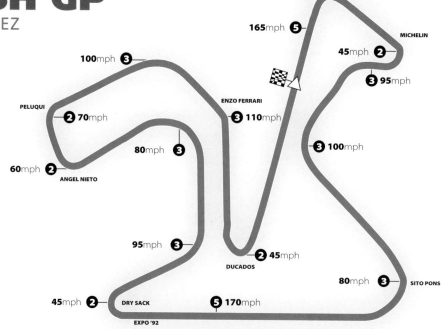

BRIDGESTONE
TYRE OPTIONS
FRONT MEDIUM (M) / HARD (H)
REAR SOFT (S) / MEDIUM (M)

OFFICIAL TIMEKEEPER

60mph ② — MICHELIN
165mph ⑤
100mph ③
45mph ②
95mph ③
ENZO FERRARI
PELUQUI
② 70mph ③ 110mph
80mph ③
100mph ③
60mph ②
ANGEL NIETO
95mph ③
② 45mph
DUCADOS
80mph ③ SITO PONS
45mph ② DRY SACK ⑤ 170mph
EXPO '92

RACE RESULTS

CIRCUIT LENGTH 2.748 miles
NO. OF LAPS 27
RACE DISTANCE 74.160 miles
WEATHER Dry, 27°C
TRACK TEMPERATURE 44°C
WINNER Jorge Lorenzo
FASTEST LAP 1m 39.731s, 98.285mph, Dani Pedrosa (record)
PREVIOUS LAP RECORD 1m 39.818s, 99.120mph, Valentino Rossi, 2009

QUALIFYING

	Rider	Nationality	Team	Qualifying	Pole +	Gap
1	Pedrosa	SPA	Repsol Honda Team	1m 39.202s		
2	Lorenzo	SPA	Fiat Yamaha Team	1m 39.487s	0.285s	0.285s
3	Stoner	AUS	Ducati Marlboro Team	1m 39.511s	0.309s	0.024s
4	Rossi	ITA	Fiat Yamaha Team	1m 39.558s	0.356s	0.047s
5	Hayden	USA	Ducati Marlboro Team	1m 39.560s	0.358s	0.002s
6	De Puniet	FRA	LCR Honda MotoGP	1m 39.591s	0.389s	0.031s
7	Edwards	USA	Monster Yamaha Tech 3	1m 39.970s	0.768s	0.379s
8	Spies	USA	Monster Yamaha Tech 3	1m 39.989s	0.787s	0.019s
9	Dovizioso	ITA	Repsol Honda Team	1m 40.021s	0.819s	0.032s
10	Melandri	ITA	San Carlo Honda Gresini	1m 40.027s	0.825s	0.006s
11	Capirossi	ITA	Rizla Suzuki MotoGP	1m 40.206s	1.004s	0.179s
12	Aoyama	JPN	Interwetten Honda MotoGP	1m 40.322s	1.120s	0.116s
13	Bautista	SPA	Rizla Suzuki MotoGP	1m 40.416s	1.214s	0.094s
14	Barbera	SPA	Paginas Amarillas Aspar	1m 40.482s	1.280s	0.066s
15	Espargaro	SPA	Pramac Racing Team	1m 40.555s	1.353s	0.073s
16	Simoncelli	ITA	San Carlo Honda Gresini	1m 40.586s	1.384s	0.031s
17	Kallio	FIN	Pramac Racing Team	1m 40.803s	1.601s	0.217s

FINISHERS

1 JORGE LORENZO An astonishing late charge after another bad start put him down in fifth on lap two. Took two seconds out of Pedrosa in the last five laps to set up a last-ditch fight that was as risky as it looked. Jorge's first win at Jerez gave him the championship lead.

2 DANI PEDROSA Pessimistic before the race despite setting pole and surprised afterwards that he was so competitive. Led for all but the final half-lap and defended his lead as hard as he could. A major improvement on the first race, but problems with the bike were still all too apparent.

3 VALENTINO ROSSI Handicapped by a motocross training injury to his shoulder and his usual Jerez problem of lack of rear grip, which made itself felt when the tyres were worn later in the race. Had no answer for Pedrosa or his team-mate – a strangely anonymous weekend.

4 NICKY HAYDEN Despite a big crash in practice, Nicky was just as competitive as in Qatar. Ran in third for much of the race, before Lorenzo's charge to the front, and had hopes of finding another tenth or two to challenge for the rostrum again.

5 CASEY STONER Never improved on his base set-up, crashed in practice and had several big moments from the front end early in the race which shot his confidence. This

was the first time he'd felt confident about being able to fight for a podium at Jerez, but sadly he was wrong.

6 ANDREA DOVIZIOSO Nowhere near as competitive as in Qatar and never threatened the Ducatis ahead of him. Rode very hard in the opening laps to make up places but realised he'd have to settle for sixth. Blamed engine electronics rather than the handling problems with which his team-mate was preoccupied.

7 MIKA KALLIO Rode brilliantly after disastrous qualifying saw him dead last on the grid. A crucial set-up gamble during warm-up (a rearwards weight shift) produced a bike he could use, especially in fending off Melandri in the closing stages

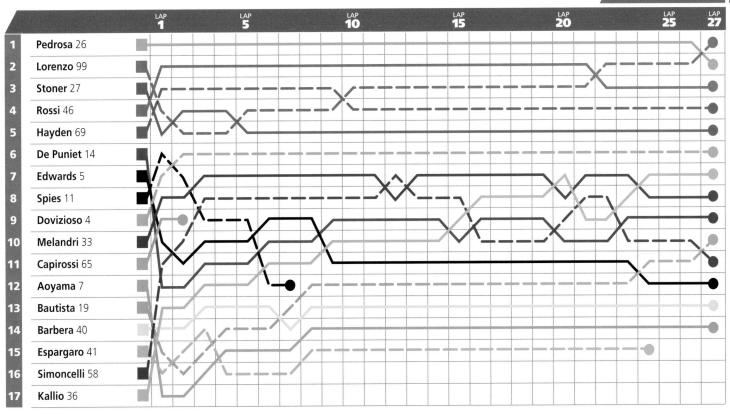

		LAP 1	LAP 5	LAP 10	LAP 15	LAP 20	LAP 25	LAP 27
1	Pedrosa 26							
2	Lorenzo 99							
3	Stoner 27							
4	Rossi 46							
5	Hayden 69							
6	De Puniet 14							
7	Edwards 5							
8	Spies 11							
9	Dovizioso 4							
10	Melandri 33							
11	Capirossi 65							
12	Aoyama 7							
13	Bautista 19							
14	Barbera 40							
15	Espargaro 41							
16	Simoncelli 58							
17	Kallio 36							

RACE

	Rider	Motorcycle	Race Time	Time +	Fastest Lap	Av Speed	B
1	Lorenzo	Yamaha	45m 17.538s		1m 40.007s	98.305mph	H/M
2	Pedrosa	Honda	45m 18.081s	0.543s	1m 39.731s	98.285mph	H/M
3	Rossi	Yamaha	45m 18.428s	0.890s	1m 39.733s	98.273mph	H/M
4	Hayden	Ducati	45m 26.553s	9.015s	1m 40.102s	97.980mph	H/M
5	Stoner	Ducati	45m 27.572s	10.034s	1m 39.988s	97.943mph	H/M
6	Dovizioso	Honda	45m 40.682s	23.144s	1m 40.405s	97.475mph	H/M
7	Kallio	Ducati	45m 52.027s	34.489s	1m 41.044s	97.073mph	H/M
8	Melandri	Honda	45m 52.225s	34.687s	1m 40.748s	97.066mph	H/M
9	De Puniet	Honda	45m 53.698s	36.160s	1m 40.992s	97.014mph	H/M
10	Bautista	Suzuki	45m 54.329s	36.791s	1m 41.274s	96.992mph	H/M
11	Simoncelli	Honda	45m 54.693s	37.155s	1m 40.758s	96.971mph	H/M
12	Edwards	Yamaha	45m 55.798s	38.260s	1m 40.974s	96.940mph	H/M
13	Barbera	Ducati	45m 55.909s	38.371s	1m 41.266s	96.936mph	H/M
14	Aoyama	Honda	46m 19.590s	1m 02.052s	1m 41.379s	96.110mph	H/M
15	Espargaro	Ducati	46m 41.784s	3 laps	1m 41.024s	84.755mph	H/S
16	Spies	Yamaha	11m 59.976s	20 laps	1m 41.102s	96.198mph	H/M
17	Capirossi	Suzuki	3m 30.104s	25 laps	1m 40.739s	94.185mph	H/M

CHAMPIONSHIP

	Rider	Team	Points
1	Lorenzo	Fiat Yamaha Team	45
2	Rossi	Fiat Yamaha Team	41
3	Pedrosa	Repsol Honda Team	29
4	Dovizioso	Repsol Honda Team	26
5	Hayden	LCR Honda MotoGP	26
6	De Puniet	LCR Honda MotoGP	17
7	Edwards	Monster Yamaha Tech 3	12
8	Stoner	Ducati Marlboro Team	11
9	Spies	Monster Yamaha Tech 3	11
10	Melandri	San Carlo Honda Gresini	11
11	Simoncelli	San Carlo Honda Gresini	10
12	Kallio	Pramac Racing Team	9
13	Aoyama	Interwetten Honda MotoGP	8
14	Capirossi	Rizla Suzuki MotoGP	7
15	Barbera	Paginas Amarillas Aspar	7
16	Bautista	Rizla Suzuki MotoGP	6
17	Espargaro	Pramac Racing Team	1
18			

to win the group dice, and also defused earlier criticism from his team owner.

8 MARCO MELANDRI Still not happy with his electronics or the stability of the bike, but this was so much better than the complete disaster of the first round. The problems were worst in the opening stages of the race.

9 RANDY DE PUNIET Another bad start after impressive qualifying. Twelfth at the end of the first lap, he was unable to run the same pace as in qualifying and then ran into front tyre problems.

10 ALVARO BAUTISTA First finish in MotoGP and top rookie in the race. Tentative at the start, as the bike felt

different from qualifying, but was right with the two Hondas in front of him at the flag, having passed Simoncelli on the last lap.

11 MARCO SIMONCELLI The same result as the first race, but a very different feeling. This time he got a good start and was in the hectic dice for seventh all race long. Lost out late on when the tyres started to slide.

12 COLIN EDWARDS Couldn't put any load on the rear tyre at full lean, which was also his problem in Qatar, despite a very different set-up. 'I've had one good race at Jerez in my entire career and this wasn't it.'

13 HECTOR BARBERA Very fast in free practice but never carried that speed into qualifying or the race.

14 HIROSHI AOYAMA Another bad start saw him running off track on the first lap, condemning himself to a lonely race.

15 ALEIX ESPARGARO Crashed on the fourth lap but was able to get the bike back to the pits for a new brake pedal. Went out again to complete the race and take the final point, three laps in arrears of the winner.

NON-FINISHERS

BEN SPIES Pulled in with what he thought was a defective front tyre, having nearly crashed several times. Decided not to throw on a new tyre and go out for a point or two, on the grounds that it would be putting miles on the engine for no reason. Bridgestone checked the tyre and found no problem.

LORIS CAPIROSSI Confident with the direction the team were taking with the bike, got a good start and moved up a couple of places, then lost the front going into the final corner on lap three.

MotoGP SEAS

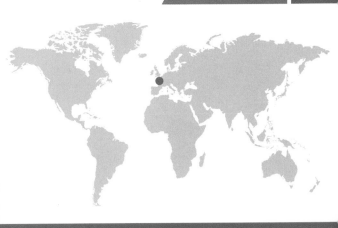

COUP DE GRACE

Back-to-back wins for Lorenzo for the first time in MotoGP – and his team-mate never laid a glove on him

The Jorge Lorenzo who celebrated victory at Le Mans was a very different person from the one who'd won at Jerez. In Spain he was a frenzy of adrenaline-fuelled posturing. In France he pulled up a chair and watched himself on one of the big trackside screens while eating popcorn. He even used the word 'easy' in describing the race. Beating Valentino Rossi on a level playing field is never easy, but Jorge made it look that way; and the man himself admitted that, not long ago, he might not have had the patience to bide his time as he had this year.

The two Fiat Yamahas went to the front on the first lap and never looked in danger. Pole-man Rossi led, with Lorenzo shadowing him, and that's how they stayed for ten laps. Valentino had expressed worries about his set-up and his shoulder before the race, but most of the paddock thought he was protesting just a little too much. Mind games, perhaps? From trackside the team-mates looked evenly matched, but Rossi was experiencing the same rear grip problems he'd suffered in Spain. Lorenzo knew he was faster in the corners, but because Valentino was so good on the brakes he couldn't find a way past. 'I try to stay as close to him as possible, I wait for one mistake of Valentino.' That doesn't sound like the Lorenzo of old. 'If this happen to me three or four years ago maybe I do some crazy things.' Three or four years? Six months ago, more like.

Jorge's patience was rewarded just before half-distance when he made a move stick at the Dunlop chicane. The first time Lorenzo went past, Rossi immediately repassed him on the exit of the corner, but he later said it was 'just for fun. I understand I don't have the pace.' He didn't use the shoulder as an excuse, although it did give him problems in the last seven or eight laps – 'but by then the race was lost'. The Rossi who made these painfully honest statements seemed tired and jaded, not even trying to put on a brave face. He looked like a man who had seen the writing on the wall. Indeed, he looked the way the other guys used to look after a race against him.

Once Jorge got in front he was able to pull away, and interest now focused on the battle for third. It looked as if Pedrosa had the measure of it, although he too was being stalked by his team-mate, with Nicky Hayden also closing in. It was all Dovizioso could do to stay with Dani, until the final four laps when Pedrosa, still with handling issues, started making mistakes. He didn't know it, but he'd worn out his rear brake pads; the rear brake is used a lot at Le Mans to control a bike's tendency to wheelie out of the slow corners. Hayden got a good look at the two Repsol Hondas during the battle for third place, reporting later that they behaved so differently he could have believed they were motorcycles from two different manufacturers. Dovi avenged last year's

final-lap overtake by his team-mate to seize third, while Nicky also pushed through on the last lap but couldn't put a pass on the Italian.

Dani Pedrosa was making so many mistakes in the last two laps he hardly hit an apex. He'd go into a corner, braking as he'd done all race, only to find himself running wildly wide on the exit. It was a superb defensive effort but the result was inevitable, not that he'd ever looked comfortable: 'I was fighting the bike the whole race.' Things are obviously tense at Repsol Honda, for Andrea's mechanics were overheard on a TV effects microphone in *parc fermé* delightedly informing their guy that 'Nicky passed him too!'

Hayden had what he called 'another solid race', but didn't know whether to be happy, notably at being two seconds quicker in qualifying than last year, or totally ticked off at missing the rostrum yet again. He had a grandstand seat for Stoner's third-lap crash – the front end again. Casey held it up on his knee and elbow for 20 metres before letting go. He'd spent practice trying to get the front to give him a problem and it never happened: the first time the front-end woes that had afflicted him in Qatar and Spain reappeared was as he crashed. 'Frustrating' was the word the Australian used. Not knowing what causes a crash is the worst possible situation for any rider – and Stoner also had to cope with the fact that the World Championship was beyond his grasp after only three races.

Things weren't any better at Suzuki. Loris Capirossi had the same crash as Stoner, and Alvaro Bautista became the season's third rider to be hurt in a motocross training accident. A heavy practice fall then

'I HAD TO BE VERY PATIENT, SOMETHING THAT I MIGHT NOT HAVE MANAGED ONE YEAR AGO'

JORGE LORENZO

Above Surprisingly, seventh was Randy de Puniet's best result at his home race

Below The Fiat Yamahas were first and second for the whole race, but not always in the same order

Above Aleix Espargaro
was part of the
entertaining and at times
fraught dice for eighth

put him out of the race and damaged his ribs. The team
left France with their riders rooted to the bottom of the
points table. The good news story concerned Marco
Melandri. A swap to Showa suspension either sorted
out the Honda to his satisfaction or sorted out Marco's
head to his team's satisfaction. Average qualifying was
followed by a great start that put him in sixth. The really
encouraging fact was that he ran with Hayden and was

not far off the pace of the factory Hondas. Team owner
Fausto Gresini's temper was also considerably improved
by a good race from Marco Simoncelli, who led the
entertaining and hectic group fight for eighth for most
of the race before losing two places on the last lap.

After the staccato start to the season, Le Mans
brought everything into focus. Clearly the Yamaha was
still the best bike – but who was now its best rider?

WHAT'S CASEY'S PROBLEM?

After his Qatar fall, Casey Stoner tempted fate by saying that he'd got his crash for the year out of the way early. He crashed again in practice at Jerez and then spent a lot of practice time in France trying to identify the problem. The team could find nothing, but then the problem reared its head again during the race, causing Casey to fall 'at the most unimportant part of the corner, probably of the whole circuit'.

As he was at pains to explain, all the top riders push the front all the time and routinely save a crash by pushing the bike back upright with their knee. The Ducati, fitted with new 2010 Ohlins forks, seemed to have two problems, the crucial one being a lack of feel that had the team moving weight on and off the front end with seemingly no effect – something about which Ducati riders other than Casey have been known to complain. Second, when the bike did let go at the front, Stoner found it simply refused to be levered back upright in the usual way. He nearly wore through his elbow protector, never mind the knee slider, trying to get his Ducati back on its wheels.

The 2007 World Champion was adamant that the new big-bang motor's characteristics were nothing to do with the problem and, as the frame was basically unchanged, he focused on the new forks. Back-to-back tests with the 2009 forks were suggested, but as testing is severely restricted this could only happen in practice for the next GP. This was a highly unusual step for a factory team and indicative of the serious nature of the problem.

Below Colin Edwards, a past pole setter and rostrum finisher at Le Mans, found himself down with the rookies

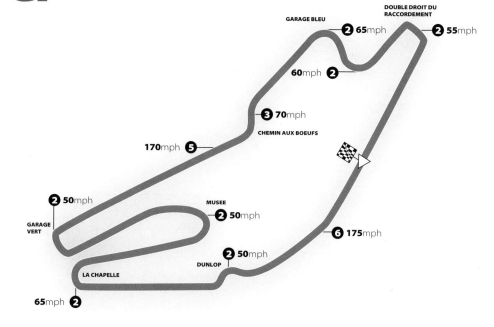

BRIDGESTONE
TYRE OPTIONS
FRONT SOFT (S) / MEDIUM (M)
REAR SOFT (S) / MEDIUM (M)

OFFICIAL TIMEKEEPER

FRENCH GP
LE MANS

ROUND 3
May 23

Circuit labels:
DOUBLE DROIT DU RACCORDEMENT
GARAGE BLEU
2 65mph
2 55mph
2 60mph
3 70mph
CHEMIN AUX BOEUFS
170mph 5
MUSEE
2 50mph
2 50mph
6 175mph
GARAGE VERT
2 50mph
DUNLOP
2 50mph
LA CHAPELLE
65mph 2

RACE RESULTS

CIRCUIT LENGTH 2.600 miles
NO. OF LAPS 28
RACE DISTANCE 72.816 miles
WEATHER Dry, 32°C
TRACK TEMPERATURE 51°C
WINNER Jorge Lorenzo
FASTEST LAP 1m 34.545s, 98.210mph, Jorge Lorenzo
LAP RECORD 1m 34.215s, 99.363mph, Valentino Rossi, 2008

QUALIFYING

	Rider	Nationality	Team	Qualifying	Pole +	Gap
1	Rossi	ITA	Fiat Yamaha Team	1m 33.408s		
2	Lorenzo	SPA	Fiat Yamaha Team	1m 33.462s	0.054	0.054s
3	Pedrosa	SPA	Repsol Honda Team	1m 33.573s	0.165s	0.111s
4	Stoner	AUS	Ducati Marlboro Team	1m 33.824s	0.416s	0.251s
5	Hayden	USA	Ducati Marlboro Team	1m 33.845s	0.437s	0.021s
6	De Puniet	FRA	LCR Honda MotoGP	1m 34.074s	0.666s	0.229s
7	Dovizioso	ITA	Repsol Honda Team	1m 34.204s	0.796s	0.130s
8	Edwards	USA	Monster Yamaha Tech 3	1m 34.304s	0.896s	0.100s
9	Capirossi	ITA	Rizla Suzuki MotoGP	1m 34.306s	0.898s	0.002s
10	Espargaro	SPA	Pramac Racing Team	1m 34.514s	1.106s	0.208s
11	Melandri	ITA	San Carlo Honda Gresini	1m 34.523s	1.115s	0.009s
12	Spies	USA	Monster Yamaha Tech 3	1m 34.920s	1.512s	0.397s
13	Simoncelli	ITA	San Carlo Honda Gresini	1m 34.942s	1.534s	0.022s
14	Aoyama	JPN	Interwetten Honda MotoGP	1m 34.979s	1.571s	0.037s
15	Barbera	SPA	Paginas Amarillas Aspar	1m 35.323s	1.915s	0.344s
16	Kallio	FIN	Pramac Racing Team	1m 35.810s	2.402s	0.487s
	Bautista	SPA	Rizla Suzuki MotoGP			

FINISHERS

1 JORGE LORENZO Back-to-back wins for the first time in his MotoGP career. Stalked Rossi for the first third of the race before making his second passing attempt stick, then pulled away as he pleased. Jorge was able to describe the victory as 'easy' and no-one laughed.

2 VALENTINO ROSSI Knew he wouldn't have the pace of Lorenzo, despite his pole position. As in Jerez, it was grip under acceleration that was the problem. Refused to blame his shoulder, saying it didn't become an issue until seven laps from the flag, 'by which time the race was lost'.

3 ANDREA DOVIZIOSO Revenge for a year ago, when it was team-mate Pedrosa who stole the final podium place on the last lap. Tailed Dani but couldn't make a pass until the closing stages when the Spanish rider started running wide. Hailed his second rostrum of the year as confirmation that Qatar wasn't a one-off.

4 NICKY HAYDEN Another fourth place, his third in three races. Did his best to appear pleased but was deeply frustrated by another rostrum slipping just out of reach, even though he said he couldn't have ridden any faster. Pleased to have found something extra for race day.

5 DANI PEDROSA Lost two places on the final lap after wearing out his rear brake pads, which caused him to run wide in corners. Used the same chassis as in Jerez but reported he was fighting the bike all race. Not the way he wanted to celebrate his 150th GP start.

6 MARCO MELANDRI A massive improvement in form after the Gresini team persuaded HRC to let him revert to Showa suspension from Ohlins. Fast from the start but lost touch with Hayden after a small mistake, so he decided to 'pull the oars in' and settle for sixth.

7 RANDY DE PUNIET His best result at Le Mans, but not where he wanted to be from sixth on the grid. Made good progress in the opening laps but several warnings from the front tyre meant he was stuck in seventh after Stoner's crash.

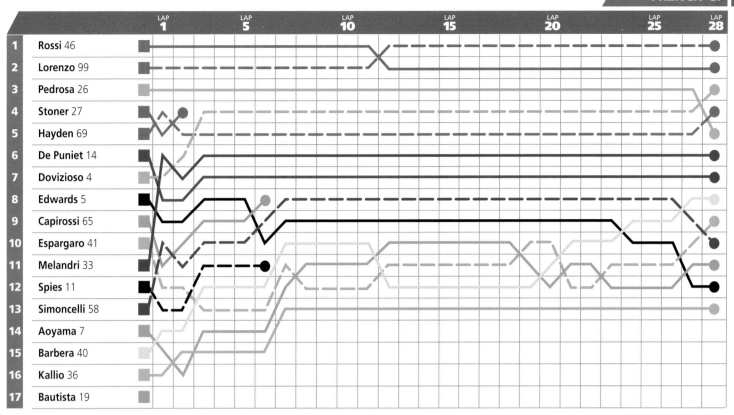

| | | | | | | LAP 1 | | | | LAP 5 | | | | | LAP 10 | | | | LAP 15 | | | | | LAP 20 | | | | LAP 25 | | LAP 28 |

1	Rossi 46
2	Lorenzo 99
3	Pedrosa 26
4	Stoner 27
5	Hayden 69
6	De Puniet 14
7	Dovizioso 4
8	Edwards 5
9	Capirossi 65
10	Espargaro 41
11	Melandri 33
12	Spies 11
13	Simoncelli 58
14	Aoyama 7
15	Barbera 40
16	Kallio 36
17	Bautista 19

RACE

	Rider	Motorcycle	Race Time	Time +	Fastest Lap	Av Speed	B
1	Lorenzo	Yamaha	44m 29.114s		1m 34.545s	98.210mph	M/M
2	Rossi	Yamaha	44m 34.786s	5.672s	1m 34.586s	98.002mph	M/M
3	Dovizioso	Honda	44m 36.986s	7.872s	1m 34.756s	97.922mph	M/M
4	Hayden	Ducati	44m 38.460s	9.346s	1m 35.006s	97.868mph	M/M
5	Pedrosa	Honda	44m 41.727s	12.613s	1m 34.632s	97.748mph	M/M
6	Melandri	Honda	44m 51.032s	21.918s	1m 35.127s	97.410mph	M/M
7	De Puniet	Honda	44m 58.402s	29.288s	1m 35.300s	97.144mph	M/M
8	Barbera	Ducati	45m 02.242s	33.128s	1m 35.611s	97.006mph	M/M
9	Espargaro	Ducati	45m 02.607s	33.493s	1m 35.667s	96.993mph	M/s
10	Simoncelli	Honda	45m 02.919s	33.805s	1m 35.738s	96.982mph	M/M
11	Aoyama	Honda	45m 03.460s	34.346s	1m 35.540s	96.963mph	M/s
12	Edwards	Yamaha	45m 06.237s	37.123s	1m 35.527s	96.863mph	M/M
13	Kallio	Ducati	45m 24.175s	55.061s	1m 36.417s	96.225mph	s/s
14	Capirossi	Suzuki	9m 44.122s	22 laps	1m 35.413s	96.164mph	M/M
15	Spies	Yamaha	9m 47.284s	22 laps	1m 35.403s	95.647mph	M/M
16	Stoner	Ducati	3m 18.638s	26 laps	1m 35.577s	94.262mph	M/M

CHAMPIONSHIP

	Rider	Team	Points
1	Lorenzo	Fiat Yamaha Team	70
2	Rossi	Fiat Yamaha Team	61
3	Dovizioso	Repsol Honda Team	42
4	Pedrosa	Repsol Honda Team	40
5	Hayden	Ducati Marlboro Team	39
6	De Puniet	LCR Honda MotoGP	26
7	Melandri	San Carlo Honda Gresini	21
8	Edwards	Monster Yamaha Tech 3	16
9	Simoncelli	San Carlo Honda Gresini	16
10	Barbera	Paginas Amarillas Aspar	15
11	Aoyama	Interwetten Honda MotoGP	13
12	Kallio	Pramac Racing Team	12
13	Stoner	Ducati Marlboro Team	11
14	Spies	Monster Yamaha Tech 3	11
15	Espargaro	Pramac Racing Team	8
16	Capirossi	Rizla Suzuki MotoGP	7
17	Bautista	Rizla Suzuki MotoGP	6

8 HECTOR BARBERA First rookie and the winner of the spectacular group fight for eighth despite an off-track excursion after a coming-together with Aoyama. Credited the Jerez test for improving front-end feel and allowing him to enjoy racing the Ducati for the first time.

9 ALEIX ESPARGARO Lost touch with the group in the early laps, then fought back to his best result in MotoGP. A coming-together with Aoyama (not their first) on the last lap prevented him from attacking Barbera.

10 MARCO SIMONCELLI Didn't feel as comfortable with the bike on race day as he had in practice. Always in the fight for seventh, running eighth for most of the race, but lost a couple of places in the last few laps.

11 HIROSHI AOYAMA Changed his front tyre on the grid, so his tentative start was understandable. Also handicapped by the after-effects of an operation on his hand after Jerez which meant he could only hold on to the bars for five laps at a time. Survived one enormous moment at the Chemin aux Boeufs chicane.

12 COLIN EDWARDS An inexplicably lacklustre performance at a track where he has been on pole and the rostrum. Found himself tangled up with all the rookies in a hectic dice, exactly where he didn't want to be. Lack of confidence in the front end seemed to be the problem.

13 MIKA KALLIO A big crash on Saturday morning put his race participation in doubt.

Had taken a massive hit to his right shoulder and was a second a lap slower than in free practice. Gritted his teeth when his crew signalled some riders had retired and made it to the finish in agony, despite painkillers.

NON-FINISHERS

LORIS CAPIROSSI Lost the front end at Turn 3 on lap seven for no reason, his third front-end crash of the year, completing a terrible weekend for Rizla Suzuki. Doubly disappointing for both team and rider as they genuinely thought they were in good shape for the race.

BEN SPIES Handicapped by a big crash on Saturday morning that left him with a swollen and sore left foot. Suffered the same crash as Capirossi a few seconds after the Italian went down, but fortunately without further injury.

CASEY STONER Got past his team-mate and was closing on the front trio when he

lost the front on lap three. Unlike Qatar, there was no explanation for the crash. Had spent practice trying to get the front to misbehave – with no result. Admitted he was frustrated, and knew that the championship was already out of reach.

NON-STARTERS

ALVARO BAUTISTA Broke a collarbone in a motocross training accident after Jerez, then crashed again on Saturday morning, aggravating the injury.

ITALIAN GP
MUGELLO

ROUND 4
June 6

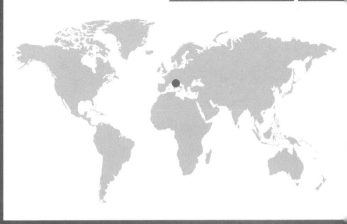

ECLIPSE OF THE SUN KING

Dani Pedrosa won in such emphatic style that it's doubtful if even the absent Valentino Rossi would have caught him

So what's wrong with the Honda? Judging by this race, not a lot. RC212Vs filled four of the first six places, thanks to the dominant Dani Pedrosa, the calculating Andrea Dovizioso, the resurgent Marco Melandri and the wild Randy de Puniet. It could be argued, though, that they were all on very different motorcycles.

The Repsol team-mates set up their bikes so differently that it's hard to compare them, while Melandi had reverted to Showa suspension at the previous race and de Puniet was using an older design of Ohlins. Pedrosa complicated the picture even further by reverting to a 2009 rear Ohlins shock. His team turned a motorcycle that on Friday felt heavy and difficult to manage in the fast changes of direction that abound at Mugello into an agile race winner – and without conjuring up the instability problems that had afflicted Dani at the start of the year: a clever trick.

Not that all the credit should go to the machinery. 'A chicane track, Mugello was always for me a difficult track,' as Dani reflected after the race, 'but I remember Mick Doohan won many times here on Repsol Honda.' He also remembered what had happened in the previous two races, losing a win and a rostrum on the last laps. 'I tried to handle the gap at the end,' said Pedrosa, and while he denied knowing who was behind him he later commented that Jorge Lorenzo was always a threat because of his consistent lap times. The real surprise was that Lorenzo didn't put in any sort of challenge for the win. As Dani pulled away to a lead of eight seconds before easing up slightly, Jorge couldn't match the pace he'd shown all through the weekend, for reasons of grip that might have been related to the slightly elevated

temperature on race day, but he was gracious enough to say he doubted if he could have caught his rival even if the Fiat Yamaha had been perfect.

In fact, Lorenzo spent the whole race worrying about protecting his runner-up spot from Andrea Dovizioso. The Italian didn't qualify well but pointed out that at Mugello, unlike some other tracks, things often change on race day. He was right, and not just about his own race. Lorenzo and Hayden, among the top men, and Aoyama and Kallio (from the satellite teams) all failed to live up to their Friday and Saturday showings while, as well as Dovi, Marco Melandri's Sunday form far exceeded most people's expectations of him. Marco was involved in the three-man dice for fourth that provided most of the race's entertainment. Casey Stoner, despite his continuing suspension problems, had enough in hand to win that fight with a well-planned and daring last-lap attack. After deciding he was making a 'good rabbit', he 'sat in' and waited. Even more than in France there were signs that Melandri's confidence, in himself as well as his bike, had been restored. Stoner was highly complimentary about Marco's riding, which he described as 'really professional', but de Puniet received a less glowing reference: 'I don't think Randy hit the same marker twice.'

The non-appearance of Valentino Rossi for the first time in a record 231 GPs was in many ways more significant than any of the on-track events. His leg-breaking crash on Saturday morning instantly altered the MotoGP world. Rossi's absence would coincide with the football World Cup in South Africa. What would his accident do to race attendances

and TV audiences? What would Yamaha do about replacing him? What would be the effect on the other riders' negotiations for 2011? The Fiat Yamaha team were not obliged to field a replacement rider until the Catalan GP, so that decision was postponed while everyone waited on news of Rossi's operation. Thankfully there were no complications. Valentino managed to joke that he had developed a great relationship with morphine and the circuit PA broadcast a phone call from him on Sunday morning.

The one thing that everyone agreed about was that Rossi should not come back until he was completely fit. Why would he do otherwise? The championship was obviously now an impossibility – and it wasn't as if he'd have trouble finding a ride for the following season. But the possibility, however faint, that Valentino might take up an offer to change to four wheels surely made Yamaha racing boss Lin Jarvis's life much more complicated. What to do, given Rossi's aversion to having Lorenzo as a team-mate? Call the Doctor's bluff or let the man most likely to take over the number-one plate go to Honda or Ducati? Whatever the decision, there would be a knock-on effect on every other team's thinking.

The missing maestro was saluted by riders and

Above The top six, split into two groups of three, on the run down from Palagio to Correntaio

Opposite Two Repsol Hondas in the top three – a rare sight in 2010

'IT LOOKS LIKE WE ARE BACK NEAR WHERE WE NEED TO BE'
DANI PEDROSA

Left The wreckage of Rossi's M1 Yamaha is brought back to the pits

Below Valentino tumbles through the Biondetti gravel trap as his M1 demonstrates how much momentum is possessed by a bike travelling at 110mph

crowd alike. Jorge Lorenzo's grid placard was particularly well judged: 'Anyone can feel pain, not everyone can be a legend.' His team wasn't so amused when he donned a number 46 T-shirt on the rostrum, denying the sponsors' logos camera time. Everyone else thought it was a fine gesture. Dani Pedrosa dutifully thanked the fans for remembering Valentino, but his pre-race thoughts were more insightful. He hoped that the operation to pin Rossi's tibia had gone well 'because the first operation is very important'. There spoke a man who knows.

Dani's win put him second in the championship, just 25 points behind Lorenzo. A couple of races ago it had been pointed out to him that his title chances were being written off, but now he was being described as a serious contender, 'probably by the same people'. The Honda man may have allowed himself a wry grin to accompany this mild dig at the Spanish media, but the picture had changed in more ways than one. Two of the four 'Aliens' were out of the championship hunt after just four races. It looked to be Pedrosa versus Lorenzo, a confrontation that never really happened in 250s – at least not for the title.

WHAT HAPPENED?

Towards the end of second free practice, Valentino Rossi came out of the pits with a new tyre, completed his out-lap and started his first flying lap, as normal. Half-way round he decided to throttle off to allow Hector Barbera, who was looking for a tow, to go past. He was over nine seconds slower than usual through the third sector, from Arrabbiata to the exit of Correntaio, a section of track with four right-handers and just one left-hand bend. Rossi got on the gas hard coming out of Correntaio, got through the first – right-handed – part of the very fast Biondetti chicane, pulled the bike over for the left and was highsided at over 110mph. The left side of the tyre had cooled down. The Bridgestones do shed heat remarkably rapidly, as other riders noted later, but it was merely one characteristic of the tyres that had to be taken into account like any other.

The crash was the result of an uncharacteristic lapse of judgement by Rossi and, as Jerry Burgess noted, remarkable only because it happened to Valentino and because he broke his leg. There's no doubt that he was charging hard.

ITALIAN GP
MUGELLO

ROUND 4
June 6

BRIDGESTONE

TYRE OPTIONS
FRONT MEDIUM (M) / HARD (H)
REAR MEDIUM (M) / HARD (H)

MotoGP

TISSOT
SWISS WATCHES SINCE 1853

OFFICIAL TIMEKEEPER

RACE RESULTS

CIRCUIT LENGTH 3.259 miles
NO. OF LAPS 23
RACE DISTANCE 74.794 miles
WEATHER Dry, 32°C
TRACK TEMPERATURE 54°C
WINNER Dani Pedrosa
FASTEST LAP 1m 49.531s, 105.909mph, Dani Pedrosa (Record)
LAP RECORD 1m 50.003s, 106.658mph, Casey Stoner, 2008

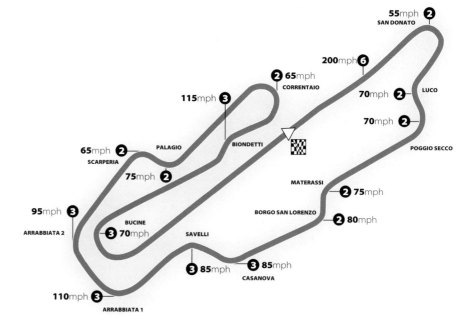

QUALIFYING

	Rider	Nationality	Team	Qualifying	Pole +	Gap
1	Pedrosa	SPA	Repsol Honda Team	1m 48.819s		
2	Lorenzo	SPA	Fiat Yamaha Team	1m 48.996s	0.177s	0.177s
3	Stoner	AUS	Ducati Marlboro Team	1m 49.432s	0.613s	0.436s
4	Hayden	USA	Ducati Marlboro Team	1m 49.546s	0.727s	0.114s
5	Edwards	USA	Monster Yamaha Tech 3	1m 49.683s	0.864s	0.137s
6	De Puniet	FRA	LCR Honda MotoGP	1m 49.737s	0.918s	0.054s
7	Spies	USA	Monster Yamaha Tech 3	1m 49.861s	1.042s	0.124s
8	Dovizioso	ITA	Repsol Honda Team	1m 50.065s	1.246s	0.204s
9	Espargaro	SPA	Pramac Racing Team	1m 50.168s	1.349s	0.103s
10	Aoyama	JPN	Interwetten Honda MotoGP	1m 50.224s	1.405s	0.056s
11	Simoncelli	ITA	San Carlo Honda Gresini	1m 50.434s	1.615s	0.210s
12	Capirossi	ITA	Rizla Suzuki MotoGP	1m 50.479s	1.660s	0.045s
13	Barbera	SPA	Paginas Amarillas Aspar	1m 50.561s	1.742s	0.082s
14	Melandri	ITA	San Carlo Honda Gresini	1m 50.664s	1.845s	0.103s
15	Kallio	FIN	Pramac Racing Team	1m 50.970s	2.151s	0.306s
16	Bautista	SPA	Rizla Suzuki MotoGP	1m 53.243s	4.424s	2.273s
	Rossi	ITA	Fiat Yamaha Team			

FINISHERS

1 DANI PEDROSA A trademark flag-to-flag victory from pole position and with the fastest lap as well – even Rossi wouldn't have stayed with him on this form. His pace in the opening laps was mightily impressive, and the lead was up to 8s before he eased to control the gap.

2 JORGE LORENZO Looked like the man to beat, despite missing out on pole, but on race day couldn't run the 1m 49s laps he'd been able to reel off in practice and qualifying – in fact he couldn't dip under 1m 50.5s. Both rider and team were puzzled, and talked vaguely about rear grip issues.

3 ANDREA DOVIZIOSO A great start after indifferent qualifying saw him third by the end of the first lap. Stayed on Lorenzo's tail for the whole of the race, never more than a second behind the Yamaha. Nearly as impressive a race as his team-mate, for this was Dovi's first MotoGP podium at Mugello.

4 CASEY STONER Tried the 2009 Ohlins forks in first practice and, despite a crash, decided he wanted to race with them. (The crash was unrelated to the bike's front end but reduced practice time with the forks.) Under the circumstances, winning the three-man fight for fourth place was an encouraging result.

5 MARCO MELANDRI A stunning race after difficult qualifying – unable to find a setting until warm-up. Gave Stoner a run for his money. A great confidence booster for Marco and Team Gresini at their home race, although all parties were well aware they have to work better in practice and qualifying.

6 RANDY DE PUNIET A fourth consecutive second-row start and a combative race which did not impress Stoner. Lost fourth on the last lap when his bike shook its head coming out of the final turn. Doubly impressive as he had his usual bad start and was 12th early on.

7 BEN SPIES In touch with the battle for fourth, but had to push hard in the turns to make up for a power deficit on the long straight. Publicly pleased with a good result after two bad races, but privately very angry about his motor's performance.

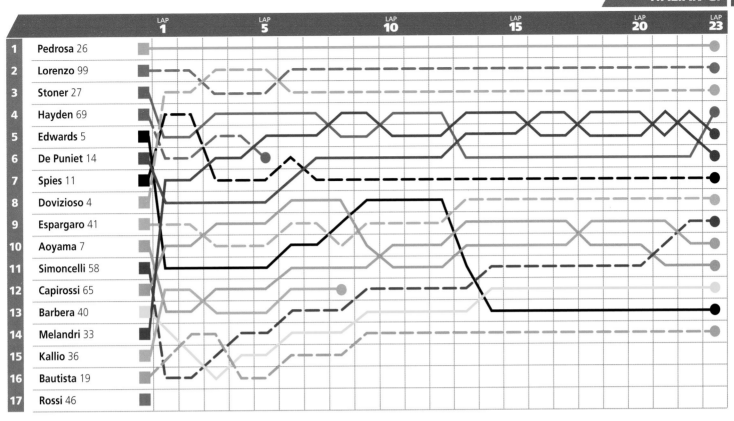

			LAP 1	LAP 5	LAP 10	LAP 15	LAP 20	LAP 23
1	Pedrosa 26							
2	Lorenzo 99							
3	Stoner 27							
4	Hayden 69							
5	Edwards 5							
6	De Puniet 14							
7	Spies 11							
8	Dovizioso 4							
9	Espargaro 41							
10	Aoyama 7							
11	Simoncelli 58							
12	Capirossi 65							
13	Barbera 40							
14	Melandri 33							
15	Kallio 36							
16	Bautista 19							
17	Rossi 46							

RACE

	Rider	Motorcycle	Race Time	Time +	Fastest Lap	Av Speed	B
1	Pedrosa	Honda	42m 28.066s		1m 49.531s	105.909mph	H/H
2	Lorenzo	Yamaha	42m 32.080s	4.014s	1m 50.418s	105.743mph	H/H
3	Dovizioso	Honda	42m 34.262s	6.196s	1m 50.293s	105.652mph	H/H
4	Stoner	Ducati	42m 53.769s	25.703s	1m 50.996s	104.851mph	H/M
5	Melandri	Honda	42m 53.801s	25.735s	1m 50.620s	104.850mph	H/M
6	De Puniet	Honda	42m 54.031s	25.965s	1m 50.971s	104.841mph	H/H
7	Spies	Yamaha	42m 56.872s	28.806s	1m 51.092s	104.725mph	H/H
8	Espargaro	Ducati	43m 08.238s	40.172s	1m 51.588s	104.265mph	H/M
9	Simoncelli	Honda	43m 09.460s	41.394s	1m 51.569s	104.216mph	H/M
10	Capirossi	Suzuki	43m 10.173s	42.107s	1m 51.557s	104.187mph	H/M
11	Aoyama	Honda	43m 11.161s	43.095s	1m 51.557s	104.147mph	H/H
12	Barbera	Ducati	43m 11.429s	43.363s	1m 51.666s	104.137mph	H/H
13	Edwards	Yamaha	43m 42.459s	1m 14.393s	1m 51.497s	102.905mph	H/H
14	Bautista	Suzuki	43m 52.455s	1m 24.389s	1m 53.171s	102.514mph	H/H
15	Kallio	Ducati	15m 06.148s	15 laps	1m 51.880s	103.588mph	H/H
16	Hayden	Ducati	9m 24.063s	18 laps	1m 51.042s	104.006mph	H/M

CHAMPIONSHIP

	Rider	Team	Points
1	Lorenzo	Fiat Yamaha Team	90
2	Pedrosa	Repsol Honda Team	65
3	Rossi	Fiat Yamaha Team	61
4	Dovizioso	Repsol Honda Team	58
5	Hayden	Ducati Marlboro Team	39
6	De Puniet	LCR Honda MotoGP	36
7	Melandri	San Carlo Honda Gresini	32
8	Stoner	Ducati Marlboro Team	24
9	Simoncelli	San Carlo Honda Gresini	23
10	Spies	Monster Yamaha Tech 3	20
11	Barbera	Paginas Amarillas Aspar	19
12	Edwards	Monster Yamaha Tech 3	19
13	Aoyama	Interwetten Honda MotoGP	18
14	Espargaro	Pramac Racing Team	16
15	Capirossi	Rizla Suzuki MotoGP	13
16	Kallio	Pramac Racing Team	12
17	Bautista	Rizla Suzuki MotoGP	8

8 ALEIX ESPARGARO The best and most impressive result of his short MotoGP career, despite a coming-together with Simoncelli early on. Good race pace and rhythm to catch and pass Capirossi in the closing stages.

9 MARCO SIMONCELLI If it hadn't been for a first-lap off-track excursion when he tried to follow Hayden past Espargaro, Marco's pace would have seen him fighting alongside team-mate Melandri in the dice for fourth place.

10 LORIS CAPIROSSI Once again, a Suzuki rider was undone by a change in conditions. Fifth fastest in morning warm-up and confident for the race, but in the higher temperatures couldn't get any feel from the front tyre. Had to seek consolation in just finishing after two DNFs.

11 HIROSHI AOYAMA Ran with Capirossi and Kallio early on, then hit problems with rear grip and the heat. Pleased that he didn't make any errors, but the team were less than impressed.

12 HECTOR BARBERA Up to eighth and looking good when he ran off track on lap three. Rejoined in last position, but managed to overhaul Edwards and Bautista before the flag.

13 COLIN EDWARDS For the first time this year Colin was fast and comfortable in practice, but then suffered from arm pump in the race, the first time in his career that he's had this problem — and, worryingly, it was allied to a general feeling of fatigue.

14 ALVARO BAUTISTA Got to the finish despite a total lack of strength in his shoulder and pain from the ribs he'd hurt in France.

NON-FINISHERS

MIKA KALLIO Problems in practice, still suffering with the shoulder he hurt at Le Mans, then crashed in the race. He'd made a good start and was up to tenth when he went out on lap nine.

NICKY HAYDEN Got away with the group fighting for fourth, but on lap six lost the front at Correntaio. Blamed himself for running wide and said it went very early in the corner, but under the circumstances another Ducati crashing off the front raised further questions about the Desmosedici's set-up for the 2010 season.

NON-STARTERS

VALENTINO ROSSI For the first time in 231 Grands Prix, they started without Valentino. He suffered a compound fracture of his right tibia in a practice crash on Saturday morning, and seemed unlikely to return until the Czech GP in August.

JORGE TAKES OFF

Lorenzo dominated, but there were satellite bikes on both the front row and the rostrum

For the first time in many years, a Grand Prix race meeting took place without Valentino Rossi. If there were any doubts about who would pick up the baton, Silverstone dispelled them. Jorge Lorenzo embarked on a run of wins in which he dominated not so much in the manner of Rossi but rather in the style of Mick Doohan. In practice and qualifying Jorge strung together long runs at race pace and then set his first pole of the year. The frightening thing from the opposition's point of view was that he made it seem easy. The Spanish rider looked unhurried and smooth and the Yamaha M1 rode the bumps better than any other machine. The question was whether anybody could give him a race.

It turned out that the answer was 'no'. Dani Pedrosa was brave and combative on the first lap but faded badly. Randy de Puniet took advantage of his grid position for once and held second in flamboyant style until Dovizioso came past. The Frenchman then ran into tyre problems and faded – but not as badly as Pedrosa, who reported a total lack of feeling with the front of his rebuilt bike, although some of the opposition reckoned a crash usually affected him. De Puniet's problem was tyre selection. He went with the harder option but didn't get the advantage he was expecting later in the race. Nevertheless, he was fast becoming the fans' favourite for his devil-may-care style that shredded tyres and opponents' nerves in equal measure.

The man who should have given Lorenzo a race was Stoner, but his clutch grabbed off the start, putting him last into the first corner. He then spent a surprising amount of time at the back of the field, thanks to

off the back of the group and was caught by Stoner half a lap after he'd passed Pedrosa.

The Aussie, now the fastest man on track, went straight across the gap to what was now the fight for third between Hayden and Spies. His progress was impeded by another new problem – arm pump – that Casey later blamed on a different undersuit that was tighter than his old version. It had struck while he was running in the new tyres at the back of the field and he'd had to adopt some unconventional riding techniques to compensate. Given the collection of difficulties he faced during the weekend, this was a stellar ride and a reminder of just how fast the Stoner–Ducati combination can be. His race pace also indicated that Casey and his crew had got the old front forks dialled in to the 2010 Desmosedici.

Once again, though, Casey was out-raced by his team-mate, Nicky Hayden, who had also bettered him in qualifying for the first time. The American was always with the leaders and went into the final laps in third and in touch with Doviziozo. Would this finally be a rostrum finish after his run of fourth places? It certainly looked likely until half-way round the last lap, when Ben Spies took advantage of a mistake going into Abbey and then held off a frantic Hayden to take a first rostrum finish in just his ninth MotoGP race. Spies's race went to his usual pattern, unobtrusive in the early laps but blazingly fast when the tyres started to wear. Given that a Saturday crash had further damaged the ankle he'd hurt at Le Mans, this was even more impressive. In fact, medical investigation revealed he'd cracked a bone in France, so make that 'doubly impressive'.

Above Dani Pedrosa had a tough weekend that included two big crashes

Opposite Jorge Lorenzo jumps to it on the rostrum, celebrating his best ride of the year

Below The fight for third place was thrilling, and was won by Ben Spies

tyres that were fresh on for the race, before starting an amazing charge through the pack. When Casey caught seventh-placed Pedrosa at half-distance there were five bikes covered by two seconds dicing for second place, with another second back to Dani and himself. By then Lorenzo was an astonishing eight seconds ahead and began to ease the pace very slightly. With de Puniet about to hit his tyre problems, Dovizioso, Hayden, Spies and Simoncelli all looked to be rostrum candidates. Dovi understood the situation perfectly and pushed past Randy for second place, then eked out a few precious tenths of a second as the rest also tried to find their way past de Puniet. At the same time, Simoncelli drifted

'ON THIS DAY I CAN SAY I WAS THE THIRD BEST RIDER IN THE WORLD AND IT IS A GOOD FEELING'

BEN SPIES

There were plenty of other talking points at Silverstone to keep everyone's mind off the absent World Champion. The new track layout met with universal approval, give or take a bump or two on the old tarmac, while the slightly chilly weather led to more muttering about tyres losing temperature quickly. Indeed, there was a rash of crashes in practice and warm-up that put Pedrosa (twice), Dovizioso, Simoncelli, Spies and Aoyama on the floor and the Japanese out of the championship for the foreseeable future. As with the spate of crashes at Le Mans, there was certainly cold rubber involved, notably for Spies and Aoyama, and the bumps caught out the other Honda riders. There were also echoes of Rossi's Mugello crash, caused by the tyres shedding heat, notably in Casey Stoner's comments. High speeds, long straights and low ambient temperatures conspired to cool the Bridgestones so rapidly that they lost grip during normal use. Fortunately, race day was considerably warmer than practice or qualifying, which didn't stop Marco Melandri crashing before the end of the first lap.

Despite the Silverstone facility as a whole being a work in progress – there will be a complete new pits complex in 2011, for instance – World Championship motorcycle racing's return after 24 years was deemed a success. The crowd was healthy, the racing was close (apart from Jorge's star turn) and the weather wasn't too bad. The only complaints were about traffic leaving – the jams were actually caused by an accident that was nothing to do with the event – and the need for a few more giant TV screens. At last, British fans and paddock personnel don't have to apologise for their home circuit.

A ROOKIE ON THE ROSTRUM

Ben Spies's rostrum was the first top-three finish of the year for a satellite-team rider – and the first since Alex de Angelis's second place at Indianapolis in 2009. The man himself had resolutely played down his chances since coming to MotoGP, repeatedly saying he was here to learn and reminding everyone how fast the field was. 'I never bought all that,' said the man whom he deprived of the rostrum place, Nicky Hayden. 'I knew he'd be up there from the start. He's been riding hard all weekend, he deserved it.' Not many people disagreed. The most impressive thing about Ben is the way he works to learn a new track: methodical, unhurried and calm. If there's a weakness it's on new or sticky tyres, plus he also has to deal with a bike that's usually the slowest thing through the speed trap.

Spies kept a lid on his complaints, at least in public, for the first few races. But after Mugello and its uphill straight, he was getting very angry behind closed doors. The satellite M1's lack of power compared to the rest of the field meant a good grid position or, failing that, a brutal first lap was vital, and so was staying with a group. Ben's speed on worn tyres generally saw him make up places in the closing laps – as at Assen, as well as Silverstone. Any race from now on that failed to follow this pattern looked like a failure, such were the expectations of him, despite his efforts. Spies's ascent through other World Championships and then to the fore in MotoGP was quicker than anyone's in recent years – with the exception of Rossi's progress through 125 and 250. If anyone was going to join Rossi, Lorenzo, Pedrosa and Stoner in the 'Aliens' club before the end of the season, it would surely be Ben Spies.

As usual, the other Tech 3 rider's opinion was trenchant. As Colin Edwards declared: 'If the bike was worth a crap he'd be on the rostrum every weekend.'

Opposite top Randy de Puniet's devil-may-care style made him the crowd's favourite

Opposite bottom A message from the Doctor: 'Back soon!'

Below Alvaro Bautista and Hector Barbera renewed their old 250-class rivalry

BRITISH GP
SILVERSTONE
ROUND 5
June 20

RACE RESULTS

CIRCUIT LENGTH 3.667 miles
NO. OF LAPS 20
RACE DISTANCE 73.340 miles
WEATHER Dry, 17°C
TRACK TEMPERATURE 29°C
WINNER Jorge Lorenzo
FASTEST LAP 2m 03.526s,
105.874mph, Jorge Lorenzo (record)

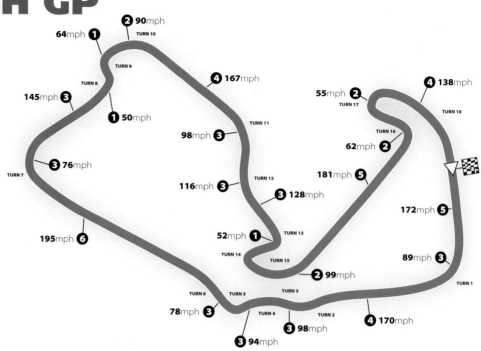

QUALIFYING

	Rider	Nationality	Team	Qualifying	Pole +	Gap
1	Lorenzo	SPA	Fiat Yamaha Team	2m 03.308s		
2	De Puniet	FRA	LCR Honda MotoGP	2m 03.434s	0.126s	0.126s
3	Pedrosa	SPA	Repsol Honda Team	2m 03.586s	0.278s	0.152s
4	Dovizioso	ITA	Repsol Honda Team	2m 03.995s	0.687s	0.409s
5	Hayden	USA	Ducati Team	2m 04.332s	1.024s	0.337s
6	Stoner	AUS	Ducati Team	2m 04.394s	1.086s	0.062s
7	Spies	USA	Monster Yamaha Tech 3	2m 04.477s	1.169s	0.083s
8	Melandri	ITA	San Carlo Honda Gresini	2m 04.555s	1.247s	0.078s
9	Simoncelli	ITA	San Carlo Honda Gresini	2m 04.868s	1.560s	0.313s
10	Edwards	USA	Monster Yamaha Tech 3	2m 05.035s	1.727s	0.167s
11	Barbera	SPA	Paginas Amarillas Aspar	2m 05.354s	2.046s	0.319s
12	Aoyama	JPN	Interwetten Honda MotoGP	2m 05.712s	2.404s	0.358s
13	Espargaro	SPA	Pramac Racing Team	2m 05.748s	2.440s	0.036s
14	Capirossi	ITA	Rizla Suzuki MotoGP	2m 05.821s	2.513s	0.073s
15	Bautista	SPA	Rizla Suzuki MotoGP	2m 06.607s	3.299s	0.786s
16	Kallio	FIN	Pramac Racing Team	2m 06.980s	3.672s	0.373s

FINISHERS

1 JORGE LORENZO As dominant a win as one could hope to see, complete with fastest lap and pole position. Only headed once, in a frantic first-lap barging match with Pedrosa, and had a lead of over 8.5s two laps from the flag before backing off a little.

2 ANDREA DOVIZIOSO Backed up his best qualifying of the year with a clever, controlled race. Involved in a serious fight for second with de Puniet and Hayden for most of the race but was able to drop back into 2m 04s lap times for the whole of the second half and pull out a slight but decisive advantage.

3 BEN SPIES First podium in his ninth MotoGP race, and the first satellite-bike rostrum finish for nearly a year. Fought with Simoncelli, then jumped the gap to the battle for second before passing Hayden on the last lap and holding off Nicky's frantic retaliation. And all with a cracked ankle aggravated by a big crash in practice.

4 NICKY HAYDEN Fourth place again, his fourth in five races. Outqualified his team-mate for the first time, and seemed to find something in warm-up. All set for the rostrum when he went past de Puniet for third, four laps from the flag, only to make a crucial mistake half-way round the last lap, giving Spies his chance to steal the place.

5 CASEY STONER A remarkable race. Clutch problems off the line saw him last into the first corner, had to get going on a tyre that had been fresh on for the warm-up lap, before battling through the field to within half a second of third. Not pleased: thought second was a racing certainty and he'd be able to give Lorenzo a fight.

6 RANDY DE PUNIET Brilliant qualifying followed by – at last – a great start and a spectacular race. In second place from lap two before being passed by, and repassing, Dovizioso, but had pushed the (softer) front so hard it was shot four laps from the finish. Slipped from third to sixth in those final laps.

7 MARCO SIMONCELLI His best result and also best race of his season so far, despite

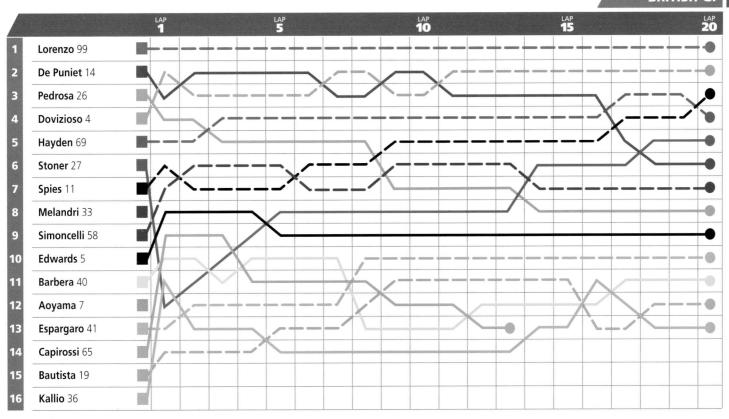

		LAP 1	LAP 5	LAP 10	LAP 15	LAP 20
1	Lorenzo 99					
2	De Puniet 14					
3	Pedrosa 26					
4	Dovizioso 4					
5	Hayden 69					
6	Stoner 27					
7	Spies 11					
8	Melandri 33					
9	Simoncelli 58					
10	Edwards 5					
11	Barbera 40					
12	Aoyama 7					
13	Espargaro 41					
14	Capirossi 65					
15	Bautista 19					
16	Kallio 36					

RACE

	Rider	Motorcycle	Race Time	Time +	Fastest Lap	Av Speed	B
1	Lorenzo	Yamaha	41m 34.083s		2m 03.526s	105.874mph	M/M
2	Dovizioso	Honda	41m 40.826s	6.743s	2m 04.117s	105.589mph	M/M
3	Spies	Yamaha	41m 41.180s	7.097s	2m 04.194s	105.573mph	M/M
4	Hayden	Ducati	41m 41.397s	7.314s	2m 04.223s	105.564mph	M/H
5	Stoner	Ducati	41m 41.577s	7.494s	2m 03.886s	105.557mph	M/M
6	De Puniet	Honda	41m 43.138s	9.055s	2m 04.135s	105.491mph	M/H
7	Simoncelli	Honda	41m 48.508s	14.425s	2m 04.521s	105.265mph	M/M
8	Pedrosa	Honda	41m 49.396s	15.313s	2m 04.191s	105.228mph	M/H
9	Edwards	Yamaha	42m 02.037s	27.954s	2m 04.666s	104.700mph	M/M
10	Espargaro	Ducati	42m 16.477s	42.394s	2m 05.510s	104.105mph	M/M
11	Barbera	Ducati	42m 17.448s	43.365s	2m 05.798s	104.065mph	M/M
12	Bautista	Suzuki	42m 17.491s	43.408s	2m 05.762s	104.063mph	M/M
13	Kallio	Ducati	42m 17.663s	43.580s	2m 05.839s	104.055mph	M/M
14	Capirossi	Suzuki	27m 33.079s	7 laps	2m 06.028s	103.829mph	M/M
15	Melandri	Honda					M/M

CHAMPIONSHIP

	Rider	Team	Points
1	Lorenzo	Fiat Yamaha Team	115
2	Dovizioso	Repsol Honda Team	78
3	Pedrosa	Repsol Honda Team	73
4	Rossi	Fiat Yamaha Team	61
5	Hayden	Ducati Team	52
6	De Puniet	LCR Honda MotoGP	46
7	Spies	Monster Yamaha Tech 3	36
8	Stoner	Ducati Team	35
9	Melandri	San Carlo Honda Gresini	32
10	Simoncelli	San Carlo Honda Gresini	32
11	Edwards	Monster Yamaha Tech 3	26
12	Barbera	Paginas Amarillas Aspar	24
13	Espargaro	Pramac Racing Team	22
	Aoyama	Interwetten Honda MotoGP	18
	Kallio	Pramac Racing Team	15
	Capirossi	Rizla Suzuki MotoGP	13
	Bautista	Rizla Suzuki MotoGP	12

a heavy crash in practice. Was able to run with the second-place scrap until a couple of laps from the end when his lack of experience with worn tyres started to tell.

8 DANI PEDROSA Two heavy falls – one in practice, one in warm-up – left Dani with a hastily rebuilt bike on which he never felt comfortable. Combative on the first lap but slipped back to his worst result of the season so far. Post-race comments focused on the bike but it emerged that he had banged his knee badly in his first crash.

9 COLIN EDWARDS Happier than expected with ninth after another difficult weekend. Still unable 'to get the bike to go where I want it to' and this lack of agility again brought on arm pump. Both problems

weren't as severe as at Mugello, and he was happy that at least things got better in the race.

10 ALEIX ESPARGARO A third top-ten finish on the run, but it could have been better. Got pushed to the back at the first corner, then quickly passed three riders, but out of range of the pack. After that it was a lonely race for the Spanish rider.

11 HECTOR BARBERA Got a good start and tried to stay with the midfield group before running wide and losing three places. Rode on his own for a while but was caught by the pursuing group, then got back on the sort of pace he'd shown in practice. Still lacking confidence on the brakes.

12 ALVARO BAUTISTA Warmer conditions on race day meant Sunday felt like first free practice as he had to learn the track at a much higher pace than he'd managed on Friday and Saturday. The shoulder injury was a handicap in the closing stages, but at least felt he was able to push for the first time since Jerez.

13 MIKA KALLIO Another discouraging race after qualifying last. Difficult to know whether it was rider confidence, the shoulder injury or his set-up that was the main problem. Lost a couple of places in the final laps which suggested the shoulder wasn't yet fixed.

NON-FINISHERS

LORIS CAPIROSSI Another crash, this time after he had to run into the gravel after outbraking himself. The combination of long corners, bumpy track and cold weather was the Suzuki's worst nightmare.

MARCO MELANDRI A first-lap crash on the brakes while trying to force past Spies.

NON-STARTERS

HIROSHI AOYAMA A nasty warm-up highside crash left the Japanese rider with a break to the T12 vertebra and out for at least three months.

VALENTINO ROSSI Absent from the paddock for the first time in 231 races following his Mugello accident.

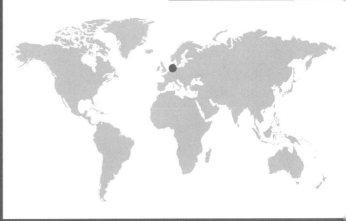

RETURN OF THE ALIENS

It looked like another Jorge Lorenzo walkover, but this time the win wasn't easy

Assen was as crowded as ever, despite the continuing absence of Valentino Rossi, but unfortunately the same could not be said for the MotoGP race. Yamaha declined to replace Rossi until obliged to do so, so there was only one Fiat Yamaha taking part. The Interwetten Honda team did get their bike on the grid, though, because HRC test rider Kousuke Akiyoshi was drafted in to replace the injured Hiro Aoyama while they searched for a long-term replacement. Unfortunately, the grid then reverted to just 15 riders when Marco Melandri dislocated his shoulder in a freakish accident on Saturday morning.

It seemed the race might be a repeat of Lorenzo's Silverstone triumph because Jorge was imperious in both practice and qualifying, but a startling improvement in Dani Pedrosa's form in warm-up on Sunday morning was a hint that things might not be as clear cut as everyone thought. Optimistic spectators also noted Ben Spies's best qualifying so far, and a solid session from Casey Stoner too. The Australian looked to be coming to terms with his decision to revert to the '09-spec Ohlins front forks. Maybe the 80th Dutch TT would be a real race, not a procession.

When Lorenzo got to the first corner and started pulling away from Spies, however, it looked likely to be another runaway win. Jorge's lead was over a second on lap two, but then the queue forming behind Ben found a way past. Pedrosa cut inside the American half-way round lap three, Stoner immediately went past on the front straight and Dovizioso repeated his team-mate's move. It only took two more laps for Dani to close right up on Lorenzo, and a lap later Casey made it a three-man fight for the lead. Or rather, it looked like

it was going to be a fight – there actually wasn't any overtaking – but the pressure kept Lorenzo honest.

The lead didn't increase significantly until half-distance, when Jorge started to take advantage of his choice of the harder tyre. Both Stoner and Pedrosa had gone for the softer option, and Dani reported afterwards that his tyres had handicapped him very slightly late on in the race, in the first, tighter part of the track. However, he was delighted with his second place, given the trouble he'd been in on Friday and Saturday. What had his team changed to alter his fortunes so dramatically? 'I don't know – all things.' It was an astonishing turnaround from his third-row qualifying, over half a second off Lorenzo's pace. Stoner was unable to push harder because he was having a repeat of his Silverstone problems with arm pump, but he was able to hang on for his – and Ducati's – first rostrum of the year. While suitably happy to be back on the podium, Casey typically remarked that it wasn't the first time he should have been there.

Lorenzo's winning margin was under three seconds. He had to wait for his harder rear tyre to come in, all the while 'keeping my mind quiet' because he was well aware that the two men behind him were a real threat. He looked comfortable after half-distance but the reality was rather different, and his tyres began sliding in the final three laps. Jorge also had one massive moment at the chicane – a rear-wheel slide so dramatic that he thought he was going to crash.

A look at the lap chart would suggest that this was a tedious race. It wasn't. It was tense, never quite catching fire in the way it threatened to do, but it was a superb illustration of the way the 800s work. Lorenzo and his crew chief Ramon Forcada understand the Yamaha M1 as well as Rossi and Burgess, and Bridgestone engineers were now looking first to Jorge as the benchmark for the performance of their tyres. That combination was proving very difficult to beat. The significant difference between the 800s and the old 990cc MotoGP bikes was that no aspect of 800

Above Lorenzo leads from the start, while Spies got his best start of the year so far; he later claimed to have been 'a mobile chicane' for Pedrosa and Stoner

Opposite Pedrosa and his crew turned around what looked like a lost cause after qualifying and Dani pressured Jorge all the way

Right The 80th running of the Dutch TT was celebrated with an appearance by Giacomo Agostini and his 1975 title-winning Yamaha; Ago won 14 GPs at Assen

Assen 2010

'THIS IS THE FIRST RACE THIS SEASON WE HAVE COME AWAY FROM WITH A DECENT RESULT'
CASEY STONER

set-up could afford to be anything less than perfect. On the 990s, the rider could make up for an imperfect setting, but not on an 800. Lorenzo's bike at the Dutch TT was near perfect and ridden by a man at the top of his form; Pedrosa's crew gave him a slightly less perfect bike and even Dani's riding couldn't make up for the grip problems in the first, slower part of the circuit. It would have needed a big mistake from Jorge to hand Dani the three seconds he needed.

Thankfully, Randy de Puniet again provided the entertainment. He started from the front row for the second race in succession and then reverted to his old habit of getting a bad start. However, he hung on to the rear of the leading group and enlivened the closing stages with a typically spirited attack on Dovizioso that was only resolved at the final corner. Equally typically, Randy and Andrea changed places at least four times in the last laps before the French rider lost fifth with an optimistic lunge on the brakes. Their dice ensured that Ben Spies wasn't troubled on his way to an impressive fourth place.

The overwhelming feeling at Assen was that the established pattern of the 2010 season had been played out again. Lorenzo looked stronger than ever; one Honda worked, the other didn't; Casey Stoner continued his gradual recovery from the disaster of Le Mans; and Ben Spies made stealthy progress. The one thing everyone did agree on was the modification to the right-hander at the end of the back straight, opening it out to take a couple of seconds off the lap time. That, at least, was a step back to the ultra-fast Assen of old, even if the racing wasn't what might have been expected at one of MotoGP's finest tracks.

Above Jorge Lorenzo welcomes Casey Stoner back to the rostrum

Below Once again, the works Suzukis found themselves dicing with the class rookies

Opposite After fading a little following a great start, Ben Spies won the fight for fourth place

SUBSTITUTE

The absence of Valentino Rossi focused attention on the size of the MotoGP grid. While the satellite Interwetten Honda team replaced Hiro Aoyama, the factory Fiat Yamaha squad declined to replace Rossi until obliged to do so by their contract with Dorna. That would be the following race in Catalunya when veteran tester Wataru Yoshikawa would ride. Of course the six-engine rule is a serious disincentive to replace a top rider, and Rossi would benefit at the end of the year. The last two engines of his allocation would be the power-up spec while Lorenzo could only take one as his sixth and final motor. There was also a definite split within Yamaha management. One faction saw a PR opportunity in putting a young charger on Rossi's bike, the other – more conservative – faction only saw the chance to reduce some engine mileage.

There is also the perennial problem of who to put on a MotoGP bike mid-season. Cal Crutchlow, still fighting in the World Superbike Championship, declined the opportunity, citing lack of testing as well as the crowded calendar and different tyres, brakes, etc. The experienced MotoGP men now in Moto2, Elias and de Angelis, had contracts, so exactly where should a team look other than to factory test riders? Twelve months earlier, Pramac Ducati had found itself in a similar situation and given the then unemployed Aleix Espargaro a temporary job. That proved an inspired choice and got Aleix his ride for 2010. However, there was no obvious candidate this time round.

Hence Honda's factory tester Kousuke Akiyoshi got to

ride the Interwetten Honda for a couple of races while the team searched for a long-term replacement. That would eventually be Alex de Angelis, who had to wait for the collapse of his Moto2 team before making himself available. Alex had been on the rostrum 12 months previously in MotoGP, but even he struggled to make an impact. What chance a youngster with no experience of the class, carbon brakes or Bridgestone tyres? Maybe the conservatives were right to play it safe.

DUTCH TT
TT CIRCUIT ASSEN

ROUND 6
June 26

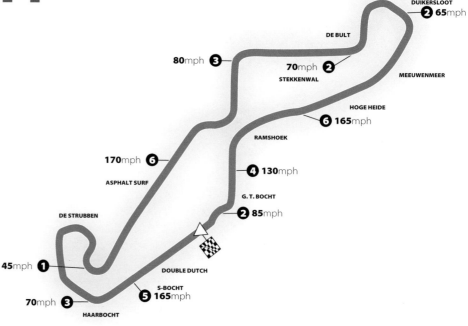

BRIDGESTONE
TYRE OPTIONS
FRONT SOFT (**S**) / MEDIUM (**M**)
REAR MEDIUM (**M**) / HARD (**H**)

OFFICIAL TIMEKEEPER
TISSOT SWISS WATCHES SINCE 1853

Circuit markers:
- MANDEVEEN
- DUIKERSLOOT ❷ 65mph
- DE BULT
- 80mph ❸
- 70mph ❷ STEKKENWAL
- MEEUWENMEER
- HOGE HEIDE ❻ 165mph
- RAMSHOEK
- 170mph ❻
- ❹ 130mph
- ASPHALT SURF
- G. T. BOCHT
- ❷ 85mph
- DE STRUBBEN
- DOUBLE DUTCH
- 45mph ❶
- S-BOCHT ❺ 165mph
- 70mph ❸
- HAARBOCHT

RACE RESULTS

CIRCUIT LENGTH 2.830 miles
NO. OF LAPS 26
RACE DISTANCE 73.592 miles
WEATHER Dry, 23°C
TRACK TEMPERATURE 48°C
WINNER Jorge Lorenzo
FASTEST LAP 1m 34.525s, 106.455mph, Dani Pedrosa (Record)
PREVIOUS LAP RECORD 1m 36.558s, 105.524mph, Valentino Rossi, 2009

QUALIFYING

	Rider	Nationality	Team	Qualifying	Pole +	Gap
1	Lorenzo	SPA	Fiat Yamaha Team	1m 34.515s		
2	De Puniet	FRA	LCR Honda MotoGP	1m 34.797s	0.282s	0.282s
3	Stoner	AUS	Ducati Team	1m 34.803s	0.288s	0.006s
4	Spies	USA	Monster Yamaha Tech 3	1m 34.926s	0.411s	0.123s
5	Hayden	USA	Ducati Team	1m 34.999s	0.484s	0.073s
6	Dovizioso	ITA	Repsol Honda Team	1m 35.015s	0.500s	0.016s
7	Pedrosa	SPA	Repsol Honda Team	1m 35.162s	0.647s	0.147s
8	Simoncelli	ITA	San Carlo Honda Gresini	1m 35.283s	0.768s	0.121s
9	Edwards	USA	Monster Yamaha Tech 3	1m 35.393s	0.878s	0.110s
10	Espargaro	SPA	Pramac Racing Team	1m 35.593s	1.078s	0.200s
11	Capirossi	ITA	Rizla Suzuki MotoGP	1m 35.664s	1.149s	0.071s
12	Bautista	SPA	Rizla Suzuki MotoGP	1m 36.344s	1.829s	0.680s
13	Kallio	FIN	Pramac Racing Team	1m 36.502s	1.987s	0.158s
14	Barbera	SPA	Paginas Amarillas Aspar	1m 36.569s	2.054s	0.067s
15	Akiyoshi	JPN	Interwetten Honda MotoGP	1m 38.198s	3.683s	1.629s
	Melandri	ITA	San Carlo Honda Gresini			

FINISHERS

1 JORGE LORENZO Win not as easy as the previous race. The harder tyre choice worked for him but he never had time to relax – the gap to Pedrosa was under half a second ten laps in. Had to keep pressing and had one big moment at the chicane in the closing laps before celebrating – and becoming an Assen winner in all three classes.

2 DANI PEDROSA Looked completely off the pace until warm-up. Changes to 'all things' produced a bike that worked – he seemed surprised – and his usual cannonball start put him in immediate contention. Used his soft tyre to pressure Lorenzo early on, setting fastest lap, but didn't provoke a mistake. Regained second in the title race.

3 CASEY STONER At last, his and Ducati's first rostrum of the year, but again had a serious problem with pump in his right forearm. Changes of direction were the biggest problem. Pleased that he now appeared to have a base set-up with the bike that should enable him to be competitive.

4 BEN SPIES Highest qualifying of the year so far followed by his best start. Tailed Lorenzo for three laps but then couldn't run at top-three pace on the soft tyre and dropped back into a superb fight for fourth. Had to work very hard to repass Dovizioso in the closing stages: a cool and calculated race.

5 ANDREA DOVIZIOSO Disappointed with his pace on race day, with front-end feel in the middle of the race getting the blame. Thought he should have been fourth, blaming the fight with de Puniet for losing touch with Spies. As in every race so far, improved on his qualifying position.

6 RANDY DE PUNIET Second front row in succession, this time followed by a bad start. Caught Dovi and Spies at mid-distance and once again provided much of the entertainment for viewers and spectators with his cavalier attacking style. Tried a big lunge at Andrea in the final chicane but went deep and was repassed.

7 NICKY HAYDEN A complicated weekend. Lost an engine due to a

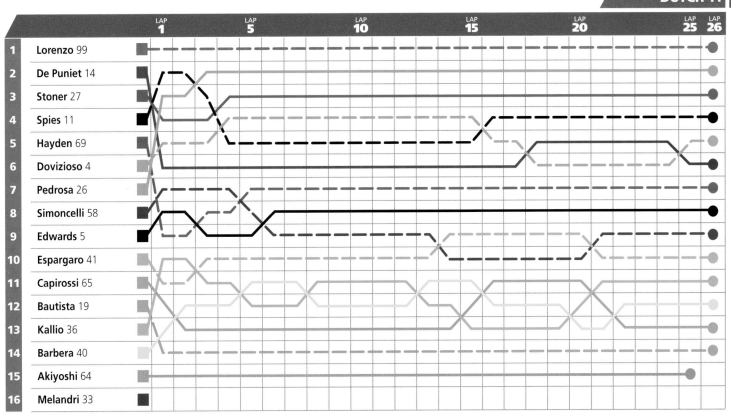

					LAP 1		LAP 5		LAP 10		LAP 15		LAP 20		LAP 25	LAP 26
1	Lorenzo 99															
2	De Puniet 14															
3	Stoner 27															
4	Spies 11															
5	Hayden 69															
6	Dovizioso 4															
7	Pedrosa 26															
8	Simoncelli 58															
9	Edwards 5															
10	Espargaro 41															
11	Capirossi 65															
12	Bautista 19															
13	Kallio 36															
14	Barbera 40															
15	Akiyoshi 64															
16	Melandri 33															

RACE

	Rider	Motorcycle	Race Time	Time +	Fastest Lap	Av Speed	B
1	Lorenzo	Yamaha	41m 18.629s		1m 34.626s	106.581mph	M/H
2	Pedrosa	Honda	41m 21.564s	2.935s	1m 34.525s	106.455mph	M/M
3	Stoner	Ducati	41m 25.651s	7.022s	1m 34.761s	106.280mph	M/M
4	Spies	Yamaha	41m 31.894s	13.265s	1m 35.068s	106.013mph	M/M
5	Dovizioso	Honda	41m 33.952s	15.323s	1m 35.063s	105.926mph	M/H
6	De Puniet	Honda	41m 34.401s	15.772s	1m 35.266s	105.907mph	M/H
7	Hayden	Ducati	41m 44.496s	25.867s	1m 35.312s	105.480mph	M/M
8	Edwards	Yamaha	41m 47.620s	28.991s	1m 35.647s	105.349mph	M/M
9	Simoncelli	Honda	41m 54.287s	35.658s	1m 35.643s	105.070mph	M/H
10	Espargaro	Ducati	41m 54.466s	35.837s	1m 35.644s	105.062mph	M/M
11	Kallio	Ducati	42m 15.398s	56.769s	1m 36.450s	104.195mph	M/M
12	Barbera	Ducati	42m 15.519s	56.890s	1m 36.281s	104.190mph	M/M
13	Capirossi	Suzuki	42m 19.244s	1m 00.615s	1m 36.219s	104.037mph	M/M
14	Bautista	Suzuki	42m 26.703s	1m 08.074s	1m 37.143s	103.732mph	M/H
15	Akiyoshi	Honda	41m 42.019s	1 lap	1m 38.056s	101.524mph	M/M

CHAMPIONSHIP

	Rider	Team	Points
1	Lorenzo	Fiat Yamaha Team	140
2	Pedrosa	Repsol Honda Team	93
3	Dovizioso	Repsol Honda Team	89
4	Rossi	Fiat Yamaha Team	61
5	Hayden	Ducati Team	61
6	De Puniet	LCR Honda MotoGP	56
7	Stoner	Ducati Team	51
8	Spies	Monster Yamaha Tech 3	49
9	Simoncelli	San Carlo Honda Gresini	39
10	Edwards	Monster Yamaha Tech 3	34
11	Melandri	San Carlo Honda Gresini	32
12	Espargaro	Pramac Racing Team	28
13	Barbera	Paginas Amarillas Aspar	28
14	Kallio	Pramac Racing Team	20
15	Aoyama	Interwetten Honda MotoGP	18
	Capirossi	Rizla Suzuki MotoGP	16
	Bautista	Rizla Suzuki MotoGP	14
	Akiyoshi	Interwetten Honda MotoGP	1

breakdown, a set of tyres through a crash on Friday and wasn't happy with the front end during the race. It all made for Nicky's worst finish of the season so far.

8 COLIN EDWARDS After recent results, Colin was pleased with both eighth place and the work he did on new front-end geometry. Reckoned he rode harder for this result than he had for fourth place 12 months previously.

9 MARCO SIMONCELLI A tough weekend. Thought he had a good set-up after qualifying but on race day found he had a totally different feel from the tyres. Took a few risks early on but then decided to 'pull the oars into the boat' and get to the finish for some points.

10 ALEIX ESPARGARO Another top-ten finish, and the smallest gap yet between himself and the race winner – and could have been even better, but for a terrible start. Regained position early on, then jumped a 3s gap to Simoncelli. Decided to let the Italian through after a few scares and couldn't retake him in the closing laps.

11 MIKA KALLIO A much better showing on a track at which he always goes well. A good start helped, but couldn't run the pace of the midfield group and spent most of the race in a fight with Capirossi and Barbera. A return to form?

12 HECTOR BARBERA Never comfortable with the Ducati, especially the electrics, and qualified last of the

championship regulars. Found 'some solutions' in the race and enjoyed a battle with Kallio and Capirossi which kept the spectators entertained.

13 LORIS CAPIROSSI The Silverstone nightmare continued: no feeling from the front meant it took at least three laps before he had any confidence in the tyre. Loris is not a man who expects to be this far back: 'It is the same to finish 11th or 13th, both positions feel the same.'

14 ALVARO BAUTISTA Thought he'd made a breakthrough after practice but had obviously overdone it because he woke on race day with severe pain in his injured shoulder which, of course, compromised his race. Like his team-mate, reported the tyres

took a long time to get up to temperature and the bike moved around a lot.

15 KOUSUKE AKIYOSHI Replacing Hiro Aoyama on the Interwetten Honda, the HRC test rider suffered a bike-destroying crash in practice but brought it home safely in the race to score the final point.

NON-STARTERS

HIROSHI AOYAMA Out long-term with broken vertebra after his Silverstone warm-up crash. Replaced by Akiyoshi.

VALENTINO ROSSI Out due to the broken leg he suffered at Mugello. Not replaced.

MARCO MELANDRI Crashed in second free practice and dislocated his left shoulder.

CATALAN GP
CIRCUIT DE CATALUNYA
ROUND 7
July 4

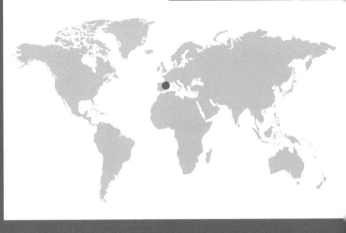

CREME CATALAN

It was three wins in a
row for Jorge Lorenzo
after all his main rivals
made major errors

After qualifying it seemed, on paper, as if Jorge Lorenzo would only have to turn up to collect the victory. However, while it's true that he put in a stellar performance on the softer tyres in the last ten minutes of qualifying, both Casey Stoner and Dani Pedrosa looked just as fast right up to the end of Saturday afternoon. As long as they chose the right rubber to cope with a track temperature of nearly 50 degrees, there was every expectation of a close race.

And for half the distance there was indeed a close race, only the man who was pressing Lorenzo wasn't either Stoner or Pedrosa – it was Andrea Dovizioso. Yet again the other Repsol Honda rider raced a lot better than his qualifying position seemed to indicate. In the first six races of the season Dovi had bettered his qualifying position every time, and he looked like doing it again in Catalunya. The Italian leapt into second place after ripping past Stoner on the second lap. He then had the temerity to take the lead, although he was deposed almost immediately. For the next ten laps Dovi was never more than half a second behind Lorenzo, and usually a lot closer. The challenge ended on lap 15 of the 25 when he crashed in the tight left that leads into the stadium section. What only he knew was that there was a problem with the Honda's rear brake that was giving him problems settling the bike on corner entry. That in turn exerted extra pressure on the front, which proved his undoing. Turning identical lap times to, and putting pressure on, Jorge Lorenzo and the M1 Yamaha puts a rider, by definition, on the limit. Andrea was able to remount and score points, but 14th place was scant reward for his gutsy race.

Left Lorenzo leads again, but this time he had to survive serious pressure, mainly from Andrea Dovizioso

Opposite Randy de Puniet got new chassis parts from HRC and had his best race of the year

Below Hector Barbera got back in the top ten for the first time in four races

There should have been two Repsol Hondas keeping Jorge honest, but Dani Pedrosa had a major scare on the way to the first corner. A serious bout of head-shaking off the start knocked the front brake pads back in their calipers, so when Dani went for the lever it didn't have any effect. 'My heart was out,' he said – the Spaniard had been staring in great trepidation at the fast-approaching fence before a few pumps of the lever got him some retardation. He rejoined in ninth place and charged back up the field, passing Bautista, Spies, Simoncelli and Capirossi on the second lap alone.

As Pedrosa caught back up to the leading quartet, Casey Stoner's chance of a win disappeared down the same slip road Dani had encountered. Going into Turn 1 on lap six the Australian caught the slipstream of Lorenzo's and Dovizioso's bikes and couldn't get his braking done in time to turn. He took an excursion off track and rejoined in fifth. Casey was able to get ahead of de Puniet next time round, but although he pressured Pedrosa for the rest of the race, he couldn't find a way past. 'He rode really well – clean and faultless, without leaving me a single gap.' The pair moved up to second and third when Dovizioso crashed.

For the third race in a row Randy de Puniet started from the front row of the grid and ended the day with a season's best result of fourth, but a gamble on the harder tyres didn't pay off at the end of the race. Neither he nor his team looked too upset, though.

There was also a startling upturn in form for Suzuki. For the first time they qualified both bikes in the top ten, and they finished fifth and seventh. The high track temperature had a lot to do with this quantum leap, but so did the return to fitness of Alvaro Bautista. Despite a machinery-induced crash in practice that tweaked his shoulder injury, Alvaro improved his best result by five places to finish fifth. The Suzuki's problem this season has always been getting enough heat into its tyres, with that particular difficulty solved

here by the weather – the riders finally got to prove what some of the competition had been saying for a while, that there wasn't too much wrong with the GSV-R. Bautista's return to form also seemed to give his much more experienced team-mate some renewed belief in the bike, although Loris's race was compromised by his choice of the harder tyre.

The most striking aspect of the Catalan GP was the number of empty seats on race day. The official crowd figure of 81,000 was far from shabby, but well down on what is usual at Catalunya. There were several possible explanations, including a clash with one of Spain's games in the knockout rounds of the World Cup, the general downturn in the Spanish economy and, of course, the absence of Valentino Rossi. Spanish fans have a lot of choice, and it would appear that they decided to stay at home and watch football on TV rather than pay to see a race with no Valentino. Despite the form of Lorenzo and Pedrosa, it seemed many fans had decided to wait for the GPs at Aragon and Valencia later in the year where they would get to see Rossi as well as their local heroes.

Valentino Rossi might not have been there, but his bike was. As Fiat Yamaha were now required by their contract with Dorna to field two bikes, tester Wataru Yoshikawa was drafted in. The likeable 41-year-old rider's job was to bring the bike home safely and not blow up any of Valentino's six engines, which he duly did. He may have been off the pace, but every time Yoshikawa came down the main straight the crowd in the main grandstand stood and cheered. The man himself might not have been there, so the fans made do with his M1.

'I THINK I RODE A CLEVER RACE TODAY'
JORGE LORENZO

Above Fiat Yamaha fielded Wataru Yoshikawa on Valentino Rossi's bike

Below But for a frightening moment at the first corner when he found he didn't have any brakes, Pedrosa would surely have challenged Lorenzo for the win

Opposite Fifth place was a season's best result for Alvaro Bautista and Suzuki

HOPE SPRINGS ETERNAL

Alvaro Bautista's stunning ride to fifth place beat Suzuki's previous best result of the year by four places. More to the point, the RSV did not look outclassed by the opposition, echoing comments from satellite team riders who'd been in close proximity to it on track and reported that there wasn't a lot wrong with it.

The Suzuki's constant bugbear has been cold tracks. It always takes time to force some heat into its tyres, with the result that Loris Capirossi and Bautista have had to wait and then try and ride through what is usually a crowded midfield. The Suzuki's other major dislike is being over on the edge of the tyre with the power on in long corners. The combination of long corners and cold tarmac, usually found in Phillip Island, is still a nightmare for the team.

However, with track temperatures above 50 degrees the main problem was suddenly gone. The other major factor was the rider's health. Alvaro was riding pain-free for the first time since the start of the year following his motocross accident before the Le Mans GP. He tried to ride in France but suffered a nasty cold-tyre crash. Although he sat out the race, the extent of Bautista's injuries was covered up. As well as the original shoulder problem, which the French crash exacerbated, he damaged several ribs. No wonder he didn't get near the top ten in the next three races. A crash, not his fault, in practice at Catalunya didn't help but Alvaro was fitter than he'd been since Qatar and was able to remind us of his potential.

Bautista's form also helped his much more experienced

team-mate. Loris Capirossi had clearly lost some confidence in the bike. Three crashes in the first five races are enough to dent the ambitions of even a trier like Loris. He finished seventh at Catalunya, handicapped by his decision to go with the harder tyre, but it was still a season's best. The question now was could Bautista carry this form into the rest of the season? The answer was 'yes', but not yet.

CATALAN GP
CIRCUIT DE CATALUNYA

ROUND 7
July 4

BRIDGESTONE
TYRE OPTIONS
FRONT MEDIUM **(M)** / HARD **(H)**
REAR HARD **(H)** / EXTRA HARD **(XH)**

OFFICIAL TIMEKEEPER

RACE RESULTS

CIRCUIT LENGTH 2.937 miles
NO. OF LAPS 25
RACE DISTANCE 73.425 miles
WEATHER Dry, 34°C
TRACK TEMPERATURE 49°C
WINNER Jorge Lorenzo
FASTEST LAP 1m 43.154s, 98.085mph, Andrea Dovizioso
LAP RECORD 1m 42.358s, 103.304mph, Dani Pedrosa, 2008

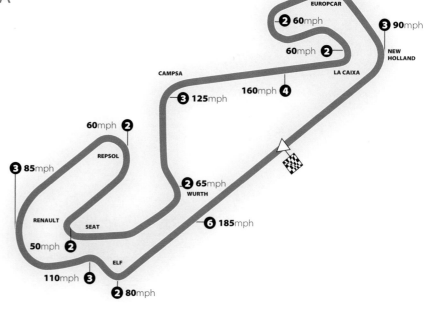

QUALIFYING

	Rider	Nationality	Team	Qualifying	Pole +	Gap
1	Lorenzo	SPA	Fiat Yamaha Team	1m 42.046s		
2	Stoner	AUS	Ducati Team	1m 42.410s	0.364s	0.364s
3	DePuniet	FRA	LCR Honda MotoGP	1m 42.512s	0.466s	0.102s
4	Pedrosa	SPA	Repsol Honda Team	1m 42.592s	0.546s	0.080s
5	Spies	USA	Monster Yamaha Tech 3	1m 42.710s	0.664s	0.118s
6	Dovizio	ITA	Repsol Honda Team	1m 42.866s	0.820s	0.156s
7	Capirossi	ITA	Rizla Suzuki MotoGP	1m 42.903s	0.857s	0.037s
8	Simoncelli	ITA	San Carlo Honda Gresini	1m 42.994s	0.948s	0.091s
9	Bautista	SPA	Rizla Suzuki MotoGP	1m 43.025s	0.979s	0.031s
10	Edwards	USA	Monster Yamaha Tech 3	1m 43.059s	1.013s	0.034s
11	Hayden	USA	Ducati Team	1m 43.068s	1.022s	0.009s
12	Espargaro	SPA	Pramac Racing Team	1m 43.380s	1.334s	0.312s
13	Barbera	SPA	Paginas Amarillas Aspar	1m 43.417s	1.371s	0.037s
14	Melandri	ITA	San Carlo Honda Gresini	1m 43.621s	1.575s	0.204s
15	Kallio	FIN	Pramac Racing Team	1m 43.685s	1.639s	0.064s
16	Akiyoshi	JPN	Interwetten Honda MotoGP	1m 45.577s	3.531s	1.892s
17	Yoshikawa	JPN	Fiat Yamaha Team	1m 45.759s	3.713s	0.182s

FINISHERS

1 JORGE LORENZO A model of consistency all weekend, at his home GP. Withstood early pressure from Stoner and Dovizioso to take his third successive win, becoming only the fourth rider in history to win three in a row in 250 and 500cc/MotoGP classes. Doubly satisfying after the last-corner defeat of 2009.

2 DANI PEDROSA Recovered superbly from a first-corner run-on with a brutal couple of laps that took him from tenth to fourth. Then profited from the mistakes of Casey and Dovi to go second, riding brilliantly in the closing stages to deny Stoner the chance of making a pass.

3 CASEY STONER The only Ducati man to have a good weekend. Lost the chance of victory at the end of the front straight on lap five after catching a two-bike slipstream. Was 'maxed out' on the brakes but had the bike turning well. Contented, but not overjoyed, with a second rostrum in two races.

4 RANDY DE PUNIET Third consecutive front-row start followed by his best result so far – with an upgraded chassis and swingarm from HRC as a reward for his form. Only Honda rider using the harder rear tyre but didn't get the hoped-for advantage in the closing stages, coming a lonely fourth, well ahead of the fight for fifth.

5 ALVARO BAUTISTA 'This fifth position is like winning.' Riding pain-free for the first time since Le Mans, he gave Suzuki their best result of the year – and, more importantly, hope. Controlled his race, with the tyres working much better on a hot track, and even held off a charging Spies in the closing stages.

6 BEN SPIES Not satisfied with what seemed a reasonable result. Felt Simoncelli's and Dovizioso's crashes made him look better than he really was. As usual, happier on worn tyres when he had the same grip levels as riders around him, so did progress in the second half, but took too long getting past Capirossi to catch Bautista.

7 LORIS CAPIROSSI Went for the harder tyre option, which gave him problems early on and in the last four laps, but in the middle part of the race Loris was more like his old self

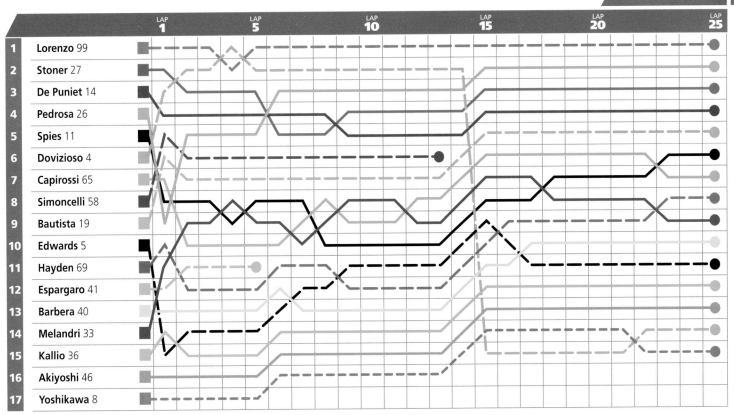

		LAP 1	LAP 5	LAP 10	LAP 15	LAP 20	LAP 25
1	Lorenzo 99						
2	Stoner 27						
3	De Puniet 14						
4	Pedrosa 26						
5	Spies 11						
6	Dovizioso 4						
7	Capirossi 65						
8	Simoncelli 58						
9	Bautista 19						
10	Edwards 5						
11	Hayden 69						
12	Espargaro 41						
13	Barbera 40						
14	Melandri 33						
15	Kallio 36						
16	Akiyoshi 46						
17	Yoshikawa 8						

RACE

	Rider	Motorcycle	Race Time	Time +	Fastest Lap	Av Speed	B
1	Lorenzo	Yamaha	42m 22.805s		1m 43.310s	101.555mph	H/H
2	Pedrosa	Honda	43m 27.559s	4.754s	1m 43.317s	101.382mph	H/H
3	Stoner	Ducati	43m 27.761s	4.956s	1m 43.276s	101.374mph	H/H
4	De Puniet	Honda	43m 40.862s	18.057s	1m 43.887s	100.868mph	H/XH
5	Bautista	Suzuki	43m 44.166s	21.361s	1m 43.929s	100.741mph	H/H
6	Spies	Yamaha	43m 44.308s	21.503s	1m 44.156s	100.735mph	H/H
7	Capirossi	Suzuki	43m 46.986s	24.181s	1m 44.190s	100.633mph	H/XH
8	Hayden	Ducati	43m 50.746s	27.941s	1m 44.390s	100.489mph	H/H
9	Melandri	Honda	43m 50.851s	28.046s	1m 44.232s	100.485mph	H/H
10	Barbera	Ducati	43m 55.244s	32.439s	1m 44.433s	100.317mph	M/H
11	Edwards	Yamaha	44m 01.211s	38.406s	1m 44.141s	100.090mph	H/H
12	Kallio	Ducati	44m 21.062s	58.257s	1m 44.952s	99.344mph	H/XH
13	Akiyoshi	Honda	44m 32.153s	1m 09.348s	1m 45.695s	98.931mph	H/H
14	Dovizioso	Honda	44m 55.207s	1m 32.402s	1m 43.154s	98.085mph	H/H
15	Yoshikawa	Yamaha	44m 58.042s	1m 35.237	1m 47.258s	97.982mph	H/XH
	Simoncelli	Honda	22m 40.799s	12 laps	1m 43.837s	101.019mph	H/H
	Espargaro	Ducati	8m 49.351s	20 laps	1m 44.326s	99.881mph	H/H

CHAMPIONSHIP

	Rider	Team	Points
1	Lorenzo	Fiat Yamaha Team	165
2	Pedrosa	Repsol Honda Team	113
3	Dovizioso	Repsol Honda Team	91
4	Hayden	Ducati Team	69
5	De Puniet	LCR Honda MotoGP	69
6	Stoner	Ducati Team	67
7	Rossi	Fiat Yamaha Team	61
8	Spies	Monster Yamaha Tech 3	59
9	Melandri	San Carlo Honda Gresini	39
10	Simoncelli	San Carlo Honda Gresini	39
11	Edwards	Monster Yamaha Tech 3	39
12	Barbera	Paginas Amarillas Aspar	34
13	Esparago	Pramac Racing Team	28
14	Bautista	Rizla Suzuki MotoGP	25
15	Capirossi	Rizla Suzuki MotoGP	25
16	Kallio	Pramac Racing Team	24
17	Aoyama	Interwetten Honda MotoGP	18
18	Akiyoshi	Interwetten Honda MotoGP	4
19	Yoshikawa	Fiat Yamaha Team	1

and visibly more confident on the bike. Getting both Suzukis in the top ten gave the team a great boost.

8 NICKY HAYDEN A chronic lack of edge grip produced his worst result of the year so far. When he did have rear grip, early in the race, it pushed the front so badly he saved it on his elbow a couple of times. Was able to push harder in the second half of the race, though, and moved up to fourth in the championship.

9 MARCO MELANDRI An astonishing result given he'd dislocated his left shoulder at Assen just a week earlier. Had also cracked his sternum, so it was no surprise he was in trouble on the brakes. Was relying totally on the right side of his body by the end of the

race, but only succumbed to Hayden three laps from the flag.

10 HECTOR BARBERA Back in the top ten for the first time in four races. Used the softer front tyre as he had no confidence in the harder option, but from lap 15 was tucking the front 'at nearly every corner' and sliding so much he reckoned he was losing half a second through the two fast rights that end the lap.

11 COLIN EDWARDS A bad start lost him five places, and although he got past Hayden, Colin immediately started having grip problems with the right side of the front tyre. Tried to carry less lean angle to avoid running wide but nothing he did could improve his lap times.

12 MIKA KALLIO Another disappointing weekend. Seemed as if he had found something in warm-up and a good start suggested the Finn was back on form, but he was a second a lap slower than the midfield group and slipped to the back of the field.

13 KOUSUKE AKIYOSHI The Honda test rider finished his two-race stint with the Interwetten team by bringing the bike home safely and beating Yamaha tester Yoshikawa. From Germany onwards the bike would be ridden by Alex de Angelis.

14 ANDREA DOVIZIOSO Pressuring Lorenzo for the lead when he slipped off at La Caixa, remounting to score a couple of points. Reported a slight problem with his thumb-operated rear brake that compromised

the last part of his corner entry and put more pressure on the front tyre. Riding at Lorenzo's pace is enough to induce a crash.

15 WATARU YOSHIKAWA Yamaha's test rider took over Rossi's bike seven years after he last raced. The double ex-Japanese Superbike Champion did what he was there for – getting through the weekend without damaging the Doctor's bike or engines.

NON-FINISHERS

MARCO SIMONCELLI Like de Puniet, had the updated frame and swingarm. Was going well, chasing the Frenchman, when he lost the front end on lap 14.

ALEIX ESPARGARO Blazingly fast all weekend but tried too hard to make up for a bad start from an average qualifying position and crashed out.

NON-STARTERS

HIROSHI AOYAMA Out long-term with a broken vertebra; replaced by Akiyoshi.

VALENTINO ROSSI Out due to the broken leg he suffered at Mugello; replaced by Yoshikawa.

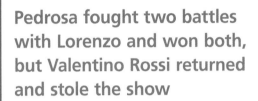

A RACE OF TWO HALVES

Pedrosa fought two battles with Lorenzo and won both, but Valentino Rossi returned and stole the show

It's hard not to feel sorry for Dani Pedrosa. The Honda man won his second race of the year in fine style, fighting off a challenge from Jorge Lorenzo both before and after a red flag led to a restart, yet all the interest centred on the battle for third place. That's because it involved Valentino Rossi.

Six weeks after he was clutching his broken leg in a Mugello gravel trap, Vale was back on the track. After a couple of tests on a Yamaha superbike he decided he was fit enough to race and, despite still using crutches, he was competitive from the off, qualifying on the second row and fighting for a rostrum finish following an understandably tentative start. The man who hadn't read the script was Casey Stoner. As well as pointing out that Rossi wasn't the first rider in history to come back from a serious injury, the Australian won the battle for third place on the very last corner with a well-planned tough pass that would have given him a deal of satisfaction. It wasn't quite revenge for Laguna Seca in 2008, but it was close.

The battle for third should have been a sideshow to the fight at the front between the two Spaniards. Pedrosa proved yet again that when he can ride as he wants to he isn't just a race winner but a World Championship contender. This wasn't one of his trademark runaway wins, however, because he had to deal with a very determined Lorenzo – and not once, but twice. Dani had swapped the lead with his countryman and was following him closely when the red flag went out because of a multi-bike crash precipitated by Randy de Puniet. It wasn't the Frenchman's first fall of the weekend. In qualifying he and Ben Spies had crashed on oil from Lorenzo's

Above Pedrosa and Lorenzo started their duel at the first corner

Opposite Randy de Puniet looks on as Espargaro and Bautista launch themselves over his fallen Honda

disintegrating engine, with Randy sliding at speed into the American's bike. His leg took a nasty blow, but not as traumatic as the one de Puniet suffered in the race. He was leading a group when he fell, and Bautista and Espargaro hit his Honda. The unsighted Mika Kallio avoided the bike but then ran over Randy's left leg: broken tibia and fibula.

When the race restarted there were only 13 bikes on the grid. Randy de Puniet was *hors de combat*, but Bautista and Espargaro weren't allowed to take part because they didn't get their bikes back to pit lane within the five minutes allowed after a red flag. This rule was introduced to prevent the instigator of an accident benefiting from the stoppage – clearly not something that applied to the two Spanish riders in this case. Nevertheless, Race Direction enforced the letter of the law and excluded them. The field was then immediately reduced even further when Kallio crashed at the first corner of the restarted race.

As in the first 'race', Pedrosa and Lorenzo swapped the lead a couple of times early on. Dani then stalked Jorge until just before half-distance before inexorably pulling away. It was a carbon copy of what had taken place before the red flag. Lorenzo realised he was on the limit just trying to stay in touch with the Honda, so he decided to settle for losing five points to his nearest championship rival.

Yet again there was the puzzling sight of one Repsol

'THIS VICTORY IS EVEN BETTER THAN THE ONE IN ITALY, BECAUSE AT MUGELLO I JUST WENT AWAY IN FRONT AND THERE WAS NO BATTLE'
DANI PEDROSA

Above Just a minor miracle: on his return from a broken leg, Valentino Rossi battles with Casey Stoner

Below There was just a bit of media interest in what Valentino had to say about his rapid comeback

Honda working perfectly while the other one struggled. Andrea Dovizioso started well but couldn't hold off Stoner and Rossi, and even in the second part of the race, which was run over 21 laps rather than the scheduled 30, he only just held off Simoncelli and Hayden. If it had gone the full distance Ben Spies would have been on his case too.

Not surprisingly, crowd and media interest centred on the final rostrum position. The only evidence of Rossi's four-race absence was a slight lack of confidence on new tyres at both starts. By the time the Doctor caught Stoner there were no inhibitions at all, and the pair swapped positions half a dozen times. Stoner then did to Rossi what Sete Gibernau had so

famously done to Valentino at the same corner in 2003. Vale rode a tight defensive line at the penultimate left but Casey was thinking further ahead. He didn't attack on the brakes – probably the most common passing move at the Sachsenring – but used all the track to carry maximum speed to the last corner, where he carved none too gently inside the Yamaha.

Rossi appeared far from displeased with fourth place and said afterwards that the shortened race hadn't affected the result: although he had some pain in both shoulder and leg, he could have raced 30 laps with no more problems. Just to show he was as competitive as ever, Valentino even got in a couple of digs. First he offered the observation that Casey would have 'cried' if their roles in the last-corner pass were reversed; he also noted that the Aussie had upped his pace considerably as soon as he reached him: 'It seems I am a great motivation for other riders.' Then, more subtly, he observed that if Dovizioso hadn't held him up he could have given Lorenzo a harder time.

Yet again Valentino Rossi had dominated a race, this time without even winning it. His comeback overshadowed issues that would otherwise have been picked over at some length. Lorenzo's spectacular engine failure in practice raised the first serious question of the year about the six-engine allowance and how or if it would affect the final races of the season. The exclusion of Bautista and Espargaro from the restarted race again highlighted the low numbers on the grid, as well as doubts about the inflexible application of the five-minute rule. And, of course, there might well have been a few more column inches devoted to Dani Pedrosa's splendid victory.

DUCATI'S WINGS

These intriguing little winglets appeared on Ducati's fairing at the Sachsenring. What were they for? The immediate assumption was that they were another attempt to generate some extra downforce as part of the search for a solution to Casey Stoner's problems with the front end of his bike. This wasn't the first time such devices have appeared on a racing motorcycle; MV, Yamaha and Suzuki have also dabbled with downforce in the past.

However, the Sachsenring is one of the slowest circuits on the calendar, so this explanation seems unlikely as any downforce generated is proportional to speed squared. Some back-of-an-envelope calculations suggest that the small surface area of the winglets would generate at most 10kg of downforce on the main straights of fast tracks like Catalunya and Mugello. Stoner said he couldn't detect any effect in Germany.

So what were they for? The clues are the vertical surfaces and the involvement of Alan Jenkins, the vastly experienced ex-F1 engineer and long-time Ducati consultant. If any realm of motorsport knows about aerodynamics, it is F1. Under Jenkins' influence, Ducati pay more attention to aerodynamics than the other factories, hence the choice of fairings for high- and low-speed circuits. Look at the positioning of the devices relative to the vents in the fairing that extract hot air that has passed through the radiator. If one thinks of them as vertically mounted aerofoils, it seems likely that the vertical fins reduce pressure at those vents, thus effectively 'sucking' more air through the radiator. With

the advent of the six-engine limit for the 2010 season, reliability is obviously of paramount importance, and increasing the efficiency of the cooling system would be a preferable alternative to increasing the size of the radiator, and with it the frontal area of the motorcycle.

The horizontal winglets may indeed generate some downforce, but the best guess is that the primary effect of the design is improved cooling.

Below A season's best for Simoncelli – sixth at the Sachsenring

BRIDGESTONE
TYRE OPTIONS
FRONT HARD (**H**) / EXTRA HARD (**XH**)
REAR HARD (**H**) / EXTRA HARD (**XH**)

OFFICIAL TIMEKEEPER

GERMAN GP
SACHSENRING CIRCUIT

ROUND 8
July 18

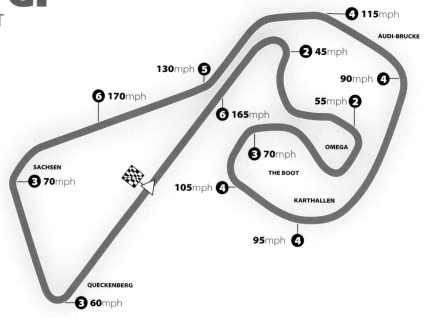

115mph **4**

AUDI-BRUCKE

45mph **2**

130mph **5**

90mph **4**

170mph **6**

55mph **2**

165mph **6**

OMEGA

70mph **3**

SACHSEN

THE BOOT

70mph **3**

105mph **4**

KARTHALLEN

95mph **4**

QUECKENBERG

60mph **3**

RACE RESULTS

CIRCUIT LENGTH 2.281 miles
NO. OF LAPS 21
RACE DISTANCE 47.901 miles
WEATHER Dry, 21°C
TRACK TEMPERATURE 31°C
WINNER Dani Pedrosa
FASTEST LAP 1m 21.882s,
99.657mph, Dani Pedrosa (record)
PREVIOUS LAP RECORD 1m 22.126s,
99.990mph, Dani Pedrosa, 2009

QUALIFYING

	Rider	Nationality	Team	Qualifying	Pole +	Gap
1	Lorenzo	SPA	Fiat Yamaha Team	1m 21.817s		
2	Stoner	AUS	Ducati Team	1m 21.841s	0.024s	0.024s
3	Pedrosa	SPA	Repsol Honda Team	1m 21.948s	0.131s	0.107s
4	Dovizioso	ITA	Repsol Honda Team	1m 22.263s	0.446s	0.315s
5	Rossi	ITA	Fiat Yamaha Team	1m 22.395s	0.578s	0.132s
6	Barbera	SPA	Paginas Amarillas Aspar	1m 22.454s	0.637s	0.059s
7	De Puniet	FRA	LCR Honda MotoGP	1m 22.610s	0.793s	0.156s
8	Simoncelli	ITA	San Carlo Honda Gresini	1m 22.624s	0.807s	0.014s
9	Espargaro	SPA	Pramac Racing Team	1m 22.910s	1.093s	0.286s
10	Melandri	ITA	San Carlo Honda Gresini	1m 22.917s	1.100s	0.007s
11	Kallio	FIN	Pramac Racing Team	1m 22.961s	1.144s	0.044s
12	Edwards	USA	Monster Yamaha Tech 3	1m 23.026s	1.209s	0.065s
13	Spies	USA	Monster Yamaha Tech 3	1m 23.028s	1.211s	0.002s
14	Capirossi	ITA	Rizla Suzuki MotoGP	1m 23.040s	1.223s	0.012s
15	Hayden	USA	Ducati Team	1m 23.090s	1.273s	0.050s
16	Bautista	SPA	Rizla Suzuki MotoGP	1m 23.193s	1.376s	0.103s
17	De Angelis	RSM	Interwetten Honda MotoGP	1m 23.515s	1.698s	0.322s

FINISHERS

1 DANI PEDROSA Not a runaway win for once, but described it as better than his Mugello victory because it involved a fight. Had to battle past Lorenzo, then take advantage of his Honda's superior corner speed to pull away. Used the same tyre as in the abandoned first start. Wore a Spanish World Cup football shirt on the rostrum.

2 JORGE LORENZO Held off Pedrosa for nine laps before succumbing to the inevitable: he'd been on the limit anyway. Realised he couldn't go with Dani so settled for second place and minor damage to his championship lead at a track he's never liked. Started from pole for the fourth time in a row.

3 CASEY STONER A third rostrum in consecutive races confirmed his renewed confidence in the Ducati. Changed to a used tyre for the restart and found a bit of extra speed to dice with Rossi. Happily played the baddie, pouring cold water on the hysteria surrounding Vale's return, putting a hard pass on him at the last corner.

4 VALENTINO ROSSI Apart from a slight lack of confidence at the start, it was almost impossible to tell he'd missed four races. Only lost third by riding a defensive line at the penultimate corner, which allowed Stoner to get a run on him. Looked happier with fourth place than he has done with some wins.

5 ANDREA DOVIZIOSO Unusually finished lower than his qualifying position. Never got his set-up right so ended up over-riding and giving both his tyres and his body a harder time than normal. Only just held off Simoncelli at the finish.

6 MARCO SIMONCELLI Best race so far in MotoGP. Changed tyres for the restart and found some more pace in the early stages, then had a scary fight with Hayden and Dovizioso in the final laps.

7 NICKY HAYDEN Made up places in the first 'race' after awful qualifying, putting himself on the second row for the restart. Lost the fight for fifth when he had a big moment at the top of the Waterfall, then the bike jumped out of gear on the last lap.

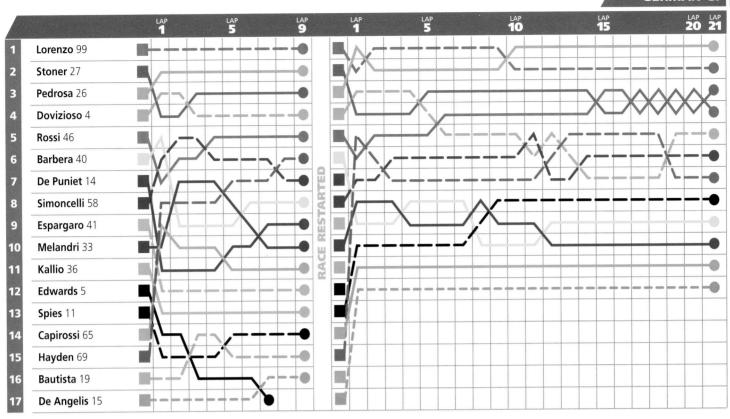

					LAP 1	LAP 5	LAP 9		LAP 1	LAP 5	LAP 10	LAP 15	LAP 20	LAP 21
1	Lorenzo 99													
2	Stoner 27													
3	Pedrosa 26													
4	Dovizioso 4													
5	Rossi 46													
6	Barbera 40													
7	De Puniet 14													
8	Simoncelli 58													
9	Espargaro 41													
10	Melandri 33													
11	Kallio 36													
12	Edwards 5													
13	Spies 11													
14	Capirossi 65													
15	Hayden 69													
16	Bautista 19													
17	De Angelis 15													

RACE RESTARTED

RACE

	Rider	Motorcycle	Race Time	Time +	Fastest Lap	Av Speed	B
1	Pedrosa	Honda	28m 50.476s		1m 21.882s	99.657mph	XH/H
2	Lorenzo	Yamaha	28m 53.831s	3.355s	1m 22.099s	99.465mph	XH/H
3	Stoner	Ducati	28m 55.733s	5.257s	1m 22.135s	99.355mph	XH/H
4	Rossi	Yamaha	28m 56.099s	5.623s	1m 22.035s	99.335mph	XH/H
5	Dovizioso	Honda	29m 07.634s	17.158s	1m 22.592s	98.678mph	XH/H
6	Simoncelli	Honda	29m 08.233s	17.757s	1m 22.644s	98.645mph	XH/H
7	Hayden	Ducati	29m 08.411s	17.935s	1m 22.604s	98.635mph	XH/XH
8	Spies	Yamaha	29m 11.433s	20.957s	1m 22.652s	98.465mph	H/H
9	Barbera	Ducati	29m 12.476s	22.000s	1m 22.983s	98.406mph	XH/H
10	Melandri	Honda	29m 25.693s	35.217s	1m 23.091s	97.669mph	H/H
11	Capirossi	Suzuki	29m 35.518s	45.042s	1m 23.965s	97.129mph	XH/H
12	De Angelis	Honda	29m 35.680s	45.204s	1m 23.865s	97.120mph	XH/H

CHAMPIONSHIP

	Rider	Team	Points
1	Lorenzo	Fiat Yamaha Team	185
2	Pedrosa	Repsol Honda Team	138
3	Dovizioso	Repsol Honda Team	102
4	Stoner	Ducati Team	83
5	Hayden	Ducati Team	78
6	Rossi	Fiat Yamaha Team	74
7	De Puniet	LCR Honda MotoGP	69
8	Spies	Monster Yamaha Tech 3	67
9	Simoncelli	San Carlo Honda Gresini	49
10	Melandri	San Carlo Honda Gresini	45
11	Barbera	Paginas Amarillas Aspar	41
12	Edwards	Monster Yamaha Tech 3	39
13	Capirossi	Rizla Suzuki MotoGP	30
14	Espargaro	Pramac Racing Team	28
15	Bautista	Rizla Suzuki MotoGP	25
16	Kallio	Pramac Racing Team	24
17	Aoyama	Interwetten Honda MotoGP	18
18	De Angelis	Interwetten Honda MotoGP	4
19	Akiyoshi	Interwetten Honda MotoGP	4
20	Yoshikawa	Fiat Yamaha Team	1

8 BEN SPIES Bad qualifying thanks to his crash, then having to avoid the tumbling Kallio at the first corner made life more difficult. In the race he closed down the group in front of him, with only the top four lapping quicker. A better result than it looked on paper.

9 HECTOR BARBERA By far his best qualifying of the year followed by a great start that put him as high as third before the red flag came out. Not quite so good in the restart but, after taking his time to get past Melandri, finished only 5s off fifth place.

10 MARCO MELANDRI A left-handed circuit was just what Marco didn't need given the dislocation he suffered in Assen. After ten laps had no strength left in his shoulder so all he could think about was getting to the finish.

11 LORIS CAPIROSSI Things looked vaguely hopeful for the restart, but a change of tyre to one used in practice resulted in 'zero grip' from start to finish. A real let-down after the confidence boost of Catalunya.

12 ALEX DE ANGELIS Riding as replacement for Hiroshi Aoyama, Alex destroyed a bike on Saturday but held it together on Sunday to chase Capirossi home. A difficult start to his MotoGP comeback.

NON-FINISHERS

MIKA KALLIO After his best qualifying of the season so far Mika gained some places following a bad start before the red flag came out. Got a little too enthusiastic at the restart and lost the rear going into the first corner.

NON-STARTERS
AFTER RACE PART 1

RANDY DE PUNIET A tale of two crashes, the first on Lorenzo's oil in qualifying, the second at Turn 4. His bike brought down Bautista and Espargaro, then Kallio ran over Randy's left leg and the red flag came out. Transported to the medical centre where he was diagnosed with a broken tibia and fibula.

ALEIX ESPARGARO An innocent victim of de Puniet's crash. Made up places after a bad start and within range of the fight for eighth when he hit the Honda, wrecking his front end. Fell foul of the rule requiring a rider to return his bike to pit lane within five minutes of a red flag. Took heavy blows to his wrist and neck and the first diagnosis was a fractured vertebra; fortunately it turned out to be an old injury.

ALVARO BAUTISTA Suffered exactly the same misfortune as Espargaro: hit de Puniet's fallen Honda and couldn't get his bike back to the pits within the required time so not allowed to take the restart.

COLIN EDWARDS A horrible weekend. Never happy, bad qualifying and crashed at the final corner when he ran wide, pushing too hard to make up on the corners what he was losing on the straights.

NON-STARTER

HIROSHI AOYAMA Replaced by Alex de Angelis as he recovered from the broken vertebra sustained at Silverstone.

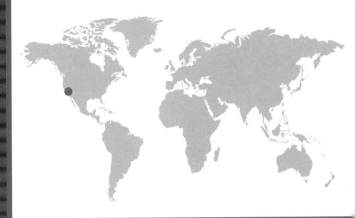

PRESSURE COOKER

Was this the race that won Jorge Lorenzo the world title? Yet again his rivals made mistakes or hit problems as he claimed his sixth victory of the season

If there's one thing that wins titles, it's consistency – and two statistics demonstrate just how astonishingly consistent Jorge Lorenzo was in the first half of the 2010 season. At the half-way mark, after the US GP, he had started every race from the front row and never finished lower than second place. He had also scored points at every round. The only other competitor to have done that – and remember there had been several races in which a rider only had to finish to score points – was Andrea Dovizioso. (There is a caveat to Dovi's record, though, because he was lucky to be able to restart when he crashed in Catalunya and went on finish 14th.)

It would be too easy to concentrate on the mistakes of the other 'Aliens' – Rossi, Stoner and Pedrosa – but it's true that all three had their problems at Laguna, as did 'Alien in waiting' Ben Spies. However, Jorge yet again put together an almost perfect weekend. It would also be simplistic to assume that he was able to adopt a risk-free strategy and think of the championship rather than race wins, but it wasn't like that either. In qualifying it looked as if Stoner had pole position and Lorenzo was in a perfectly acceptable second place. However, the Yamaha man put in two astonishing laps at the end of the session to take pole by nearly two-tenths of a second on the shortest circuit of the year. It was faster than Stoner's pole record set two years previously using qualifying tyres. Not exactly playing it safe, was he?

In the race, Jorge had no choice but to fight. He made a terrible start and found his 'Round the Outside' motto being thrown back in his face when Dani Pedrosa shot off the second row and outgunned them all, with Stoner, Spies and Dovizioso also getting past Lorenzo. Dovi was put in his place immediately, Spies was dealt

Above Pedrosa tries to pull away, Lorenzo piles on the pressure

Below Spies' race was compromised by a wardrobe malfunction – his visor kept coming open

with first time round at the Corkscrew, and Jorge ended the first lap in third but three-quarters of a second behind Pedrosa, who was clearly intent on running away from the field as he'd done a year previously. Stoner knew the danger of letting Pedrosa open a gap and he started to close up too, setting the fastest lap of the race fourth time round. The gap was below half a second a lap later, before Casey's problems began: it was the front end tucking again,

and just like earlier in the season there had been no warning on Friday or Saturday. With the 2009 forks the Australian was able to rescue the situation and was keen to point out later that he felt a lot 'safer' than with the 2010 forks. The first big moment sent him very wide and cost him second place and, unfortunately, every time he tried to raise his game he hit the same problem; it was enough to ensure Casey never challenged for the win.

That left Pedrosa pressing hard at the front, but coming under serious pressure from Lorenzo – and Jorge had a plan. He could see clearly that Dani was on the limit, but by lap eight the Honda's lead was over a second. Over the next couple of laps Jorge took a quarter of a second out of the gap, saying later that Pedrosa was racing at '110%' and he thought a mistake was likely. Lorenzo was right. With his lead reduced to fractionally over half a second, Pedrosa crashed on lap 12 while braking for Turn 5. He blamed a bump for his crash, and indeed both Marco Simoncelli and Aleix Espargaro had similar crashes at the same corner.

Pedrosa's exit left Lorenzo and Stoner uncatchable, but it did have an unforeseen effect further down the field. Valentino Rossi was part of an entertaining group that was squabbling for fourth. Rossi was stalking Dovizioso, with local heroes Ben Spies and Nicky Hayden in close attendance, but Vale discovered some extra motivation when he saw Dani in the gravel trap. 'Fourth or fifth, more or less is same, but fourth or third change a lot,' he said afterwards. It changed enough for Rossi to cross a gap of two-and-a-half seconds and take third place five laps from the flag. As

Below Ben Spies and
Nicky Hayden plummet
down the Corkscrew

everyone who has been around them has noted, the Yamahas are impeccably stable on the brakes and the Honda isn't. Rossi duly went past on the brakes going into Turn 11 and Dovi couldn't respond. In fact, the Italian only just fended off a late charge from Hayden, and he would doubtless have been troubled by Spies as well, had the Tech 3 Yamaha rider not had problems with the visor of his helmet that led to uncharacteristic errors, especially a run-on at the very final corner. A lot of observers thought that Rossi would have had trouble from Spies if the Texan had been able to run his usual race.

Rossi isn't the first racer to return from a horrible injury in an unfeasibly short time, but there was no denying he's still the biggest draw in motorsport. Laguna Seca reckoned they took $250,000 in ticket receipts in short order after it was known he would be racing. Never at a loss for a meaningful gesture, Valentino arrived on the rostrum using one crutch, which he promptly threw into the crowd. Biblical or what? Then the PA played the Italian national anthem instead of Spain's. It was the only time all weekend that Jorge Lorenzo looked seriously unhappy.

Top Casey Stoner's challenge for the lead foundered on the old problem of pushing the front

Left Rossi upstaging the winner on the rostrum by throwing his crutches to the crowd

Right Jorge Lorenzo carves through Laguna's scary first corner in glorious isolation

HALF TIME

At the half-way point of the season the six-engine rule hadn't really made itself felt but, as Jerry Burgess pointed out at the start of the year, the difference from previous seasons was that teams were planning for the last race before the first one had started.

Thinking ahead, the most noticeable trend on engine usage was that the factory Honda riders – Dani Pedrosa, Andrea Dovizioso and Marco Simoncelli – had only taken three engines from their allocation, as had Randy de Puniet. Hiroshi Aoyama and Marco Melandri took their fourth motors at Laguna. Only one Honda engine had been withdrawn, Aoyama's first, and there were suggestions that the move was down to HRC's curiosity rather than any serious problem.

At Yamaha, Valentino Rossi's enforced absence meant he was only on his third motor while the other three M1 riders were on their fourth. Ben Spies took his fourth at Laguna; Jorge Lorenzo and Colin Edwards took theirs at the Sachsenring. Two motors had been withdrawn: the one Lorenzo blew up in Germany that had been used in 21 sessions, including two races, and an engine Edwards had used in 26 sessions, including two races.

All Ducati's satellite riders were still on their third motors, with only one withdrawal – a unit Hector Barbera had used in 24 sessions, including the first four races of the year. Works riders Casey Stoner and Nicky Hayden both took their fourth motors for warm-up at the Sachsenring. Casey had had two engines withdrawn under very different circumstances, one going very early thanks to the crash at Losail, the other after being used in 30 sessions, although that might not be as extreme as it looked given his habit of doing many fewer laps than anyone else in both practice and qualifying. The engine Nicky lost in a smoky haze at Assen had done 17 sessions, including three races.

The only factory already looking to be in serious trouble was Suzuki. Loris Capirossi was still on his fourth motor; Alvaro Bautista took his fifth in Germany. More worrying was the rate of attrition. Four motors, two from each rider, had already gone back to the factory after 19, 5, 11 and 15 sessions, including four, zero, one and two races respectively.

Above At the season's mid-point, Honda were best-placed on engine usage with the factory riders still on the third motor of six allowed for the year

'I KNEW THAT DANI WAS PUSHING SO HARD, BRAKING AT THE LIMIT'
JORGE LORENZO

BRIDGESTONE
TYRE OPTIONS
FRONT MEDIUM (M) / HARD (H)
REAR MEDIUM (M) / HARD (H)

motoGP | **TISSOT** SWISS WATCHES SINCE 1853
OFFICIAL TIMEKEEPER

UNITED STATES GP
LAGUNA SECA

ROUND 9
July 28

RACE RESULTS

CIRCUIT LENGTH 2.243 miles
NO. OF LAPS 32
RACE DISTANCE 71.776 miles
WEATHER Dry, 23°C
TRACK TEMPERATURE 40°C
WINNER Jorge Lorenzo
FASTEST LAP 1m 21.376s, 97.946mph, Casey Stoner (Record)
PREVIOUS LAP RECORD 1m 21.488s, 99.098mph, Casey Stoner, 2008

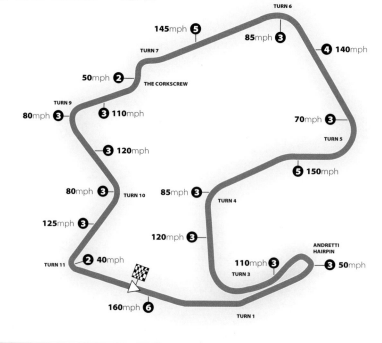

Circuit map:
TURN 6 — 145mph 5 — TURN 7 — 85mph 3 — 4 140mph — 50mph 2 — THE CORKSCREW — TURN 9 — 80mph 3 — 3 110mph — 70mph 3 — TURN 5 — 3 120mph — 5 150mph — 80mph 3 — TURN 10 — 85mph 3 — TURN 4 — 125mph 3 — 120mph 3 — ANDRETTI HAIRPIN — TURN 11 — 2 40mph — 110mph 3 — TURN 3 — 3 50mph — 160mph 6 — TURN 1

QUALIFYING

	Rider	Nationality	Team	Qualifying	Pole +	Gap
1	Lorenzo	SPA	Fiat Yamaha Team	1m 20.978s		
2	Stoner	AUS	Ducati Team	1m 21.169s	0.191s	0.191s
3	Dovizioso	ITA	Repsol Honda Team	1m 21.617s	0.639s	0.448s
4	Pedrosa	SPA	Repsol Honda Team	1m 21.655s	0.677s	0.038s
5	Spies	USA	Monster Yamaha Tech 3	1m 21.679s	0.701s	0.024s
6	Rossi	ITA	Fiat Yamaha Team	1m 21.688s	0.710s	0.009s
7	Hayden N	USA	Ducati Team	1m 21.920s	0.942s	0.232s
8	Edwards	USA	Monster Yamaha Tech 3	1m 22.217s	1.239s	0.297s
9	Simoncelli	ITA	San Carlo Honda Gresini	1m 22.300s	1.322s	0.083s
10	Barbera	SPA	Paginas Amarillas Aspar	1m 22.366s	1.388s	0.066s
11	Melandri	ITA	San Carlo Honda Gresini	1m 22.407s	1.429s	0.041s
12	Capirossi	ITA	Rizla Suzuki MotoGP	1m 22.647s	1.669s	0.240s
13	Espargaro	SPA	Pramac Racing Team	1m 22.712s	1.734s	0.065s
14	Bautista	SPA	Rizla Suzuki MotoGP	1m 22.770s	1.792s	0.058s
15	Kallio	FIN	Pramac Racing Team	1m 23.127s	2.149s	0.357s
16	De Angelis	RSM	Interwetten Honda MotoGP	1m 23.226s	2.248s	0.099s
17	Hayden R	USA	LCR Honda MotoGP	1m 23.764s	2.786s	0.538s

FINISHERS

1 JORGE LORENZO Another perfect weekend – with the exception of the start. Once he'd pressured Pedrosa into his mistake, Jorge was able to convert his fifth consecutive pole position into his sixth win of the year to take a 72-point lead in the championship. Celebrated with another spaceman act.

2 CASEY STONER Looked a potential winner until he challenged for the lead, and pushed the front. And every time he tried to push hard again he lost the front on a couple of corners, so decided that second place – his best result of the season so far – wasn't a bad idea. Puzzled and a little frustrated by his Ducati's behaviour.

3 VALENTINO ROSSI As in Germany, lacked confidence at the start but seemed to gain momentum when Pedrosa crashed and the rostrum became a distinct possibility. Closed Dovizioso down quickly and outbraked him easily at Turn 11, but suffered much more from his leg and shoulder injuries than in his comeback race.

4 ANDREA DOVIZIOSO Looked a certainty for third until Rossi's late charge. Blamed his Honda's lack of stability on the brakes and exiting corners for the loss of a 2.5s advantage. Stayed with the Yamaha for the last five laps but never looked like he could make a pass.

5 NICKY HAYDEN Average qualifying followed by a bad start thanks to a glitch with the clutch, but combative in the race and only a second away from a rostrum finish. Much faster in the closing stages of the race than he'd been all weekend.

6 BEN SPIES A stunning start put him third on the first lap, then slid to the rear of the leading group before fighting back, as usual when comfortable on worn tyres. Could have been a rostrum contender, but his visor opened when his helmet banged on the tank, causing him to run on at Turn 11 while dicing with Hayden in the closing laps.

7 COLIN EDWARDS His best weekend of the year, although refused to get excited about his finishing position. Caught and passed both Honda Gresini riders before half-distance. Slightly happier with his bike after some minor upgrades.

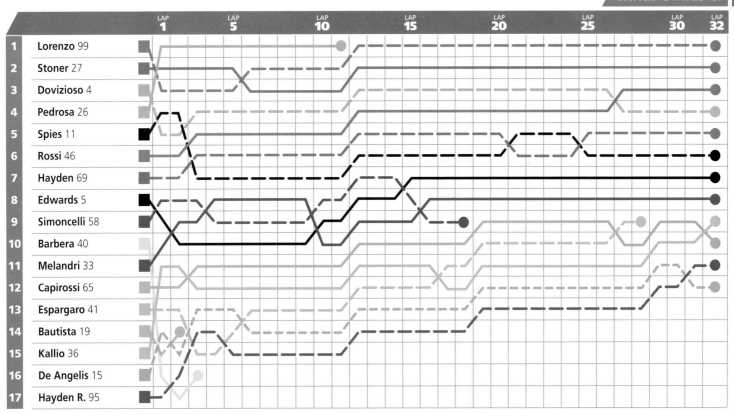

		LAP 1	LAP 5	LAP 10	LAP 15	LAP 20	LAP 25	LAP 30	LAP 32
1	Lorenzo 99								
2	Stoner 27								
3	Dovizioso 4								
4	Pedrosa 26								
5	Spies 11								
6	Rossi 46								
7	Hayden 69								
8	Edwards 5								
9	Simoncelli 58								
10	Barbera 40								
11	Melandri 33								
12	Capirossi 65								
13	Espargaro 41								
14	Bautista 19								
15	Kallio 36								
16	De Angelis 15								
17	Hayden R. 95								

RACE

	Rider	Motorcycle	Race Time	Time +	Fastest Lap	Av Speed	B
1	Lorenzo	Yamaha	43m 54.873s		1m 21.487s	98.077mph	H/M
2	Stoner	Ducati	43m 58.390s	3.517s	1m 21.376s	97.946mph	H/M
3	Rossi	Yamaha	44m 08.293s	13.420s	1m 22.116s	97.580mph	H/M
4	Dovizioso	Honda	44m 09.061s	14.188s	1m 22.039s	97.552mph	H/M
5	Hayden N	Ducati	44m 09.474s	14.601s	1m 22.112s	97.536mph	H/M
6	Spies	Yamaha	44m 13.910s	19.037s	1m 22.055s	97.374mph	H/M
7	Edwards	Yamaha	44m 35.594s	40.721s	1m 22.772s	96.584mph	H/M
8	Melandri	Honda	44m 42.092s	47.219s	1m 22.706s	96.351mph	H/M
9	Kallio	Ducati	44m 47.686s	52.813s	1m 23.318s	96.150mph	M/M
10	Capirossi	Suzuki	44m 47.687s	52.814s	1m 23.125s	96.150mph	H/M
11	Hayden R	Honda	45m 08.962s	1m 14.089s	1m 23.673s	95.395mph	H/M
12	De Angelis	Honda	45m 09.539s	1m 14.666s	1m 23.455s	95.374mph	M/M
	Espargaro	Ducati	39m 12.758s	4 laps	1m 23.029s	96.108mph	H/M
	Simoncelli	Honda	25m 05.284s	14 laps	1m 22.736s	96.568mph	H/M
	Pedrosa	Honda	15m 07.225s	21 laps	1m 21.602s	97.917mph	H/M
	Barbera	Ducati	4m 24.713s	29 laps	1m 24.472s	91.522mph	H/M
	Bautista	Suzuki	2m 58.025s	30 laps	1m 24.198s	90.725mph	M/M

CHAMPIONSHIP

	Rider	Team	Points
1	Lorenzo	Fiat Yamaha Team	210
2	Pedrosa	Repsol Honda Team	138
3	Dovizioso	Repsol Honda Team	115
4	Stoner	Ducati Team	103
5	Rossi	Fiat Yamaha Team	90
6	Hayden N	Ducati Team	89
7	Spies	Monster Yamaha Tech 3	77
8	De Puniet	LCR Honda MotoGP	69
9	Melandri	San Carlo Honda Gresini	53
10	Simoncelli	San Carlo Honda Gresini	49
11	Edwards	Monster Yamaha Tech 3	48
12	Barbera	Paginas Amarillas Aspar	41
13	Capirossi	Rizla Suzuki MotoGP	36
14	Kallio	Pramac Racing Team	31
15	Espargaro	Pramac Racing Team	28
16	Bautista	Rizla Suzuki MotoGP	25
17	Aoyama	Interwetten Honda MotoGP	18
18	De Angelis	Interwetten Honda MotoGP	8
19	Hayden R	LCR Honda MotoGP	5
20	Akiyoshi	Interwetten Honda MotoGP	4
21	Yoshikawa	Fiat Yamaha Team	1

8 MARCO MELANDRI Expected his physical condition wouldn't let him press hard for more than half the race, and that's exactly what happened. His shoulder and sternum injuries from Assen meant he struggled with braking, especially in the left-handers.

9 MIKA KALLIO Came back from crashes in practice and qualifying to make a good start and get into a dice with Capirossi. Latched on to Espargaro when he came past, then finally beat Loris to the line in a drag race out of the final corner. His most hopeful race since Jerez.

10 LORIS CAPIROSSI Had difficulties in the early laps, then tried 'a different line every lap' in the third sector – from Turn 5 to the exit of the Corkscrew – in an effort to improve his lap time, without success. Lost ninth place by a thousandth of a second, on photographic evidence.

11 ROGER LEE HAYDEN Stood in for de Puniet on the LCR Honda and did all that was expected of him. Improved his times through every session and set his best lap of the weekend making up for a tentative start. Caught and passed fellow replacement de Angelis with two laps to go.

12 ALEX DE ANGELIS Struggled badly to find any set-up that would work for him, then had tyre trouble after about one-third distance. Didn't attack Lee Hayden on the last lap when marshals started waving flags after the winner had crossed the line as he didn't know what they were for.

NON-FINISHERS

ALEIX ESPARGARO Another victim of Turn 5. Got on the white line while lying ninth, a second ahead of Capirossi, and lost the front on the brakes. Had ridden across big gaps after a bad start to catch and pass both the Suzuki rider and team-mate Kallio.

MARCO SIMONCELLI Crashed on the brakes at Turn 5 while dicing with Edwards and Melandri. It was his third crash of the weekend.

DANI PEDROSA Pushed hard while leading, after a seriously brave round-the-outside move from the second row. Was under extreme pressure from Lorenzo when he became the first of the crashers at Turn 5. Hit a bump on the brakes and lost not just a potential race victory but also his chance of challenging for the championship.

HECTOR BARBERA Went out on the third lap when his chain came off. Like Nicky Hayden, Barbera had problems with his Ducati's clutch off the start, just as Stoner had at Silverstone – the juddering may have been enough to stretch the chain.

ALVARO BAUTISTA Put out by circumstances beyond his control for the second race running when he was knocked off by Espargaro at the start of the third lap.

NON-STARTERS

RANDY DE PUNIET Recovering from the broken leg sustained a week previously at the Sachsenring. Replaced by Roger Lee Hayden.

HIROSHI AOYAMA Recovering from the back injury sustained at Silverstone. Replaced by Alex de Angelis.

TROUBLE-FREE

Once again Jorge Lorenzo didn't make any mistakes, not in the race anyway, and all his major rivals had problems

Just for a while it looked as if Jorge Lorenzo might have cracked at last. He only just scraped on to the front row of the grid, ending his run of five pole positions, and he had a big crash at the end of qualifying. Unsurprisingly, he wasn't happy with either his riding or his set-up, reckoning it was the worst session of his year 'technically speaking and for my riding style'. Sunday morning warm-up was wet, so that didn't help, and on the grid Jorge's crew chief, Ramon Forcada, could be seen giving his rider a stern lecture. Forcada was telling Lorenzo in no uncertain terms that there was nothing he could do about his front fork setting, and he should start thinking about his race.

Jorge wasn't the only one concerned about the behaviour of his bike. 'A bunch of drama' was the best description of the closing stages of qualifying, and it was delivered deadpan by Ben Spies, who ended the day as fastest Yamaha rider. First Lorenzo had thrown his Fiat Yamaha at the scenery with enough force to park it on top of a tyre wall. It was his first flying lap on a new tyre and the left side hadn't got enough heat in it. 'At least I put my bike in a comfortable place,' he said afterwards. There was more than a little worry about the engine, with Jorge saying before the race that he was one nasty incident away from being in trouble with the six-bike rule, but it seems as if he got away with it.

Then the shocks continued when Valentino Rossi crashed at the end of the session, fortunately without further damage to his leg or shoulder. It was a gentle lowside caused by too much lean angle, and he was properly angry as he walked away. This wasn't usual for

Left Lorenzo flat-out past one of the packed spectator bankings – the crowd figure was very healthy

Vale, who normally accepts a crash philosophically, but he was trying to steal a couple of tenths because he thought he had 'the potential for pole'.

Three minutes from the flag and Spies was fastest. Both Fiat Yamahas were on the floor and it looked as if the American's first front-row start in MotoGP might be from pole. Then Dani Pedrosa slammed in a time over a third of a second quicker than Ben's and the Texan had to settle for second on the grid. He didn't seem too upset – although it can be difficult to tell for those of us who haven't been observing him for years. He was positively effusive in praise of his crew, however, reporting that 'every change made the bike better'. Spies didn't think his World Superbike victory here last year had much effect, because the difference in riding style was so great. He spent Friday working that out and on Saturday was trying to get off the brakes early and let the bike run through the corners, but he found 'there was nowhere to put my elbows' so they ended up dragging on the ground.

A look at the timing sheet suggested that Pedrosa should run away with the race, but by his own admission he 'didn't put so many laps together' – and his doubts turned out to be well founded. Once Lorenzo and Spies had gone past the Honda rider in Turn 3 on the first lap, it was game over. Dani hung on to second despite wheelspin, while Stoner's now habitual front-end worries forced him to settle for third and Ben Spies was fourth. There were some heroics back down the field from the still injured Randy de Puniet – delighted to finish tenth – and an angry and disappointed Rossi was fifth.

Valentino didn't know what to blame. Where most people lost a tenth or two on race day compared with practice, the World Champion had lost a second a lap. And he knew right from the first bend that he was in trouble: it was, he said, as though he was riding in the wet and everyone else was in the dry. He had a coming-together with Capirossi in the first corner and got in far too hot on the second lap. Despite the bike being unchanged, the problem was with the front

Above Ben Spies started from the front row for the first time and didn't lose time worrying about cold tyres

Below Andrea Dovizioso looked to be making up for disappointing qualifying when he crashed out of the race

Above Brno is one of the best spectator tracks on the MotoGP calendar and attracts fans from all over Europe

Below Dani Pedrosa holds court after setting pole position

Opposite Valentino Rossi leads his future Ducati team-mate Nicky Hayden

tyre's grip, and Vale wasn't the only one having front-end problems. Andrea Dovizioso tried to hang on to a tucking front end for about 20 metres before giving in to the inevitable right in front of Edwards, Hayden and Rossi. Dovi ended up standing in the middle of the track wondering which way to jump. Valentino later reported seeing Andrea's bulging eyes behind his visor.

Rossi had experienced similar problems at Laguna, but after seven or eight laps there he'd been able to get back up to lap speeds that he thought matched his potential. This time he didn't get out of the 1m 58s bracket and his best lap was 0.7s slower than Lorenzo's best. The inquest continued at the Monday test without coming to a firm conclusion. Bridgestone blamed the surprisingly slow race and lap times on the mixed conditions, including very heavy overnight rain, and the track temperature being ten degrees down on 2009.

Despite protestations that he was now focused on the title and would take no risks, Jorge's race didn't look any different from his domination of the six other races he'd won up to this point in the season. 'Sometimes it's better to be angry,' said Jorge. 'I race so quick.' He certainly did that, although he denied that he'd forgotten about his Thursday promise to think about the championship: he wasn't going crazy, he claimed, it was all under control. Everyone laughed and the post-race press conference dispersed and immediately reconvened outside Rossi's race truck for an alfresco analysis of his unsatisfactory race. Then it was time to read his handwritten goodbye letter to Yamaha and listen to Ducati's CEO talk about the new partnership of two Italian icons. That got a lot more column inches on Monday than the race did.

AT LAST...

The worst-kept secret in motorsport was finally revealed after the Czech Republic GP. Valentino Rossi would indeed be leaving Yamaha at the end of the year, after seven seasons and four titles, and would join Ducati for 2011. Typically, Valentino's comments were delivered as a handwritten love letter to his M1, complete with crossings-out and other corrections. Yamaha's press officer was told to distribute it just as it was, totally unaltered.

The pending retirement of Masao Furusawa, the father of the M1's cross-plane crank engine, was cited as one of the reasons for the decision. As was Valentino's relationship with Filippo Preziosi when Ducati CEO Gabriele del Torchio later officially announced that Rossi would be riding in red in 2011. Rossi said he saw in Preziosi what he'd seen in Furusawa back in 2004, but, as usual with Valentino's pronouncements, there were several layers of meaning discernible.

After the Monday test he explained that he now saw 'flexibility' in Ducati's approach. There were also signs of friction with Yamaha. Rossi didn't test the 2011 prototype, but neither was he offered the modified Ohlins front fork. Yamaha said it was a 2011 component; Valentino said he would know if this were true or not as the differences were obvious. Not very diplomatic...

Perhaps the key sentence in Valentino's goodbye letter was 'My work here at Yamaha is finished.' He detailed how he, Furusawa and Burgess had turned the M1 from an also-ran into the best bike on the grid, the unspoken insinuation being 'Let's see what Jorge can do on his own.'

Another departure was crucial to Rossi's decision, namely Livio Suppo's move from Ducati to Honda. Paddock gossip made the connection between Rossi's remark about Ducati's new-found flexibility and the departure of Suppo; the two are known not to see eye to eye.

And finally, of course, there is the matter of Rossi's place in history. No rider has ever won the premier title on three different makes of motorcycle. Indeed, only four racers have even won Grands Prix on three different marques: Mike Hailwood, Randy Mamola, Eddie Lawson and Loris Capirossi. This was just another challenge that Valentino couldn't resist.

CZECH REPUBLIC GP
AUTOMOTODROM BRNO

ROUND 10
August 15

BRIDGESTONE
TYRE OPTIONS
FRONT HARD (**H**) / EXTRA HARD (**XH**)
REAR MEDIUM (**M**) / HARD (**H**)

TISSOT SWISS WATCHES SINCE 1853
OFFICIAL TIMEKEEPER

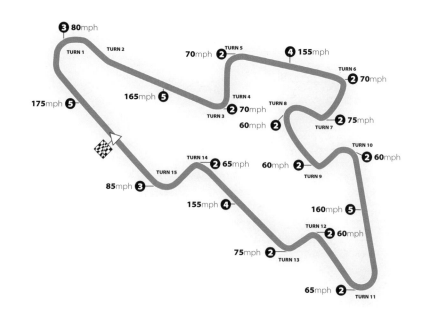

RACE RESULTS

CIRCUIT LENGTH 3.357 miles
NO. OF LAPS 22
RACE DISTANCE 73.854 miles
WEATHER Dry, 26°C
TRACK TEMPERATURE 40°C
WINNER Jorge Lorenzo
FASTEST LAP 1m 57.524s, 102.168mph, Jorge Lorenzo
LAP RECORD 1m 56.670s, 103.592mph, Jorge Lorenzo, 2009

QUALIFYING

	Rider	Nationality	Team	Qualifying	Pole +	Gap
1	Pedrosa	SPA	Repsol Honda Team	1m 56.508s		
2	Spies	USA	Monster Yamaha Tech 3	1m 56.846s	0.338s	0.338s
3	Lorenzo	SPA	Fiat Yamaha Team	1m 56.865s	0.357s	0.019s
4	Stoner	AUS	Ducati Team	1m 56.868s	0.360s	0.003s
5	Rossi	ITA	Fiat Yamaha Team	1m 57.059s	0.551s	0.191s
6	Dovizioso	ITA	Repsol Honda Team	1m 57.117s	0.609s	0.058s
7	Edwards	USA	Monster Yamaha Tech 3	1m 57.222s	0.714s	0.105s
8	Hayden	USA	Ducati Team	1m 57.635s	1.127s	0.413s
9	Barbera	SPA	Paginas Amarillas Aspar	1m 57.960s	1.452s	0.325s
10	Capirossi	ITA	Rizla Suzuki MotoGP	1m 57.981s	1.473s	0.021s
11	De Puniet	FRA	LCR Honda MotoGP	1m 58.089s	1.581s	1.108s
12	Simoncelli	ITA	San Carlo Honda Gresini	1m 58.169s	1.661s	0.080s
13	Kallio	FIN	Pramac Racing Team	1m 58.182s	1.674s	0.013s
14	Melandri	ITA	San Carlo Honda Gresini	1m 58.430s	1.922s	0.248s
15	De Angelis	RSM	Interwetten Honda MotoGP	1m 58.522s	2.014s	0.092s
16	Espargaro	SPA	Pramac Racing Team	1m 58.700s	2.192s	0.178s
	Bautista	SPA	Rizla Suzuki MotoGP			

FINISHERS

1 JORGE LORENZO Worries after qualifying but this was another convincing win, the 50th by a Spanish rider in the top class. Blasted past a hesitant Pedrosa in the third corner and was never headed. Took ten laps to get the lead up to a second, then it was a matter of maintaining concentration. The win extended his title lead to 77 points.

2 DANI PEDROSA Got the holeshot from pole but was 'too concerned about tyre temperature' and was shuffled back. Set a very fast time on lap seven trying to stay with Jorge, then had problems with 'too much spinning' on corner exit

compromising his drive. Relieved to be back on the rostrum after his Laguna disaster, but not happy.

3 CASEY STONER His fifth consecutive rostrum, but not overjoyed: the usual front-end problems slowed him at the start and when things got better he was too far from the leaders to mount a challenge. 'Seems about it, the weekend always ends up the same.' Tested a new Ohlins front fork on the Monday.

4 BEN SPIES First front row and able to run with the leaders from the start for the first time: he saw it as a big step forward. Hit a set-up problem with the front – not the tyre – tucking on the throttle. Only had a second on Stoner and reckoned the problem cost a half-second a lap, so had to settle for fourth.

5 VALENTINO ROSSI A very strange weekend at a track Vale loves. A crash in qualifying, then a bad start; mistakes at Turn 1 on the first two laps and a front-end problem that put him back to eighth for five laps, lapping a second slower than he'd been in qualifying. Did get past Edwards and Hayden.

6 NICKY HAYDEN Broke the tip off his radius in practice, so this has to be seen as a good result. Held on to Rossi for a few laps, but after that had a lonely race. Adrenaline kept the pain at bay, but it kicked in as soon as he crossed the line, although amazingly he managed to test on the Monday.

7 COLIN EDWARDS Happier than expected with seventh place. New front-end geometry helped him turn the bike and he

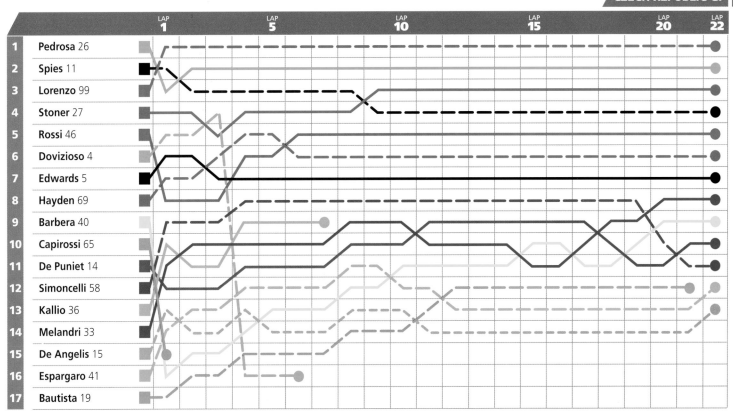

		LAP 1	LAP 5	LAP 10	LAP 15	LAP 20	LAP 22
1	Pedrosa 26						
2	Spies 11						
3	Lorenzo 99						
4	Stoner 27						
5	Rossi 46						
6	Dovizioso 4						
7	Edwards 5						
8	Hayden 69						
9	Barbera 40						
10	Capirossi 65						
11	De Puniet 14						
12	Simoncelli 58						
13	Kallio 36						
14	Melandri 33						
15	De Angelis 15						
16	Espargaro 41						
17	Bautista 19						

RACE

	Rider	Motorcycle	Race Time	Time +	Fastest Lap	Av Speed	B
1	Lorenzo	Yamaha	43m 22.638s		1m 57.524s	102.168mph	XH/M
2	Pedrosa	Honda	43m 28.132s	5.494s	1m 57.712s	101.953mph	XH/M
3	Stoner	Ducati	43m 34.064s	11.426s	1m 58.121s	101.721mph	XH/M
4	Spies	Yamaha	43m 36.361s	13.723s	1m 58.001s	101.632mph	XH/M
5	Rossi	Yamaha	43m 40.568s	17.930s	1m 58.240s	101.469mph	XH/M
6	Hayden	Ducati	43m 49.453s	26.815s	1m 58.433s	101.126mph	XH/M
7	Edwards	Yamaha	43m 56.034s	33.396s	1m 58.469s	100.873mph	XH/M
8	Melandri	Honda	44m 02.044s	39.406s	1m 59.328s	100.644mph	XH/M
9	Barbera	Ducati	44m 02.277s	39.639s	1m 59.251s	100.635mph	XH/M
10	De Puniet	Honda	44m 03.531s	40.893s	1m 59.416s	100.587mph	XH/M
11	Simoncelli	Honda	44m 04.670s	42.032s	1m 58.630s	100.544mph	XH/M
12	Espargaro	Ducati	44m 09.729s	47.091s	1m 59.611s	100.352mph	XH/M
13	De Angelis	Honda	44m 14.006s	51.368s	1m 59.487s	100.190mph	XH/M
	Bautista	Suzuki	42m 04.519s	1 lap	1m 59.197s	100.541mph	XH/M
	Kallio	Ducati	14m 06.189s	15 laps	1m 59.524s	99.985mph	XH/M
	Dovizioso	Honda	12m 59.533s	16 laps	1m 58.045s	93.030mph	XH/M
	Capirossi	Suzuki	2m 08.360s	21 laps	2m 08.360s	94.162mph	XH/M

CHAMPIONSHIP

	Rider	Team	Points
1	Lorenzo	Fiat Yamaha Team	235
2	Pedrosa	Repsol Honda Team	158
3	Stoner	Ducati Team	119
4	Dovizioso	Repsol Honda Team	115
5	Rossi	Fiat Yamaha Team	101
6	Hayden N	Ducati Team	99
7	Spies	Monster Yamaha Tech 3	90
8	De Puniet	LCR Honda MotoGP	75
9	Melandri	San Carlo Honda Gresini	61
10	Edwards	Monster Yamaha Tech 3	57
11	Simoncelli	San Carlo Honda Gresini	54
12	Barbera	Paginas Amarillas Aspar	48
13	Capirossi	Rizla Suzuki MotoGP	36
14	Espargaro	Pramac Racing Team	32
15	Kallio	Pramac Racing Team	31
16	Bautista	Rizla Suzuki MotoGP	25
17	Aoyama	Interwetten Honda MotoGP	18
18	De Angelis	Interwetten Honda MotoGP	11
19	Hayden R	LCR Honda MotoGP	5
20	Akiyoshi	Interwetten Honda MotoGP	4
21	Yoshikawa	Fiat Yamaha Team	1

was hoping for his first top-six finish of the year at a track where he's never been higher than sixth. Like many others, didn't have the same feel with the front tyre on race day as he'd had in practice.

8 MARCO MELANDRI Came out on top of a spectacular group dice despite terrible qualifying and a bad start. Struggled at the beginning, and his ongoing problems with electronics made it difficult for him to overtake, but looked more like his old self in the closing stages.

9 HECTOR BARBERA Started the race with a new clutch to avoid a repeat of his Laguna problems, but made a complete hash of it and was almost last off the line. A controlled and spirited fight saw him join the group dice. Said his lap times in the race showed he could have caught Edwards but for his bad start.

10 RANDY DE PUNIET Racing a remarkable four weeks after his accident in Germany. Banged his injured leg on Friday, crashed on Saturday, but after painkilling injections got involved in the dice and beat Simoncelli. Exhausted, with seven laps to go, he was passed by Barbera and Melandri, but delighted to be so competitive.

11 MARCO SIMONCELLI Looked to be in a safe eighth place until the final laps when caught by the group 'as if I was on a bike from a different category'. Lost the front a few times, then couldn't get the power down in the higher gears. The team had changed the set-up overnight, but wet warm-up meant they didn't get to test it.

12 ALEIX ESPARGARO Found a set-up that enabled him to get into corners much better than in qualifying and started the race impressively – getting up to 11th from 16th on the grid – then ran into problems with arm pump. Decided finishing was a better idea than trying to catch the group in front, after crashing in the last three races.

13 ALEX DE ANGELIS Replaced Aoyama for the third time. Put on the grass by Espargaro early on, then hit stability problems in the closing stages, which resulted in another off-track excursion.

NON-FINISHERS

ALVARO BAUTISTA Raced despite not taking part in qualifying after a big crash in second free practice. Caught the group but fell at the final corner when he lost the front trying to pass Simoncelli.

MIKA KALLIO Another front-end crash victim. Looked much better than in qualifying but crashed while chasing Simoncelli, shortly after passing Melandri.

ANDREA DOVIZIOSO Had just taken fourth place when he lost the front at Turn 9. Held the bike up on his knee for so long that he ended up in the middle of the track and was very lucky not to be hit by following riders who dodged either side of him.

LORIS CAPIROSSI Hit by Rossi in the first corner after which he had to push his clutch lever back into place. Immediately repassed four riders before losing the front at Turn 12 on the second lap.

NON-STARTERS

HIROSHI AOYAMA Recovering from injuries sustained at Silverstone. Replaced by Alex de Angelis.

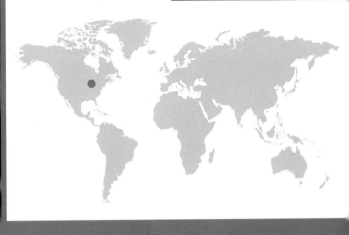

THREE AT LAST

Pedrosa reminded everyone he was a contender, while Lorenzo had his worst weekend of the year but still finished on the rostrum

Twelve months previously Dani Pedrosa had looked an odds-on winner of the Indianapolis GP. He had been fastest in every session, set pole position by a substantial margin and was leading at the end of lap four when he fell at the final corner. Despite significant damage to the bike he got back on and was the fastest man on track in the closing stages. This year things didn't look so good. Dani didn't even make the front row and was very worried about having to use the harder tyre option for the race; the other Repsol Honda man, Andrea Dovizioso, also had to go for the hard tyre, a choice made by only two other riders.

For once, Pedrosa didn't get his usual cannonball start. He was fourth into the first corner, with local heroes Ben Spies and Nicky Hayden in front of him as well as team-mate Dovizioso. Dani started making progress on the third lap when Hayden ripped off his left kneeslider on a drain cover, ruining what had looked like a promising race after his first front-row qualification as a Ducati rider. Pedrosa passed Dovi next time round, and now with some confidence in his tyres he started closing down Spies. The Texan had started from his first pole position in MotoGP, the first time a satellite bike has been fastest in qualifying since the Chinese GP of 2008. The inevitable happened at the end of lap seven. Dani's Honda was getting out of the tight final corner and down the front straight much quicker than the Yamaha and he powered past just as the pair crossed the yard of bricks. He then pulled inexorably away, setting the fastest lap of the race on lap 11.

Significantly, this was Pedrosa's third victory of the year. In all his previous four seasons as a MotoGP rider he'd only managed two wins per year and in 2009 he only achieved his second victory at the final race of the

Right When was the last time Rossi crashed three times in a weekend? He couldn't remember either

Opposite The Indianapolis Motor Speedway is built on a different scale to most tracks

Below Ben Spies leads the field across one of the Speedway's many changes of surface

'IF YOU JUST MISS ONE LINE IN ONE CORNER, YOU CAN BE IMMEDIATELY ON THE GROUND'
DANI PEDROSA

championship. This win, at this stage in the season, removed a very large monkey from Dani's back – and it hadn't been easy. The Spanish rider was working very hard in vicious conditions, pushing the Honda upright and on to the fat part of the tyre as he came onto the straights and visibly fighting the bike. In temperatures of over 35° Centigrade and tarmac temperatures above 55° it would have been all too easy to make a mistake. Get off line on to the dirty part of the track and you were down, said Dani, especially on worn tyres.

No-one was arguing with that statement. Valentino Rossi crashed three times over the weekend; he couldn't remember even crashing twice in one race meeting at any time in his GP career. Casey Stoner crashed in the race as well as in practice – those front-end problems again – and both men were vociferous in their complaints about the track. Not only are there four different surfaces but there are also some very big bumps, while the final right-hander seemed to be seriously lacking in grip. The big bump at Turn 6 got both Rossi and Spies in practice, Valentino pointing out that the riders had asked for that particular crater to be filled in two years ago. Stoner told a local newspaper that 70% of the track needed to be resurfaced.

Of course the temperature also made things more difficult because the track wasn't just bumpy – as it has been for the past two years – but it was very greasy as well, as the plethora of crashes in the 125 and Moto2 races demonstrated. TV cameras caught Ben Spies having a massive slide going into the first corner late in the race. There was also the matter of the drain covers, installed after the flooding of 2008. Not only was

Hayden's race ruined when his kneeslider was ripped off by one, Stoner had two similar incidents in practice and the matter was brought to the attention of officials on Friday.

The race wasn't just about avoiding the bumps and coping with the surface, however; it concerned physical endurance too. The only man who didn't look like he'd had a hard day was Spies. Pedrosa was shattered – the water supply in the hump of his leathers hadn't been working; Lorenzo had to sit down afterwards in *parc fermé*; and Valentino Rossi said he'd started seeing visions of St Peter between Turns 2 and 3. The patron saint of travellers obviously convinced him that fourth place was good enough. Rossi said his lack of fitness told towards the end of the race, although he was pleased with his pace and set-up. He wasn't alone. Hiro Aoyama and Randy de Puniet struggled at the back of the field with their injuries.

Pedrosa's win closed the gap at the top of the championship slightly, with Lorenzo's lead shrinking by nine points, although he still had a healthy 68-point margin. Jorge wasn't at all pleased with his weekend. A bad start meant he couldn't get on terms with the front two, and third place was his worst result of the year so far. Finishing behind another Yamaha wasn't something he was used to. Not only was this Spies's first pole, it was the first time he was first Yamaha man home – and all in front of his home fans on the weekend Yamaha officially confirmed he would be in the factory team for 2011. After qualifying, Rossi had remarked that 'Lorenzo will have his own Jorge in the garage next year.' Pedrosa might have won more than two races in a season for the first time in his five-year MotoGP career, but just over half-way through his rookie year as a full-time MotoGP rider Ben Spies had served warning that he would be a threat for the foreseeable future.

Above Only Spies looked cool in parc fermé; the two Spaniards were severely affected by the heat

Below Check the left knee of Hayden's leathers: his kneeslider was ripped off by a drain cover on lap 3

Opposite Lorenzo sported a special helmet design inspired by the film *Iron Man*

COMING SOON

The 2011 season will be the last year of the 800cc MotoGP formula. From 2012, the technical regulations will allow engines of up to 1,000cc with a maximum of four cylinders and a maximum bore of 81mm. The big change will be the introduction of a distinction between factory teams, who will have to stick to the current limits of 21 litres of fuel and six engines for the season, and Claiming Rule Teams – CRTs.

What are CRTs? Basically, these are private teams that will be allowed to use engines based on street motorcycles – much like the old TT F1 championship, precursor of Superbikes, which specified that bikes must use main engine cases from homologated street bikes. Bikes like the Honda RVF therefore used VFR750 cases, barrels and heads with highly tuned internals in prototype chassis. CRT bikes will be allowed to use three more litres of fuel per race and double the number of engines per season.

The Grand Prix Commission will decide which squads qualify as CRTs, and will obviously be wary of thinly disguised factory efforts. The GPC will also have the right to reclassify teams if they over-perform. However, any new manufacturer entering the championship will be allowed nine motors, rather than six, for their first season. This is clearly an invitation to BMW and Aprilia.

Next year will also be the last season of the 125cc formula. From 2012 the junior class of MotoGP will be called Moto3. Details have still to be worked out, but the basic engine specification will be a single-cylinder four-stroke with, like MotoGP, a maximum bore of 81mm. Unlike Moto2,

Above This is what Moto3 will look like: the Moriwaki MD250H used in junior racing in the USA features a Honda CRF250X engine plus RS125 suspension and brakes

this class is not going to start life with a control motor. However, engines must not cost more than €10,000 and they will be required to last for at least three races. Any manufacturer must be able to supply at least 15 riders, if required. As for Moto2, it will see out its three-year contract with Honda before the control-engine rule is scrapped in 2014.

BRIDGESTONE

TYRE OPTIONS
FRONT MEDIUM (M) / HARD (H)
REAR HARD (H) / EXTRA HARD (XH)

motoGP T+ TISSOT
SWISS WATCHES SINCE 1853
OFFICIAL TIMEKEEPER

INDIANAPOLIS GP
INDIANAPOLIS MOTOR SPEEDWAY

ROUND 11
August 29

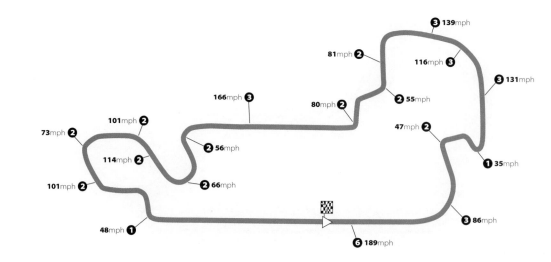

RACE RESULTS

CIRCUIT LENGTH 2.620 miles
NO. OF LAPS 28
RACE DISTANCE 73.360 miles
WEATHER Dry, 35°C
TRACK TEMPERATURE 56°C
WINNER Dani Pedrosa
FASTEST LAP 1m 40.896s, 92.605mph, Dani Pedrosa
LAP RECORD 1m 40.152s, 94.166mph, Jorge Lorenzo, 2009

QUALIFYING

	Rider	Nationality	Team	Qualifying	Pole +	Gap
1	Spies	USA	Monster Yamaha Tech 3	1m 40.105s		
2	Lorenzo	SPA	Fiat Yamaha Team	1m 40.325s	0.220s	0.220s
3	Hayden N	USA	Ducati Team	1m 40.336s	0.231s	0.011s
4	Dovizioso	ITA	Repsol Honda Team	1m 40.559s	0.454s	0.223s
5	Pedrosa	SPA	Repsol Honda Team	1m 40.637s	0.532s	0.078s
6	Stoner	AUS	Ducati Team	1m 40.664s	0.559s	0.027s
7	Rossi	ITA	Fiat Yamaha Team	1m 41.005s	0.900s	0.341s
8	Simoncelli	ITA	San Carlo Honda Gresini	1m 41.092s	0.987s	0.087s
9	Edwards	USA	Monster Yamaha Tech 3	1m 41.232s	1.127s	0.140s
10	Capirossi	ITA	Rizla Suzuki MotoGP	1m 41.512s	1.407s	0.280s
11	Bautista	SPA	Rizla Suzuki MotoGP	1m 41.534s	1.429s	0.022s
12	Melandri	ITA	San Carlo Honda Gresini	1m 41.623s	1.518s	0.089s
13	Aoyama	JPN	Interwetten Honda MotoGP	1m 41.631s	1.526s	0.008s
14	Espargaro	SPA	Pramac Racing Team	1m 41.649s	1.544s	0.018s
15	Kallio	FIN	Pramac Racing Team	1m 41.856s	1.751s	0.207s
16	Barbera	SPA	Paginas Amarillas Aspar	1m 41.896s	1.791s	0.040s
17	De Puniet	FRA	LCR Honda MotoGP	1m 41.923s	1.818s	0.027s

FINISHERS

1 DANI PEDROSA Three wins in a season for the first time. Overcame disappointing qualifying to work his way past the leaders and pull away despite having to use the harder tyre. Used the Honda's acceleration on the front straight but also had the handling well sorted.

2 BEN SPIES First pole position, led a race for the first time, a season's best finish and first Yamaha home for the first time. Laconically remarked that he didn't make too many mistakes and it was a 'big race' – and all on the weekend where he was confirmed as a factory rider for the 2011 season.

3 JORGE LORENZO Not bad for his worst race of the season so far. Qualified well but didn't get a good start and was then held up by Dovizioso. Wasn't happy with his race: 'I didn't have the physical strength. It was like in Malaysia last year.'

4 VALENTINO ROSSI An unheard-of three crashes in a weekend for Vale: he managed to fall off every day. Luckily his Sunday crash was in warm-up. Suffered from his lack of fitness in the race, deciding fourth place wasn't too bad a reward.

5 ANDREA DOVIZIOSO Like his team-mate, had to start on the harder tyre. Began well but shuffled back in the early stages. Not happy after the race and commented that his radically different set-up from Pedrosa's, and even how he sat on the bike, might need to be worked on.

6 NICKY HAYDEN After his first front-row start as a Ducati rider and promising pace in practice, Nicky's race was ruined when he tore his left kneeslider and its Velcro off his leg on the third lap. All prospects of a third rostrum finish at Indy vanished immediately.

7 MARCO SIMONCELLI Pleased with his race, if not his finishing position. Realised he couldn't push as he had in practice but held off a spirited attack from Bautista in the closing stages.

8 ALVARO BAUTISTA First finish since Catalunya and third top-ten placing. Boxed

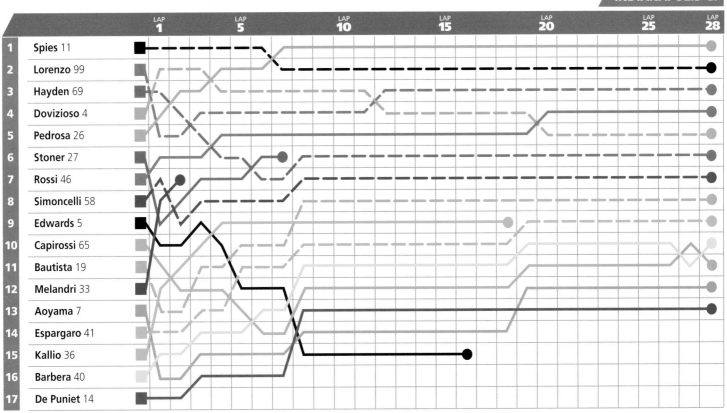

		LAP 1	LAP 5	LAP 10	LAP 15	LAP 20	LAP 25	LAP 28
1	Spies 11							
2	Lorenzo 99							
3	Hayden 69							
4	Dovizioso 4							
5	Pedrosa 26							
6	Stoner 27							
7	Rossi 46							
8	Simoncelli 58							
9	Edwards 5							
10	Capirossi 65							
11	Bautista 19							
12	Melandri 33							
13	Aoyama 7							
14	Espargaro 41							
15	Kallio 36							
16	Barbera 40							
17	De Puniet 14							

RACE

	Rider	Motorcycle	Race Time	Time +	Fastest Lap	Av Speed	B
1	Pedrosa	Honda	47m 31.615s		1m 40.896s	92.605mph	H/XH
2	Spies	Yamaha	47m 35.190s	3.575s	1m 41.417s	92.490mph	H/H
3	Lorenzo	Yamaha	47m 38.427s	6.812s	1m 41.490s	92.385mph	H/H
4	Rossi	Yamaha	47m 44.248s	12.633s	1m 41.436s	92.197mph	H/H
5	Dovizioso	Honda	47m 53.500s	21.885s	1m 41.569s	91.900mph	H/XH
6	Hayden	Ducati	48m 06.753s	35.138s	1m 42.182s	91.478mph	H/H
7	Simoncelli	Honda	48m 08.355s	36.740s	1m 42.450s	91.354mph	H/H
8	Bautista	Suzuki	48m 08.440s	36.825s	1m 42.288s	91.425mph	H/H
9	Espargaro	Ducati	48m 16.520s	44.905s	1m 42.416s	91.170mph	H/H
10	Barbera	Ducati	48m 22.983s	51.368s	1m 42.708s	90.967mph	H/H
11	Capirossi	Suzuki	48m 27.001s	55.386s	1m 42.757s	90.841mph	H/H
12	Aoyama	Honda	48m 29.518s	57.903s	1m 42.917s	90.762mph	H/H
13	De Puniet	Honda	48m 35.754s	1m 04.139s	1m 42.866s	90.569mph	H/H
	Kallio	Ducati	30m 57.694s	10 laps	1m 42.299s	91.384mph	H/H
	Edwards	Yamaha	30m 09.466s	12 laps	1m 42.435s	83.395mph	H/XH
	Stoner	Ducati	12m 01.423s	21 laps	1m 41.417s	91.512mph	H/XH
	Melandri	Honda	3m 31.585s	26 laps	1m 42.010s	89.149mph	H/H

CHAMPIONSHIP

	Rider	Team	Points
1	Lorenzo	Fiat Yamaha Team	251
2	Pedrosa	Repsol Honda Team	183
3	Dovizioso	Repsol Honda Team	126
4	Stoner	Ducati Team	119
5	Rossi	Fiat Yamaha Team	114
6	Spies	Monster Yamaha Tech 3	110
7	Hayden N	Ducati Team	109
8	De Puniet	LCR Honda MotoGP	78
9	Simoncelli	San Carlo Honda Gresini	63
10	Melandri	San Carlo Honda Gresini	61
11	Edwards	Monster Yamaha Tech 3	57
12	Barbera	Paginas Amarillas Aspar	54
13	Capirossi	Rizla Suzuki MotoGP	41
14	Espargaro	Pramac Racing Team	39
15	Bautista	Rizla Suzuki MotoGP	33
16	Kallio	Pramac Racing Team	31
17	Aoyama	Interwetten Honda MotoGP	22
18	De Angelis	Interwetten Honda MotoGP	11
19	Hayden R	LCR Honda MotoGP	5
20	Akiyoshi	Interwetten Honda MotoGP	4
21	Yoshikawa	Fiat Yamaha Team	1

in on the first lap, came back strongly but thought better of attacking Simoncelli on the two likely passing corners because of the bumps. Pleased to prove his fitness under the most extreme of conditions.

9 ALEIX ESPARGARO Best finish since Mugello. Got a good start for once and passed Edwards and Capirossi on the fifth lap before closing on team-mate Kallio. Then found track conditions wouldn't let him up the pace to try to catch the Bautista–Simoncelli dice.

10 HECTOR BARBERA Improved on his qualifying by six places despite the front tucking on every corner. Had to 'pay attention in every corner to stay upright' and 'didn't have much fun out there',

but still raised the enthusiasm to barge Capirossi out of the way on the last lap.

11 LORIS CAPIROSSI Another weekend when Loris struggled to find any feel with the Suzuki's front end. Took tenth off Barbera two laps from the flag only to have the Spaniard put him on the grass on the final lap.

12 HIROSHI AOYAMA Hiro's first race back after two months off, one of them spent flat on his back, following his Silverstone crash. Not surprisingly, he found the 28 laps physically demanding and adopted a risk-free race strategy.

13 RANDY DE PUNIET Has never liked Indy and the ten left-hand turns put added

pressure on his injured leg when changing direction: described it as even more punishing than Brno. Never found a good set-up, was at the back in both qualifying and the race, but happy to keep his grip on eighth in the title chase.

NON-FINISHERS

MIKA KALLIO A good start meant three positions picked up on the first lap, then he and Bautista closed the 4s gap to Simoncelli. Looked like being the Finn's best race of the season, and in an entertaining dice for seventh when he lost the front 'instantly' thanks to what he called 'a hole in the asphalt'.

COLIN EDWARDS Devastated by the death of family friend Peter Lenz in a support race. Went for the harder tyre but pitted to change back to the soft option, ostensibly because of edge grip issues – but it's difficult to believe his mind was on the race.

CASEY STONER After a run of five rostrums, Casey was right back in the grip of the problem that afflicted him early in the season: front-end feel. Only qualified sixth and crashed in practice. Lost the front on lap eight while closing on Rossi.

MARCO MELANDRI Not the way he wanted to celebrate being the youngest rider ever to line up for 200 GPs. Made a great start from 12th and was trying to pass Rossi for sixth when he lost the front 'without warning' on the third lap.

SAN MARINO GP

MISANO WORLD CIRCUIT

ROUND **12**

September 5

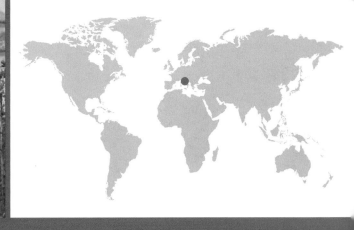

DANI DOMINATES

Dani Pedrosa won easily and set new personal records on a tragic day at Misano

The 2010 San Marino Grand Prix will be remembered for all the wrong reasons, chief among them the death of Shoya Tomizawa after a multi-bike crash in the Moto2 race. The loss of the universally popular young Japanese rider affected the whole paddock. The news was imparted to the MotoGP rostrum finishers by Dorna CEO Carmelo Ezpeleta in *parc fermé*, after which no-one felt like celebrating.

In truth there was little memorable about the race, unless you were Dani Pedrosa. Just as at Mugello, he started from pole, was never headed and set fastest lap. The difference between that race, back at the beginning of June, and the Misano GP was that there had been two other Pedrosa victories in between, including his triumph at Indianapolis a week previously. Dani had never won more than two races in a season before. This one made it four and gave him his first back-to-back victories.

At last the factory Honda team seemed to have found a base setting that worked at most tracks. The improvement over the start of the year, when the RCV wobbled frighteningly down the straight at Qatar, was nigh on miraculous. Not that the improvement had spread to the other side of the garage; Andrea Dovizioso had been on the podium in four of the first five rounds of the year, but since Silverstone had managed a best of only fifth. More worryingly, he had stopped improving on his qualifying position in races, which had been his pattern up to the crash in Catalunya. Now it was back to business as usual, albeit in a rather extreme way. Andrea qualified down in eighth and looked out of it until Sunday morning warm-up when he was third fastest, right behind Pedrosa and Lorenzo and in front of Valentino Rossi. This was very much the story of his races earlier in the season and, sure

enough, history repeated itself, with Dovi getting a great start and then pulling off a decent result, following Rossi home and just a couple of seconds off a rostrum finish.

In total contrast to Repsol Honda, Ducati had a disastrous weekend. Although Casey Stoner qualified on the front row he had a downbeat race, while Nicky Hayden's Misano hoodoo struck again. In four years the American has finished just once, and that was in 2007 when he was put off track on the first lap by de Puniet and ended up 13th. He missed 2008 through injury and last year was the victim of yet another first-lap crash. This time he qualified way down in 14th and astonishingly again failed to make it through Turn 2. As he tried to carve through the pack, Nicky's line crossed that of Loris Capirossi and both went down. Most observers thought it was a racing incident; Loris certainly didn't. The Suzuki man suffered a nasty injury to the little finger of his right hand, which required an operation and put him out of the next race.

Casey crashed in qualifying, losing the front end at one of the slowest corners on the track, but he reckoned the bike was improving as the day went on and said he felt confident. Was he desperate for a win? 'I've been desperate all year – I'm learning to live with it.' Desperation turned to resignation after the race. Although he got away in third he only managed to hold on to his place for ten laps. Pedrosa and Lorenzo pulled away from him and then Rossi and Dovizioso came past on successive laps. A depressed-looking Aussie talked after the race about Ducati being unable to change the situation before the end of the season. Paddock gossips started wondering about his motivation for the six remaining rounds.

Above Would the whole field get round the first corner for the first time at Misano?

Below The answer was 'no' – Nicky Hayden failed to get round the first corner for the second year in a row

Opposite Hiro Aoyama's return from injury was steady, and very welcome

Right Rossi's special helmet for his home GP featured an alarm clock, a reference to his inability to get up in the morning and a reminder that it was time to get some results on track

Below No joy on the rostrum after the MotoGP riders were told the sad news

'WE ARE ALL BROTHERS HERE'
NICKY HAYDEN

Home-town hero Rossi gave his fans what they wanted: a rostrum finish. Valentino was seriously happy with his pace, especially at the end of the race, doing his fastest lap three laps from the flag when he had to fend off a charging Andrea Dovizioso. Just to show how hard he was pushing, Vale's M1 ran out of petrol a couple of corners into the slow-down lap. However, Misano is a predominantly right-handed track and that gave Rossi's shoulder a really hard time. He was in serious pain for two days afterwards.

For the first time in a while Ben Spies didn't threaten the front runners. His race was compromised when he was pushed back to tenth place in the first-lap barging at Turn 2. By the time he got up to sixth, the leaders were ten seconds ahead.

The star of the now customary downfield dice was again Alvaro Bautista, who went from 16th on the grid to eighth at the flag despite being held up by the Capirossi–Hayden crash. Since his return to full fitness the Spaniard had started to show his real form. He'd ridden through the midfield pack in the previous two races as well, and from last-row grid positions on both occasions. Bautista's form perked up the beleaguered Suzuki team considerably and proved what other riders had been saying for a while, that the Suzuki wasn't that far from being competitive. The new frame he'd been using since the Brno test also seemed to help, but the real job was about getting Alvaro to perform to his potential in practice and qualifying, not just during the race.

Not many people were thinking about such details on Sunday afternoon, however.

SHOYA TOMIZAWA

Shoya Tomizawa's place in history is assured. The 19-year-old rider, from the Japanese seaside town of Asahi-shi in Chiba province, was the winner of the first ever Moto2 GP. He went on to set pole position and claim second place on the rostrum at the next round. For a rider who had only finished tenth in a GP before, on a very private 250 Honda, those results would have been enough to guarantee him some new fans. However, it wasn't just his committed and spectacular riding style that endeared him to crowds and TV audiences, but the way in which he conducted himself. Shoya had a smile for everyone, a compliment for every rival and a wave for every camera.

Tomizawa left Japan for the first time at the start of 2009 to join the Technomag-CIP team in the south of France, where he was lucky to have Giles Bigot as his race engineer, the man who took Alex Criville to the 1999 500cc world title. Shoya campaigned a 250 Honda in a BBR chassis, a bike that cost around 30,000 Euros and was on average about 0.3s slower than the million-Euro Aprilias.

Bigot recalled picking Shoya up from Marseille airport in January '09 and driving him through the ancient seaside area of La Ciotat. Much to Giles' amusement, the youngster's cameraphone never stopped clicking: 'Just like us in Japan.' Bigot is not given to long speeches, but when asked about Shoya he was hard to shut up. If he enquired whether the bike was chattering – the usual complaint in Moto2 – Shoya said, 'Yes, two corners, but no crisis.' Most teenage riders would be moaning the second they got off the bike.

After every GP the top three riders do TV interviews. This was another new experience for Shoya, but he was a natural. At Jerez he used his TV time to apologise for causing the mass crash that entailed the race having to be restarted, and he then apologised for causing his mechanics so much work. Apparently, he also apologised to the team for only finishing second.

Like most Europeans, I expect Japanese people to be polite, even if my Japanese friends think I am living in the past. Shoya's calm attitude was striking in its maturity and authority. It is impossible to define star quality, but when you see it, you recognise it. Shoya Tomizawa had it; but more importantly he was a really nice lad.

Above & below Always smiling off the track, always stylish and fast on it

SAN MARINO GP
MISANO WORLD CIRCUIT

ROUND 12
September 5

RACE RESULTS

CIRCUIT LENGTH 2.626 miles
NO. OF LAPS 28
RACE DISTANCE 73.529 miles
WEATHER Dry, 27°C
TRACK TEMPERATURE 39°C
WINNER Dani Pedrosa
FASTEST LAP 1m 34.340s, 99.435mph, Dani Pedrosa (record)
PREVIOUS LAP RECORD 1m 34.746s, 99.575mph, Valentino Rossi, 2009

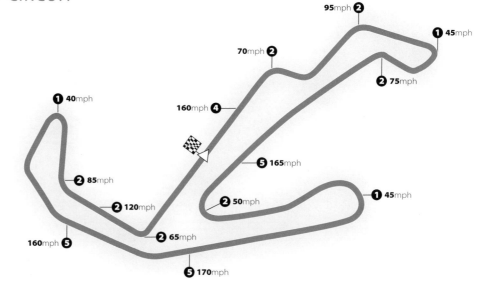

QUALIFYING

	Rider	Nationality	Team	Qualifying	Pole +	Gap
1	Pedrosa	SPA	Repsol Honda Team	1m 33.948s		
2	Lorenzo	SPA	Fiat Yamaha Team	1m 34.256s	0.308s	0.308s
3	Stoner	AUS	Ducati Team	1m 34.397s	0.449s	0.141s
4	Rossi	ITA	Fiat Yamaha Team	1m 34.470s	0.522s	0.073s
5	Spies	USA	Monster Yamaha Tech 3	1m 34.472s	0.524s	0.002s
6	De Puniet	FRA	LCR Honda MotoGP	1m 34.751s	0.803s	0.279s
7	Edwards	USA	Monster Yamaha Tech 3	1m 34.782s	0.834s	0.031s
8	Dovizioso	ITA	Repsol Honda Team	1m 34.826s	0.878s	0.044s
9	Simoncelli	ITA	San Carlo Honda Gresini	1m 34.934s	0.986s	0.108s
10	Melandri	ITA	San Carlo Honda Gresini	1m 35.018s	1.070s	0.084s
11	Capirossi	ITA	Rizla Suzuki MotoGP	1m 35.096s	1.148s	0.078s
12	Barbera	SPA	Paginas Amarillas Aspar	1m 35.259s	1.311s	0.163s
13	Aoyama	JPN	Interwetten Honda MotoGP	1m 35.286s	1.338s	0.027s
14	Hayden N	USA	Ducati Team	1m 35.303s	1.355s	0.017s
15	Espargaro	SPA	Pramac Racing Team	1m 35.438s	1.490s	0.135s
16	Bautista	SPA	Rizla Suzuki MotoGP	1m 35.629s	1.681s	0.191s
17	Kallio	FIN	Pramac Racing Team	1m 35.724s	1.776s	0.095s

FINISHERS

1 DANI PEDROSA As dominating a weekend as possible: pole position (Honda's first at Misano), fastest lap and never headed to win consecutive races for the first time in the top class. Took the lead up to five seconds before easing in the closing laps, which always worries his team.

2 JORGE LORENZO Had to scrap with Stoner on the opening lap but once in second realised he couldn't run at Pedrosa's pace and had an untroubled race. This was Jorge's 13th podium finish in succession and limited the damage to his points lead in the championship.

3 VALENTINO ROSSI Very happy with a rostrum finish in his own backyard, but especially with his pace at the end of the race when he had to hold off a challenge from Dovizioso. However, his shoulder gave Valentino severe pain for two days after the race.

4 ANDREA DOVIZIOSO A great improvement on qualifying. Again found a major improvement in Sunday warm-up. Able to run the same pace as Rossi but couldn't get close enough to make a pass stick. Mused on the set-up differences between the Hondas and whether he should make some changes.

5 CASEY STONER Very disappointed, especially considering his form right up to the race. Again it was the front end that caused problems and he was grateful just to finish on two wheels. A really disheartening weekend not just for Casey but for the whole Ducati squad.

6 BEN SPIES Race compromised by a shoving match in the second corner that put him back to tenth. Took a few laps to get confidence in the front before passing Melandri and de Puniet in one lap, and then Edwards. Over 10s behind Stoner so, despite comparable lap times, couldn't make up any more places.

7 COLIN EDWARDS Happier with his form, with only a slight front-end problem stopping Colin from going with his team-mate when he came past. Nevertheless, one of his best finishes of the season so far.

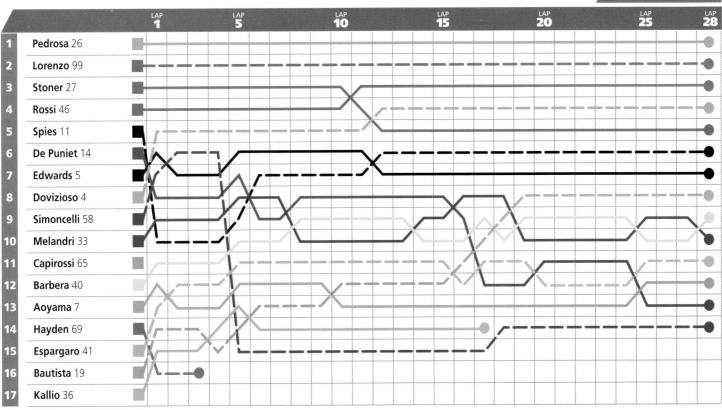

							LAP 1	LAP 5	LAP 10	LAP 15	LAP 20	LAP 25	LAP 28
1	Pedrosa 26												
2	Lorenzo 99												
3	Stoner 27												
4	Rossi 46												
5	Spies 11												
6	De Puniet 14												
7	Edwards 5												
8	Dovizioso 4												
9	Simoncelli 58												
10	Melandri 33												
11	Capirossi 65												
12	Barbera 40												
13	Aoyama 7												
14	Hayden 69												
15	Espargaro 41												
16	Bautista 19												
17	Kallio 36												

RACE

	Rider	Motorcycle	Race Time	Time +	Fastest Lap	Av Speed	B
1	Pedrosa	Honda	44m 22.059s		1m 34.340s	99.435mph	H/M
2	Lorenzo	Yamaha	44m 23.959s	1.900s	1m 34.613s	99.364mph	H/M
3	Rossi	Yamaha	44m 25.242s	3.183s	1m 34.461s	99.317mph	H/M
4	Dovizioso	Honda	44m 28.513s	6.454s	1m 34.562s	99.195mph	H/M
5	Stoner	Ducati	44m 40.538s	18.479s	1m 34.835s	98.750mph	H/M
6	Spies	Yamaha	44m 50.444s	28.385s	1m 35.357s	98.386mph	H/M
7	Edwards	Yamaha	44m 56.993s	34.934s	1m 35.546s	98.147mph	H/M
8	Bautista	Suzuki	45m 00.216s	38.157s	1m 35.240s	98.030mph	M/M
9	Barbera	Ducati	45m 03.002s	40.943s	1m 35.644s	97.929mph	H/M
10	Melandri	Honda	45m 04.436s	42.377s	1m 35.727s	97.877mph	H/M
11	Espargaro	Ducati	45m 07.965s	45.906s	1m 35.694s	97.749mph	H/M
12	Aoyama	Honda	45m 08.453s	46.394s	1m 35.834s	97.732mph	H/M
13	De Puniet	Honda	45m 12.540s	50.481s	1m 35.905s	97.585mph	H/M
14	Simoncelli	Honda	45m 45.202s	1m 23.143s	1m 35.553s	96.423mph	H/M
	Kallio	Ducati	27m 45.043s	11 laps	1m 36.240s	96.522mph	H/M
	Hayden N	Ducati	6m 11.244s	25 laps	1m 52.418s	76.394mph	H/M

CHAMPIONSHIP

	Rider	Team	Points
1	Lorenzo	Fiat Yamaha Team	271
2	Pedrosa	Repsol Honda Team	208
3	Dovizioso	Repsol Honda Team	139
4	Rossi	Fiat Yamaha Team	130
5	Stoner	Ducati Team	130
6	Spies	Monster Yamaha Tech 3	120
7	Hayden N	Ducati Team	109
8	De Puniet	LCR Honda MotoGP	81
9	Melandri	San Carlo Honda Gresini	67
10	Edwards	Monster Yamaha Tech 3	66
11	Simoncelli	San Carlo Honda Gresini	65
12	Barbera	Paginas Amarillas Aspar	61
13	Espargaro	Pramac Racing Team	44
14	Bautista	Rizla Suzuki MotoGP	41
15	Capirossi	Rizla Suzuki MotoGP	41
16	Kallio	Pramac Racing Team	31
17	Aoyama	Interwetten Honda MotoGP	26
18	De Angelis	Interwetten Honda MotoGP	11
19	Hayden R	LCR Honda MotoGP	5
20	Akiyoshi	Interwetten Honda MotoGP	4
21	Yoshikawa	Fiat Yamaha Team	1

8 ALVARO BAUTISTA Great start but held up by the second-corner crash and was 16s off the leader at the end of the first lap. Took five laps to regain his rhythm, then moved up eight places – without anyone in front falling off. Closed on Edwards at nearly a second a lap but ran out laps.

9 HECTOR BARBERA Another excellent result, this time from a bad qualifying position (16th) on a circuit where he always goes well.

10 MARCO MELANDRI Not a good race – as usual no confidence with the bike on the brakes and going into corners, the same problems he'd had since the start of the season. Good start but shuffled towards the back of the top ten as the race went on.

11 ALEIX ESPARGARO Part of the entertaining dice for eighth, but had problems in the second sector. Let Bautista past, intending the Suzuki rider would give him a tow, then got well off line trying to pass Melandri and lost contact with the group. Managed to get back past de Puniet before the flag.

12 HIROSHI AOYAMA Still recovering from his injury and with only the Indy race under his belt, Hiro never found a good feeling with his front tyre and simply couldn't close on the group in front. Improved on his qualifying position and generally felt happier with his fitness and set-up.

13 RANDY DE PUNIET Paid the price for the rapid recovery from his broken leg

and racing at Indianapolis. No problem with qualifying – his best since Catalunya – but lasting race distance was another matter.

14 MARCO SIMONCELLI The new electronics gave a completely different feeling from Indy. Marco qualified and started well, but a small mistake put him off track and at the back of the field. His feeling with the bike was much improved, though, and he was happy with everything except the result.

NON-FINISHERS

MIKA KALLIO Pushed hard at the start to try and make up places, then hit major problems with rear grip. Persevered for ten laps but realised he was risking another fall for no reason and pulled in just after half-distance.

NICKY HAYDEN Tried hard to make up for dreadful qualifying but only got as far as the second corner – for the second year in a row – before coming together with Capirossi. Able to pick up the bike, only to find the gear shifter was damaged. Unlike Loris, he saw the crash as a racing incident.

LORIS CAPIROSSI An unpleasant 200th race in the top class. The clash with Hayden

on the second corner of the first lap not only ruined what looked like a promising race but also did enough damage to Loris's right-hand little finger to put him out of the next race. Blamed Nicky for the coming-together.

ARAGON GP
MOTORLAND ARAGON
ROUND **13**
September 19

DUCATI DOUBLE

Casey Stoner finally found his form and Nicky Hayden backed him up, on a bad day for Yamaha and Lorenzo

If anyone wanted to know why Spain now had four Grands Prix, one look at Motorland Aragon provided the answer. The new facility instantly became a rider favourite, with only Casey Stoner refusing to join the chorus of approval. He described it as 'nothing special' although he did admit the last corner – a third-gear sweeper with an uphill exit – was quite interesting. By the end of the weekend the Aussie wasn't much more effusive, but he was very relieved. It was like a replay of 2007. Casey started from pole and, apart from some frantic exchanges with Jorge Lorenzo in the first few corners, he was never headed. To make Ducati's day complete, Nicky Hayden also got on the rostrum after a last-lap pass on Lorenzo.

Casey's season-long search for a set-up he could trust seemed finally to have unearthed a magic bullet. He had realised he couldn't get as close to the screen as he wanted in corners – a result of his old wrist injury – so the seat was modified to push him forward and the engine was shifted back to keep weight distribution right. That necessitated a shorter swinging arm. At last the Ducati rider had the feel and confidence he needed.

'Are you back?' said a nice Italian lady journo to him after qualifying.

'I've never been away,' he replied, with a rather charming grin.

Just as the whispers were starting to get louder, suggesting he and/or Ducati had lost interest in each other, Stoner looked like his old self. He did have a crash during Sunday morning warm-up when he touched a white line, and that made him a little

concerned for the race, but he was able to control Dani Pedrosa's challenge and win for the first time in nearly a year. The Honda man might have got closer but for a massive moment coming out of the first corner. Turn 1 is a right-angled left-hander unpleasantly close to the grid, and Dani was quite cautious going in. He was third coming out when a near-highside pinged him out of the saddle and put him back to fifth. He did set the fastest lap of the race, getting Casey's lead down to under a second, but he'd asked too much of his tyre. However, he still turned in astonishingly regular lap times to keep Stoner honest. Pedrosa's winning streak might have come to an end, but he took another seven points out of Lorenzo's lead, and his second place ensured there would definitely be a Spanish world champion.

Jorge Lorenzo ended the race crying with frustration. If the bike had just been slow on the long back straight, as usual, he could have coped, but Yamaha's problems went deeper than that. They just couldn't get the power down coming out of corners, where the Hondas and Ducatis were jumping away from them and then extending their advantage on the straights.

For reasons the team didn't yet understand, Hayden's Ducati didn't have the same top speed as the others, including the satellite teams' bikes, so although Nicky managed to close up on Lorenzo, and stick to his rear wheel for most of the race, he couldn't find a way past until the very last lap. Some attempts, particularly at the big chicane in front of the giant wall, started to look desperate, but to the joy of the Ducati garage he finally went past coming out of the bus stop. Hayden referred to it as an 'AMA-type' section of the track and the

'THIS WIN IS A BIG RELIEF, TO BE HONEST'
CASEY STONER

Above Just like old times: Casey Stoner out at the front of the field

Right Valentino Rossi found himself dicing with, and being overtaken by, riders he rarely sees in a race

Opposite Marco Simoncelli really got to grips with MotoGP in the second half of the season, but his aggressive style was very hard on tyres

move as 'a little bit hokey, kind of a backyard move you use on your brothers'. It wasn't clear whether Spanish speakers got his drift, but Jorge's view was 'what he has done is allowed'.

Lorenzo wasn't just disappointed about the end of his run of podium finishes. He'd worn a replica of Shoya Tomizawa's crash helmet and had been desperate to take it to the rostrum. As for Nicky, he seemed more relieved than exhilarated; no doubt both he and Ducati felt they had redeemed the disaster of the previous race at Misano.

It looked for a while as if Ben Spies was going to join the fight for third. Like Pedrosa, he got within a second of his target before a couple of small mistakes halted his progress and put him into Dovizioso's clutches. The American combated the Honda's significant top-end

advantage with some stunning late braking, especially at the end of the back straight, after which he carried astonishing amounts of corner speed on a wide line. The last four laps were fabulous. Dovi blew past on the penultimate lap, only for Ben to retake fifth on the brakes at Turn 1. They then swapped places at nearly every corner before Spies ran wide going into the chicane. Dovi dived underneath but highsided when he tried to change direction. Afterwards both men said how enjoyable the race had been. Andrea emphasised how clean the battle had been, and there was even the first sighting of a Ben Spies joke in MotoGP. When he got off his bike he said to his crew: 'You might want to look at the brakes. I used them a bit. Ha ha.'

As for Valentino Rossi, he was strangely invisible all weekend and described himself as 'sad but not desperate'. The need to set up the bike to turn easily in order to give his shoulder some relief didn't help the situation, and led Valentino to hint for the first time that he might opt for surgery before the end of the season. He didn't think his Yamaha had suddenly slowed down, just that the opposition had finally sorted out their front-end worries: 'Honda and Ducati fix their problems, it's not us getting worse.' The good news for Jorge and Valentino was that they were expecting an uprated motor for the next race; the bad news was that it would be the last of their six.

Was Casey Stoner really back? Ducati refused to be too upbeat. There was the lingering suspicion that this could have been a one-off result on a track that was new to everyone. The three races coming up in the Far East, all on circuits where Casey has dominated in the past, would answer that question.

SPANISH SUCCESS STORY

Casey Stoner's win at the new Aragon circuit ended a run of 11 consecutive victories by Spanish riders in the MotoGP class, while Andrea Iannone's triumph in the Moto2 class put an end to an even more amazing sequence of successes that demonstrated the strength of Spain and Spanish riders in the sport this season. Spanish riders had won the last 15 races across all three classes; the last non-Spanish GP winner was Yuki Takahashi in the Moto2 race at Catalunya. This is the highest total of successive solo GP wins by riders from a single nation in the 62-year history of Grand Prix racing. The previous record for successive wins across all classes was nine, achieved by riders from Great Britain back in 1951.

The run of 11 MotoGP victories by Lorenzo and Pedrosa, from Jerez to Misano, was the longest ever sequence of successive premier-class Grand Prix wins by Spanish riders, and was also the longest sequence of successive wins by a single nation since Italian MotoGP riders Rossi, Capirossi and Melandri took 12 successive wins in the 2005 and 2006 seasons.

At this point in the season, Spanish riders had won 29 GPs, including every 125 race – the highest number of wins that nation's riders had taken in a single season of racing.

After the Aragon round, Spanish riders were lying first and second in both the MotoGP and Moto2 championship standings, and occupying the top three places in the 125cc class. Spanish riders had won the previous 22 125cc races, the last non-Spanish victor in the 125cc class being a certain Andrea Iannone at the Catalan Grand Prix in 2009. This was the longest sequence of successive 125cc GP wins by one nation in Grand Prix history.

On six occasions already in 2010 Spanish riders had won all three classes. Prior to this season, Spain had only won the 125cc, 250cc and MotoGP races three times on the same day.

Above Three Spaniards on the rostrum – not a rare sight in 2010. This time it's 125 aces Terol, Marquez and Espargaro at Mugello

BRIDGESTONE
TYRE OPTIONS
FRONT   MEDIUM (M) / EXTRA HARD (XH)
REAR   SOFT (S) / MEDIUM (M)

motoGP   TISSOT
SWISS WATCHES SINCE 1853
OFFICIAL TIMEKEEPER

ARAGON GP
MOTORLAND ARAGON

ROUND 13
September 19

RACE RESULTS

CIRCUIT LENGTH 3.155 miles
NO. OF LAPS 23
RACE DISTANCE 72.565 miles
WEATHER Dry, 23°C
TRACK TEMPERATURE 39°C
WINNER Casey Stoner
FASTEST LAP 1m 49.521s, 102.795mph, Dani Pedrosa (Record)

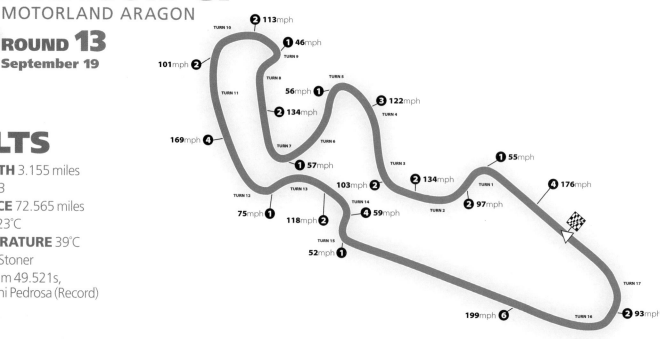

QUALIFYING

	Rider	Nationality	Team	Qualifying	Pole +	Gap
1	Stoner	AUS	Ducati Team	1m 48.942s		
2	Lorenzo	SPA	Fiat Yamaha Team	1m 49.251s	0.309s	0.309s
3	Pedrosa	SPA	Repsol Honda Team	1m 49.343s	0.401s	0.092s
4	Hayden N	USA	Ducati Team	1m 49.506s	0.564s	0.163s
5	Spies	USA	Monster Yamaha Tech 3	1m 49.565s	0.623s	0.059s
6	De Puniet	FRA	LCR Honda MotoGP	1m 49.952s	1.010s	0.387s
7	Rossi	ITA	Fiat Yamaha Team	1m 50.017s	1.075s	0.065s
8	Dovizioso	ITA	Repsol Honda Team	1m 50.046s	1.104s	0.029s
9	Simoncelli	ITA	San Carlo Honda Gresini	1m 50.088s	1.146s	0.042s
10	Barbera	SPA	Paginas Amarillas Aspar	1m 50.323s	1.381s	0.235s
11	Edwards	USA	Monster Yamaha Tech 3	1m 50.440s	1.498s	0.117s
12	Bautista	SPA	Rizla Suzuki MotoGP	1m 50.523s	1.581s	0.083s
13	Espargaro	SPA	Pramac Racing Team	1m 50.537s	1.595s	0.014s
14	Melandri	ITA	San Carlo Honda Gresini	1m 50.580s	1.638s	0.043s
15	Aoyama	JPN	Interwetten Honda MotoGP	1m 50.836s	1.894s	0.256s
16	Kallio	FIN	Pramac Racing Team	1m 51.490s	2.548s	0.654s

FINISHERS

1 CASEY STONER An adjustment to his body position on the bike seemed to be the magic bullet he'd been looking for. Started from pole for the first time since Qatar and led all the way after a frantic first-lap fight with Lorenzo for his first win since Malaysia nearly 12 months previously.

2 DANI PEDROSA The chance of going with Stoner was compromised by a near-highside coming out of the first corner, putting him back to sixth. Up to second on lap three but was 1.5s behind the Aussie, reduced the gap, then ran into rear-tyre wear issues, so settled for 20 points and beating Jorge for the third race in a row.

3 NICKY HAYDEN Took third off Lorenzo on the last lap, after shadowing him for the second half of the race, for his first rostrum since Indy over a year ago. Strong right from the first session but seemed more relieved than ecstatic to be back in the top three, maybe because of his disastrous Misano race.

4 JORGE LORENZO Extended his run of front-row starts but off the rostrum for the first time all season. Frustrated at his Yamaha's performance, not just the top speed but especially the lack of grip coming out of corners, and also being unable to take his Tomizawa replica helmet to the podium.

5 BEN SPIES Not his best finish of the year but probably his best race, closing on the dice for fourth until a mistake put him out of touch. Then fought off a strong challenge from Dovizioso, especially over an action-packed last four laps. Simply amazing on the brakes at the end of the back straight.

6 VALENTINO ROSSI Suffered from the same difficulties as the other Yamaha riders, exacerbated by his shoulder problem, and found himself fighting with Barbera and Simoncelli. Very unhappy after the race and openly discussing the idea of having an operation before the end of the season.

7 MARCO SIMONCELLI Two mistakes cost him dearly, the first after he lost touch with the Spies–Dovizioso dice, the second when he was behind Rossi and

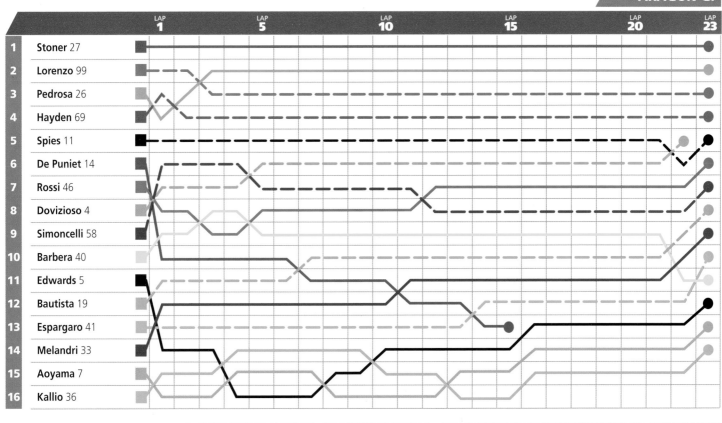

		LAP 1	LAP 5	LAP 10	LAP 15	LAP 20	LAP 23
1	Stoner 27						
2	Lorenzo 99						
3	Pedrosa 26						
4	Hayden 69						
5	Spies 11						
6	De Puniet 14						
7	Rossi 46						
8	Dovizioso 4						
9	Simoncelli 58						
10	Barbera 40						
11	Edwards 5						
12	Bautista 19						
13	Espargaro 41						
14	Melandri 33						
15	Aoyama 7						
16	Kallio 36						

RACE

	Rider	Motorcycle	Race Time	Time +	Fastest Lap	Av Speed	B
1	Stoner	Ducati	42m 16.530s		1m 49.555s	103.003mph	XH/M
2	Pedrosa	Honda	42m 21.678s	5.148s	1m 49.521s	102.795mph	XH/M
3	Hayden N	Ducati	42m 26.026s	9.496s	1m 49.935s	102.619mph	XH/M
4	Lorenzo	Yamaha	42m 26.110s	9.580s	1m 50.273s	102.616mph	XH/M
5	Spies	Yamaha	42m 30.301s	13.771s	1m 50.116s	102.447mph	XH/M
6	Rossi	Yamaha	42m 43.860s	27.330s	1m 50.701s	101.905mph	XH/M
7	Simoncelli	Honda	42m 45.041s	28.511s	1m 50.688s	101.858mph	XH/M
8	Bautista	Suzuki	42m 51.784s	35.254s	1m 50.958s	101.592mph	M/M
9	Melandri	Honda	42m 51.923s	35.393s	1m 51.145s	101.586mph	XH/M
10	Espargaro	Ducati	42m 51.997s	35.467s	1m 51.035s	101.583mph	XH/M
11	Barbera	Ducati	42m 52.052s	35.522s	1m 50.999s	101.580mph	XH/M
12	Edwards	Yamaha	43m 01.890s	45.360s	1m 51.292s	101.194mph	M/M
13	Aoyama	Honda	43m 04.849s	48.319s	1m 51.306s	101.078mph	XH/M
14	Kallio	Ducati	43m 14.577s	58.047s	1m 51.818s	100.699mph	M/M
15	Dovizioso	Honda	40m 38.333s	1 lap	1m 50.234s	102.493mph	XH/M
16	De Puniet	Honda	27m 59.238s	8 laps	1m 51.327s	101.471mph	XH/M

CHAMPIONSHIP

	Rider	Team	Points
1	Lorenzo	Fiat Yamaha Team	284
2	Pedrosa	Repsol Honda Team	228
3	Stoner	Ducati Team	155
4	Rossi	Fiat Yamaha Team	140
5	Dovizioso	Repsol Honda Team	139
6	Spies	Monster Yamaha Tech 3	131
7	Hayden N	Ducati Team	125
8	De Puniet	LCR Honda MotoGP	81
9	Melandri	San Carlo Honda Gresini	74
10	Simoncelli	San Carlo Honda Gresini	74
11	Edwards	Monster Yamaha Tech 3	70
12	Barbera	Paginas Amarillas Aspar	66
13	Espargaro	Pramac Racing Team	50
14	Bautista	Rizla Suzuki MotoGP	49
15	Capirossi	Rizla Suzuki MotoGP	41
16	Kallio	Pramac Racing Team	33
17	Aoyama	Interwetten Honda MotoGP	29
18	De Angelis	Interwetten Honda MotoGP	11
19	Hayden R	LCR Honda MotoGP	5
20	Akiyoshi	Interwetten Honda MotoGP	4
21	Yoshikawa	Fiat Yamaha Team	1

contemplating making a move. Marco's aggressive style again exacerbated tyre wear and slowed him in the closing stages.

8 ALVARO BAUTISTA A third successive eighth-place finish after another hard-fought race. Had to pass de Puniet, deal with Barbera's very fast Ducati and finally hold off Melandri's last-lap challenge. Tyre problems in the second half meant he was further from the top six than in the previous three races.

9 MARCO MELANDRI The usual story: no confidence in the front end and an inability to out-brake anyone even when he was running good lap times.

10 ALEIX ESPARGARO A better result than qualifying suggested. Diced with de

Puniet for the first half of the race, then closed on the group in front and just managed to pass Barbera on the last lap.

11 HECTOR BARBERA A difficult race after a good start. Had power delivery problems from the third lap so switched settings, only to find he had too much power and was spinning everywhere. Switched back to the original setting to try to save the tyre, but was 'clinging on' for the last half-dozen laps.

12 COLIN EDWARDS A bad start and a difficult race. Couldn't find his rhythm and dropped to the back of the field before passing Kallio and Aoyama. At least had the consolation of re-signing with the Tech 3 team for another season.

13 HIROSHI AOYAMA Spent too long stuck behind Kallio and only passed the Finn when he made a mistake. No particular problems with the bike, but Hiro wasn't happy with the result.

14 MIKA KALLIO Lost out to Edwards and Aoyama in the fight at the back of the field, but at least Mika saw the chequered flag for the first time in four races.

NON-FINISHERS

ANDREA DOVIZIOSO Crashed at the bus-stop chicane on the last lap while battling with Ben Spies for fifth place.

RANDY DE PUNIET It all looked good after he qualified sixth – by far the best performance since his return from injury – but the race didn't go well. Got his usual bad start, the front tyre started losing grip and he lost places. Made a mistake eight laps from the flag in Turn 7 and was highsided, luckily without injury.

NON-STARTERS

LORIS CAPIROSSI Recovering from an operation on the finger injured at Misano. Only expected to miss this race, so wasn't replaced.

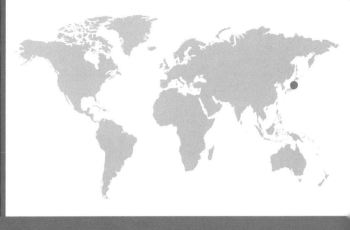

BLUE ON BLUE

The title might have been all but decided, but it felt like the 2011 season had started here

The 2010 World Championship was delivered into the hands of Jorge Lorenzo less than ten minutes into Friday morning's first free practice session when Dani Pedrosa's throttle stuck open going into V-Corner. In the inevitable crash that ensued, Dani suffered a multiple break to his left collarbone. He flew home to Barcelona and had the break plated before the race had got under way. Mathematically Pedrosa could still be champion, but only if he was able to race at Sepang in seven days' time. That looked a highly unlikely prospect.

The Repsol Honda team's remaining rider, Andrea Dovizioso, lightened the gloom in the pit garage with his most competitive weekend of the year. He'd made a habit of racing much better than he qualified, but this time he was fast from the initial session and qualified on pole for the first time in his MotoGP career. The man who nearly beat him to the spot was Valentino Rossi, surprising everyone including himself. Yamahas had won at Motegi for the previous two years but this predominantly right-handed circuit, with four very heavy braking efforts, was supposed to give his injured shoulder more stress than anywhere else. Apparently not; Vale reckoned the fact that the hard braking was mainly with the bike upright rather than on the side of the tyre gave his shoulder an easier time. Rossi put in his best qualifying since round three and his most thrillingly competitive race since the 2008 showdown with Stoner at Laguna Seca.

However, it was the third front-row qualifier who dominated the race. Casey Stoner and the Ducati team left Aragon, which they'd dominated two weeks earlier, wondering if the radical new set-up that had given them their first victory of the year would transfer to

another circuit. The answer appeared to be 'no', as the team had to trade off stability with traction: it was one or the other. Every other Ducati rider struggled in both qualifying and the race, yet Casey made it work – and, as usual, with an astonishingly small number of laps in practice and qualifying. He led from the first corner, under constant pressure from Andrea Dovizioso, the Honda man amazed by Casey's pace and willingness to ride on the edge for an entire race. Dovi was hardly risk-averse himself. Only a big moment, a near-highside three laps from the flag, finally detached him from the Ducati's rear wheel.

The race for the win was tense, but it was the fight for third that will be remembered. The two Fiat Yamaha riders nearly exchanged paint on the first lap as Lorenzo muscled past into third. It took Valentino five laps to get past Jorge, by which time the leaders were almost two seconds up the road. On lap seven Rossi set the fastest lap of the race, the first time he'd done that this season, but it wasn't enough to close the gap significantly. As he ran into tyre wear, and maybe a bit of fatigue, Lorenzo attacked. This was the first time he'd qualified off the front row all year and, unlike Valentino, he'd chosen to race with an old motor. Jorge was also the only front runner to go with the softer front tyre option, something he later said was a mistake. Neither man appeared to be thinking of injury, the championship or Yamaha's quest for team and constructors' titles.

The last three laps weren't quite up there with Rossi's famous treatment of Gibernau and Stoner, but they were close. The battle got rough on the penultimate lap when they touched at least twice. Lorenzo went past at the right-hander at Turn 5 that takes the track under

Right Dovizioso and crew try not to worry about being on pole for the first time

Opposite Team orders? What team orders? Rossi and Lorenzo go for it on the final lap

Below Ben Spies in the tunnel that brings the road circuit back under the oval

the oval. Rossi ripped back inside on the exit, barging the Spaniard towards the edge of the track. Jorge immediately attacked on the inside at the next left-hander, the V-Corner, but unfortunately that put him on the outside for the next right. Rossi conceded not an inch and shoved his rival aside once more. Jorge got past again, half-way round the last lap, but Valentino immediately retook third to achieve a couple of bike lengths' advantage, which he held to the flag.

It all got really interesting afterwards. Rossi adopted his normal tactic of saying what a great race it had been, how tough his opponent was and congratulating him. Then he mentioned that if he hadn't been held up early on by Lorenzo he would have been able to get to Stoner and Dovizioso. Not surprisingly, Jorge didn't see it in quite the same way. Even his official press release

complained about Valentino's riding, and he was more vocal to individual journalists when talking face to face. He even managed to get the team management to say that they thought Rossi shouldn't have ridden as he did. Lorenzo also threatened to take the gloves off in future. Rossi's mask slipped when he talked to the press: 'He's been saying all year he wanted a last-lap battle with me;

'THE LAST LAP WAS FUN; FUN BECAUSE I FINISHED AHEAD'
VALENTINO ROSSI

Right Colour
co-ordination
in the crowd

Opposite Nicky Hayden
rode hard to come back
from an early off-track
excursion

Below Dovi was quick in the
race, not just qualifying

well today he got it.' Jorge responded on his blog that next
time he knew what to expect and that Rossi would find
him 'hotter' than Stoner or Gibernau. He also resurrected
the subject of perceived special treatment for the Doctor, a
theme the Spanish media later ran with when they noticed
Rossi had moved on the start-line before the lights went
out but was not penalised.

Just when it looked as if interest in the championship
was fading, several intriguing sub-plots had emerged to
enliven the 2010 season's final four races. Dovizioso might
have been Honda's best man, but he was beaten by the
guy who would be on his bike in 2011. The Italian was
still unsure about the team he'd be riding for – which is
probably why he didn't look too happy with second place.
Stoner, now the winner of two races in a row, was hitting
the sort of form he'd shown on his return to racing 12
months previously, while Rossi was intent on reminding
everyone who was top gun. On *and* off the track.

ENGINE ENGINEERING

Would the new regulation restricting riders to six engines for the season have an effect over the last five races of the championship? Motegi threw up some interesting clues.

Yamaha brought in a new uprated motor for the factory team and Valentino Rossi used it in every session. He was delighted with the extra grunt in the higher gears: he took his second bike out with an old-spec engine and said it 'made me cry'. Jorge Lorenzo took a new motor for qualifying but didn't use it for the race – why? Because Lorenzo's motor was the sixth and last of his allocation and his team decided to keep it for the fast tracks coming up at Sepang and Phillip Island. Rossi's four-race absence through injury in the middle of the season meant he hadn't used up his allocation, so the motor he took at Motegi was only the fifth of his six. Colin Edwards and Ben Spies didn't get

new engines; both had one of their allocation left.

Andrea Dovizioso also had a new motor at Motegi, his fifth, which he used in both qualifying and the race. All the Honda satellite riders, except Randy de Puniet, had taken their sixth motors at Aragon.

Over at Ducati, Casey Stoner had taken his fifth motor back at San Marino, using it in warm-up as well as the race. He then used it to set pole and win at Aragon; at Motegi he used it in every session except first free practice. No Ducati rider, in fact, had yet taken his sixth engine.

The exception to the six-motor rule was Suzuki. As the team hadn't won a dry-weather race for two seasons, they were allowed nine engines. Alvaro Bautista took his seventh motor for second free practice and used it in qualifying and the race. Loris Capirossi took his sixth but only used it in warm-up.

Above Alvaro Bautista used a new exception to the six-engine rule to race with his seventh engine of the season

JAPANESE GP
TWIN-RING MOTEGI

ROUND 14
October 3

RACE RESULTS

CIRCUIT LENGTH 2.983 miles
NO. OF LAPS 24
RACE DISTANCE 71.597 miles
WEATHER Dry, 23°C
TRACK TEMPERATURE 34°C
WINNER Casey Stoner
FASTEST LAP 1m 47.395s, 99.215mph, Valentino Rossi
LAP RECORD 1m 47.091s, 100.288mph, Casey Stoner, 2008

BRIDGESTONE
TYRE OPTIONS
FRONT MEDIUM (M) / HARD (H)
REAR MEDIUM (M) / HARD (H)

OFFICIAL TIMEKEEPER

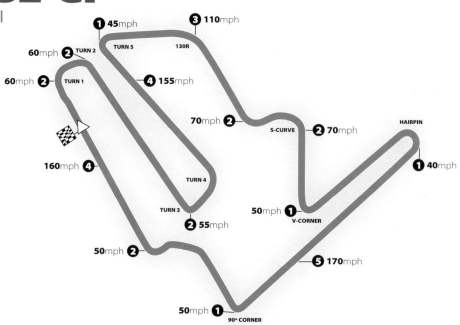

① 45mph
③ 110mph
TURN 5
130R
60mph ② TURN 2
60mph ② TURN 1
④ 155mph
70mph ②
S-CURVE
② 70mph
HAIRPIN
160mph ④
① 40mph
TURN 4
50mph ①
V-CORNER
② 55mph
TURN 3
⑤ 170mph
50mph ②
50mph ①
90° CORNER

QUALIFYING

	Rider	Nationality	Team	Qualifying	Pole +	Gap
1	Dovizioso	ITA	Repsol Honda Team	1m 47.001s		
2	Rossi	ITA	Fiat Yamaha Team	1m 47.055s	0.054s	0.054s
3	Stoner	AUS	Ducati Team	1m 47.105s	0.104s	0.050s
4	Lorenzo	SPA	Fiat Yamaha Team	1m 47.206s	0.205s	0.101s
5	Edwards	USA	Monster Yamaha Tech 3	1m 47.464s	0.463s	0.258s
6	Spies	USA	Monster Yamaha Tech 3	1m 47.648s	0.647s	0.184s
7	De Puniet	FRA	LCR Honda MotoGP	1m 47.752s	0.751s	0.104s
8	Simoncelli	ITA	San Carlo Honda Gresini	1m 47.914s	0.913s	0.162s
9	Bautista	SPA	Rizla Suzuki MotoGP	1m 48.002s	1.001s	0.088s
10	Capirossi	ITA	Rizla Suzuki MotoGP	1m 48.068s	1.067s	0.066s
11	Hayden N	USA	Ducati Team	1m 48.182s	1.181s	0.114s
12	Melandri	ITA	San Carlo Honda Gresini	1m 48.238s	1.237s	0.056s
13	Espargaro	SPA	Pramac Racing Team	1m 48.371s	1.370s	0.133s
14	Aoyama	JPN	Interwetten Honda MotoGP	1m 48.396s	1.395s	0.025s
15	Barbera	SPA	Paginas Amarillas Aspar	1m 48.535s	1.534s	0.139s
16	Kallio	FIN	Pramac Racing Team	1m 49.480s	2.479s	0.945s
	Pedrosa	SPA	Repsol Honda Team			

FINISHERS

1 CASEY STONER Led from the first corner for his second win in succession, but his team had to work hard to find a set-up that worked under braking going into corners and controlled wheelies coming out. His 22nd win in the top class moved him up to joint eighth in the all-time winners' list.

2 ANDREA DOVIZIOSO Started from pole for the first time in his MotoGP career. Followed Stoner for most of the race, rarely more than half a second behind, until a near-highside three laps from the flag when pushing hard on worn tyres. Didn't seem overjoyed with his first rostrum since Silverstone.

3 VALENTINO ROSSI His shoulder didn't give him the expected problems and a new uprated motor also helped. Qualified on the front row for the first time since Le Mans. Tangled with Lorenzo at the start and end of the race, repulsing Jorge's attack over the last two laps without mercy.

4 JORGE LORENZO Effectively handed the title by Pedrosa's crash. Failed to qualify on the front row for the first time all season and then finished off the rostrum for the second race in succession. Not at all happy with Rossi's riding in the final laps.

5 COLIN EDWARDS His best race of the year. On the pace from first practice, started well and spent the race stalking Simoncelli before going past seven laps from the flag

and pulling away. Happy with his qualifying relative to pole time, but not with the 27s gap to the race winner.

6 MARCO SIMONCELLI Equalled his best result of the year, and ran in fifth for much of the race. Developed arm pump in the closing stages, which prevented him from trying to repass Edwards.

7 ALVARO BAUTISTA His equal-best qualifying of the year (ninth), but got boxed in at the first corner and put back to 12th. The Suzuki still needs time to get heat in its tyres so he had to wait before pushing hard, which he did to good effect, and was right behind team-mate Capirossi when his bike stopped.

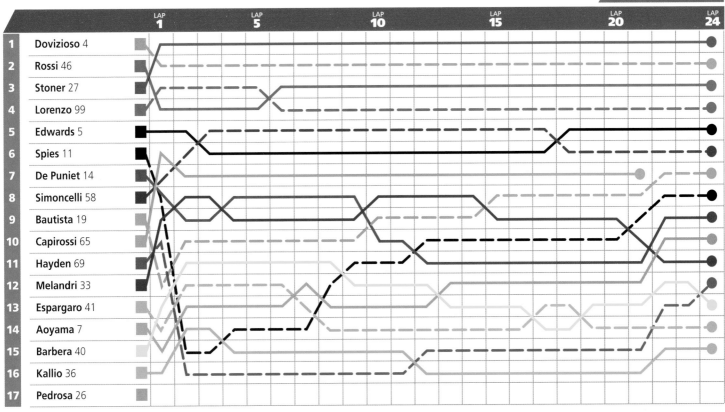

			LAP 1	LAP 5	LAP 10	LAP 15	LAP 20	LAP 24
1	Dovizioso	4						
2	Rossi	46						
3	Stoner	27						
4	Lorenzo	99						
5	Edwards	5						
6	Spies	11						
7	De Puniet	14						
8	Simoncelli	58						
9	Bautista	19						
10	Capirossi	65						
11	Hayden	69						
12	Melandri	33						
13	Espargaro	41						
14	Aoyama	7						
15	Barbera	40						
16	Kallio	36						
17	Pedrosa	26						

RACE

	Rider	Motorcycle	Race Time	Time +	Fastest Lap	Av Speed	B
1	Stoner	Ducati	43m 12.266s		1m 47.410s	99.433mph	H/M
2	Dovizioso	Honda	43m 16.134s	3.868s	1m 47.428s	99.286mph	H/M
3	Rossi	Yamaha	43m 17.973s	5.707s	1m 47.395s	99.215mph	H/M
4	Lorenzo	Yamaha	43m 18.487s	6.221s	1m 47.561s	99.195mph	M/M
5	Edwards	Yamaha	43m 39.358s	27.092s	1m 48.424s	98.405mph	H/M
6	Simoncelli	Honda	43m 42.287s	30.021s	1m 48.433s	98.295mph	H/M
7	Bautista	Suzuki	43m 44.092s	31.826s	1m 48.307s	98.228mph	H/M
8	Spies	Yamaha	43m 47.838s	35.572s	1m 48.394s	98.087mph	H/M
9	De Puniet	Honda	43m 59.830s	47.564s	1m 48.276s	97.642mph	H/M
10	Aoyama	Honda	44m 01.864s	49.598s	1m 49.133s	97.567mph	H/M
11	Melandri	Honda	44m 02.265s	49.999s	1m 48.713s	97.552mph	H/M
12	Hayden	Ducati	44m 02.969s	50.703s	1m 48.793s	97.526mph	M/M
13	Barbera	Ducati	44m 03.688s	51.422s	1m 49.131s	97.500mph	H/M
14	Espargaro	Ducati	44m 05.109s	52.843s	1m 49.244s	97.447mph	H/M
15	Kallio	Ducati	44m 26.934s	1m 14.668s	1m 49.832s	96.650mph	H/M
	Capirossi	Suzuki	38m 16.692s	3 laps	1m 48.434s	98.202mph	H/M

CHAMPIONSHIP

	Rider	Team	Points
1	Lorenzo	Fiat Yamaha Team	297
2	Pedrosa	Repsol Honda Team	228
3	Stoner	Ducati Team	180
4	Dovizioso	Repsol Honda Team	159
5	Rossi	Fiat Yamaha Team	156
6	Spies	Monster Yamaha Tech 3	139
7	Hayden N	Ducati Team	129
8	De Puniet	LCR Honda MotoGP	88
9	Simoncelli	San Carlo Honda Gresini	84
10	Edwards	Monster Yamaha Tech 3	81
11	Melandri	San Carlo Honda Gresini	79
12	Barbera	Paginas Amarillas Aspar	69
13	Bautista	Rizla Suzuki MotoGP	58
14	Espargaro	Pramac Racing Team	52
15	Capirossi	Rizla Suzuki MotoGP	41
16	Aoyama	Interwetten Honda MotoGP	35
17	Kallio	Pramac Racing Team	34
18	De Angelis	Interwetten Honda MotoGP	11
19	Hayden R	LCR Honda MotoGP	5
20	Akiyoshi	Interwetten Honda MotoGP	4
21	Yoshikawa	Fiat Yamaha Team	1

8 BEN SPIES Didn't find a practice set-up he liked and his crew tried a front geometry change and different rear shock for the race. Top rookie in qualifying but dead last after a second-lap incident at Turn 5 put him and Hayden on the grass. Back in the top ten by lap 12; his race pace was good enough for fifth.

9 RANDY DE PUNIET Running in eighth when he ran off track at Turn 5 after missing a downshift, blaming it on his injured leg. That mistake left him a lonely tenth, which became ninth when Capirossi stopped. Pleased to retain eighth place in the championship.

10 HIROSHI AOYAMA Happier with his form and fitness. Very fast early in free practice but cautious at the start of the race, waiting for his tyres to warm up. Ended the first lap in 15th before making some impressive passes. Equalled his best finish of the year.

11 MARCO MELANDRI Another sad weekend. Marco complained about traction and stability as well as the fact that Honda had 'forgotten' him. His team manager saw it differently.

12 NICKY HAYDEN A crash on Friday hindered the team in their search for traction. Followed Spies off track on lap two and took a long time to get back to the action. Made up a few places but lacked confidence on the brakes.

13 HECTOR BARBERA Like all the Ducati riders he struggled with traction in practice and qualifying. Only Stoner found a solution, the rest – including Hector – went into the race knowing they'd have problems opening the throttle. His joint worst finish of the year.

14 ALEIX ESPARGARO The worst weekend of his year, said Aleix. Handling problems all weekend and for once he couldn't find extra pace in the race.

15 MIKA KALLIO Like his fellow satellite Ducati riders he had a painful weekend. Only managed to put in two laps under 1m 50s during 'one of the worst races ever'.

NON-FINISHERS

LORIS CAPIROSSI Raced in pain from the operation to repair his little finger and looked to be on for a good result. Involved in the dice for fifth when what the team described as 'an electrical issue' caused him to lose power. Stopped shortly afterwards when the fail-safe system cut the motor.

NON-STARTERS

DANI PEDROSA Crashed six minutes into first practice when his throttle stuck open, suffering a triple fracture of the left collarbone and effectively ending his slim title hopes. Flew directly to Barcelona to have the break plated at the Dexeus clinic.

LORENZO LANDS IT

Jorge Lorenzo took his first MotoGP title with a safe third place while Valentino Rossi reminded everyone who was boss

For a series that some would have us believe is in crisis, MotoGP looked in rude health. The 20th Malaysian Grand Prix saw the coronation of a new champion and the resurgence of the outgoing one, plus some great dices down the field – and all in front of a record crowd. The absence of Dani Pedrosa, thankfully prevented from making a premature return by Honda's team management, might have put a damper on proceedings, as could the early exit of Casey Stoner from the race, but instead we were treated to a gem.

The drama started in qualifying. Jorge Lorenzo calmly took his sixth pole of the year, just edging out Nicky Hayden, while Rossi's gloom looked set to continue as he qualified at the end of the second row. His problem was the old bugbear of rear traction. There were no clues of what was to come at the start of the race, Lorenzo duly getting the holeshot, with Andrea Dovizioso in close attendance, and the pair starting to pull away from the field. Dovi put his return to form down to two factors. First, the chassis geometry change that he used at Aragon and, second, the wheelie-control electronics settings introduced at Motegi. His form had never dipped, he claimed, it was just that the opposition had improved.

Rossi's situation had actually worsened. A terrible start saw him 11th into the first corner, but he wasn't panicking. He already understood that the modifications Jerry Burgess and his crew had come up with for warm-up were working, and he launched into an astonishing destruction of the field. He went past Bautista on the first lap; Melandri, Edwards and Capirossi on lap two; Spies and Hayden on lap three;

and Simoncelli on lap four. That put him into third place. Six laps later he was past Lorenzo and next time round he took the lead off Dovizioso. Andrea fought back, and he did lead the race for a couple of laps before Valentino battled to the front again, but rather surprisingly the Honda didn't manage to gallop away from the Yamaha on Sepang's long straights. Crucially, the race had been shortened by a lap, effectively giving all the engineers an extra litre of fuel to play with – that, and the power-up motor introduced at Motegi, negated the Honda's usual advantage.

Valentino also set fastest lap for the first time this year, but it wasn't that easy for him. Dovizioso was riding as well as he'd ever done, and Rossi's lack of fitness and his shoulder injury combined with the usual Malaysian heat and humidity to make it very hard work indeed.

At the flag one would have been forgiven for thinking that Valentino Rossi had retained his world title. The outgoing champion was ecstatic about the win: 'One of the best of my career, because coming from 11th to win in MotoGP now is something great.' It was, he said, one of his best ever races. It also happened to be his 46th victory on a Yamaha, and everyone knows that that is an important number for Valentino. Was some of his pleasure with the win down to upstaging Jorge? Lorenzo did lead off pole but declined to take too many risks in the race. His celebration was comparatively simple: a sign saying 'Game Over', which at least explained the Super Mario Brothers computer-game figure

Opposite Valentino Rossi's flailing leg shows he's trying hard as he fends off Andrea Dovizioso

Above Hotter than Texas: Tom Houseworth snaps his rider for the family album

Below Hiro Aoyama had his best race in MotoGP; Marco Simoncelli looked like doing the same but faded in the heat

Above Fifth-placed Alvaro Bautista equalled his best result in MotoGP and this was definitely his best race

Opposite Lorenzo celebrates the title; for some bizarre reason the Super Mario Brothers were also involved

he'd been waving around earlier. Jorge then got in a bit of upstaging of his own. When the champagne was handed out he left the rostrum to go down to pit lane and celebrate the World Championship with his team – taking the TV cameras with him.

It would be all too easy to ignore some stirring rides behind the two champions and the very impressive Dovizioso. Marco Simoncelli seemed on for the best ride of his season until the heat got to him, and yet again it was Ben Spies who emerged from a cracking midfield dice to be the best of the rest. Alvaro Bautista continued his run of form with fifth, but both he and Spies again took time to get heat into, and confidence in, their tyres and they were never going to get on terms with the top three. It was also encouraging to see Hiro Aoyama having his best race of the season and nearing full fitness. His result might have been better but for a couple of sideswipes from Simoncelli.

No Ducati rider had a good time. Cold tyres, a difficult concept to grasp in the tropics, ended Stoner's race before a lap was over and Hayden

couldn't get any feel from his front tyre, despite his sterling qualifying performance. He was most handicapped in the braking zones, an area where he thought he'd be strong after qualifying. Nicky's sixth-place finish could have been worse, but he was the prime beneficiary of Simoncelli running wide and taking Aoyama with him. As for the satellite Ducatis, it was a horrible weekend for all of them.

While the entertainment on view was excellent, the remark at the start of this report about MotoGP being in good health was perhaps less than accurate. The optimism over the survival of the Interwetten Honda team evaporated, and the prospect of one-bike teams in 2011 for Pramac Ducati and Suzuki hardened. Not that many people outside the paddock will be too bothered if the entertainment at the front of the field is as good as it was at Motegi and Sepang, and while one of the world's most recognisable sportsmen is still competing and winning in the manner he did at Sepang, then TV audiences will also hold up. And motorcycle racing is lucky to have an equally fascinating personality succeeding him as champion.

'HE HAS BEEN FAST ALL SEASON, AT ALL TRACKS AND IN ALL CONDITIONS, AND HE DESERVES TO BE THE WORLD CHAMPION'
VALENTINO ROSSI

LORENZO'S LANDED

It has taken Jorge Lorenzo eight years to transform himself from a teenage prodigy into the complete motorcycle racer. He arrived at Jerez on a Saturday in 2002, the day he turned 15 – he'd had to miss first practice because he was too young. In truth, the young Lorenzo was not a likeable specimen. Hothoused from an early age by his father, Chico, to become a champion, Jorge came across as arrogant and sullen. The turnaround in Jorge Lorenzo as a person is just as remarkable as his passage to the MotoGP title.

Lorenzo came to MotoGP in 2008 and was an immediate sensation: pole at his first race, victory at the third. Then the bike bit back, and a succession of big, injurious crashes knocked the stuffing out of him. He'd been to a very dark place and he was frighteningly honest about it, with talk about being afraid of the bike, of wondering if he would be able to win again – the sort of admission rarely heard from a racer.

Jorge had realised that, under his father's influence, he had missed out on an education so he'd cut his ties and gone to live in Barcelona and, for a year, in London, where he perfected his English. He also developed a keen interest in cinema and reading, and even did a bit of acting. Next he split from his manager, Dani Amatriain, amid lurid rumours and restraining orders, and the world began to see Jorge's potential. In 2009 he won four races and even led the championship for a while but, as he often said, he didn't have the experience of his team-mate and he finished second to Rossi. This year, he applied all those lessons to put together a near-perfect season.

Kenny Roberts Senior was asked a few years ago whether a

rider was 'lucky' to have won his title. His answer was unequivocal. At this level no-one is ever handed a race win, let alone a championship. Jorge Lorenzo's main rivals feel exactly the same way. Rossi has praised Lorenzo's consistency, Stoner his error-free season. It was Jorge's pace, said Casey, which forced 'the rest of us' into mistakes. They certainly didn't enjoy saying those things – Rossi definitely had to take a deep breath first – but they recognise reality.

BRIDGESTONE
TYRE OPTIONS
FRONT HARD (H) / EXTRA HARD (XH)
REAR MEDIUM (M) / HARD (H)

motoGP
TISSOT SWISS WATCHES SINCE 1853
OFFICIAL TIMEKEEPER

MALAYSIAN GP
SEPANG INTERNATIONAL CIRCUIT

ROUND 15
October 10

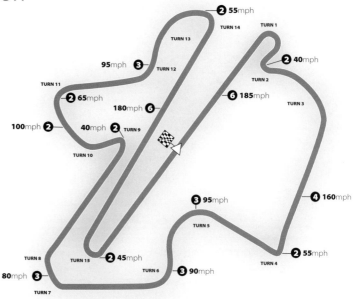

Circuit map markings:
- 2 55mph
- TURN 14 TURN 13 TURN 1
- 95mph 3 TURN 12 TURN 2
- 2 40mph
- TURN 11 TURN 2
- 2 65mph 6 185mph TURN 3
- 180mph 6
- 100mph 2 40mph 2 TURN 9
- TURN 10
- 4 160mph
- 3 95mph TURN 5
- TURN 8 2 45mph TURN 6 3 90mph 2 55mph TURN 4
- 80mph 3 TURN 15
- TURN 7

RACE RESULTS

CIRCUIT LENGTH 3.447 miles
NO. OF LAPS 20
RACE DISTANCE 68.940 miles
WEATHER Dry, 33°C
TRACK TEMPERATURE 43°C
WINNER Valentino Rossi
FASTEST LAP 2m 02.117s, 100.761mph, Valentino Rossi
LAP RECORD 2m 02.108s, 101.635mph, Casey Stoner, 2007

QUALIFYING

	Rider	Nationality	Team	Qualifying	Pole +	Gap
1	Lorenzo	SPA	Fiat Yamaha Team	2m 01.537s		
2	Hayden	USA	Ducati Team	2m 01.637s	0.100s	0.100s
3	Dovizioso	ITA	Repsol Honda Team	2m 01.829s	0.292s	0.192s
4	Spies	USA	Monster Yamaha Tech 3	2m 01.993s	0.456s	0.164s
5	Stoner	AUS	Ducati Team	2m 02.023s	0.486s	0.030s
6	Rossi	ITA	Fiat Yamaha Team	2m 02.030s	0.493s	0.007s
7	Edwards	USA	Monster Yamaha Tech 3	2m 02.097s	0.560s	0.067s
8	Bautista	SPA	Rizla Suzuki MotoGP	2m 02.394s	0.857s	0.297s
9	Capirossi	ITA	Rizla Suzuki MotoGP	2m 02.522s	0.985s	0.128s
10	Melandri	ITA	San Carlo Honda Gresini	2m 02.624s	1.087s	0.102s
11	Simoncelli	ITA	San Carlo Honda Gresini	2m 02.690s	1.153s	0.066s
12	Esparago	SPA	Pramac Racing Team	2m 02.723s	1.186s	0.033s
13	De Puniet	FRA	LCR Honda MotoGP	2m 02.775s	1.238s	0.052s
14	Aoyama	JPN	Interwetten Honda MotoGP	2m 02.778s	1.241s	0.003s
15	Barbera	SPA	Paginas Amarillas Aspar	2m 02.928s	1.391s	0.150s
16	Kallio	FIN	Pramac Racing Team	2m 04.167s	2.630s	1.239s

FINISHERS

1 VALENTINO ROSSI First win since Qatar and his 46th for Yamaha after disappointing qualifying, then one of Burgess's inspired overnight fixes. Pushed back to 11th at the first corner but realised the bike was capable of more. Later confessed to feeling shattered and had to work hard to keep Dovi behind him.

2 ANDREA DOVIZIOSO Back-to-back front-row starts and rostrum finishes marked a new level of consistency. Led the race briefly three times: into the first corner; at mid-distance from Lorenzo, just before Rossi came past; and four laps from the end when he pushed past Vale – just 0.25s behind him at the flag.

3 JORGE LORENZO Third place was enough to crown him World Champion. Started from pole and led for nine laps before Dovi and Rossi came past. Decided that winning the race 'wasn't the most important thing this time' so he 'switched to autopilot' and cruised home for the title.

4 BEN SPIES Tentative in the first four laps as he gained confidence in the left side of the harder-option front tyre, then made another trademark charge through the field, passing Hayden and Simoncelli, before putting a couple of seconds between himself and the pursuers. Only the top three lapped quicker.

5 ALVARO BAUTISTA Equalled his season's best result at Catalunya, but this was a better race. Came back from 11th, after being pushed wide in the second corner, quickly working his way up to dice with old 250 adversary Simoncelli. Finally took both Marco and Aoyama in one move, but was too late to catch Spies.

6 NICKY HAYDEN Only a tenth of a second off pole, but second was still his best qualifying on a Ducati thanks to a set-up learnt from pre-season tests here at Sepang. Had no feeling from the front tyre in the race, though, and couldn't brake as he wanted, making life difficult for him in the midfield dice.

7 HIROSHI AOYAMA Best result of the season and it might have been even better had he not got his usual awful start and then been pushed wide a couple of times by Simoncelli in the group battle behind

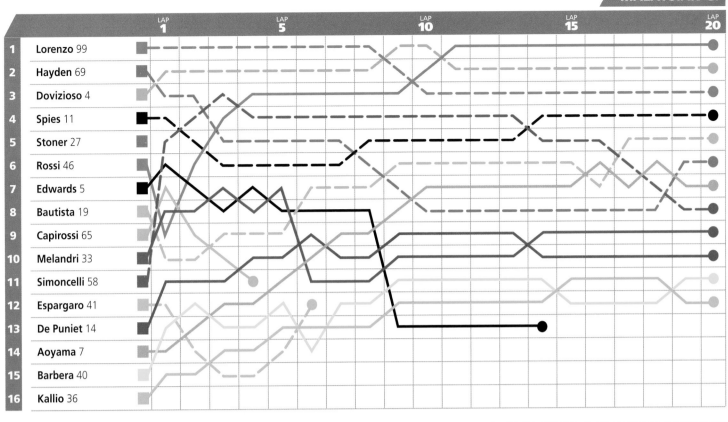

			LAP 1	LAP 5	LAP 10	LAP 15	LAP 20
1	Lorenzo 99						
2	Hayden 69						
3	Dovizioso 4						
4	Spies 11						
5	Stoner 27						
6	Rossi 46						
7	Edwards 5						
8	Bautista 19						
9	Capirossi 65						
10	Melandri 33						
11	Simoncelli 58						
12	Espargaro 41						
13	De Puniet 14						
14	Aoyama 7						
15	Barbera 40						
16	Kallio 36						

RACE

	Rider	Motorcycle	Race Time	Time +	Fastest Lap	Av Speed	🅱
1	Rossi	Yamaha	41m 03.448s		2m 02.117s	100.761mph	H/H
2	Dovizioso	Honda	41m 03.672s	0.224s	2m 02.427s	100.752mph	XH/H
3	Lorenzo	Yamaha	41m 09.483s	6.035s	2m 02.624s	100.515mph	H/H
4	Spies	Yamaha	41m 17.124s	13.676s	2m 02.773s	100.205mph	H/H
5	Bautista	Suzuki	41m 18.850s	15.402s	2m 02.895s	100.135mph	H/M
6	Hayden	Ducati	41m 22.274s	18.826s	2m 03.062s	99.997mph	XH/M
7	Aoyama	Honda	41m 23.666s	20.218s	2m 02.683s	99.941mph	XH/M
8	Simoncelli	Honda	41m 27.022s	23.574s	2m 02.898s	99.806mph	XH/H
9	Melandri	Honda	41m 27.412s	23.964s	2m 03.418s	99.791mph	XH/H
10	De Puniet	Honda	41m 35.298s	31.850s	2m 03.366s	99.475mph	XH/H
11	Barbera	Ducati	41m 42.027s	38.579s	2m 03.819s	98.802mph	XH/H
12	Kallio	Ducati	41m 42.297s	38.849s	2m 04.152s	99.197mph	XH/M
	Espargaro	Ducati	12m 37.164s	14 laps	2m 04.270s	98.348mph	XH/H
	Capirossi	Suzuki	8m 25.612s	16 laps	2m 04.425s	98.186mph	H/M
	Edwards	Yamaha	41m 58.835s	6 laps	2m 03.363s	68.982mph	H/H
	Stoner	Ducati					XH/H

CHAMPIONSHIP

	Rider	Team	Points
1	Lorenzo	Fiat Yamaha Team	313
2	Pedrosa	Repsol Honda Team	228
3	Rossi	Fiat Yamaha Team	181
4	Stoner	Ducati Team	180
5	Dovizioso	Repsol Honda Team	179
6	Spies	Monster Yamaha Tech 3	152
7	Hayden N	Ducati Team	139
8	De Puniet	LCR Honda MotoGP	94
9	Simoncelli	San Carlo Honda Gresini	92
10	Melandri	San Carlo Honda Gresini	86
11	Edwards	Monster Yamaha Tech 3	81
12	Barbera	Paginas Amarillas Aspar	74
13	Bautista	Rizla Suzuki MotoGP	69
14	Espargaro	Pramac Racing Team	52
15	Aoyama	Interwetten Honda MotoGP	44
16	Capirossi	Rizla Suzuki MotoGP	41
17	Kallio	Pramac Racing Team	38
18	De Angelis	Interwetten Honda MotoGP	11
19	Hayden R	LCR Honda MotoGP	5
20	Akiyoshi	Interwetten Honda MotoGP	4
21	Yoshikawa	Fiat Yamaha Team	1

the top three. Felt he had the pace to lead the dice and certainly proved he was back to race fitness.

8 MARCO SIMONCELLI Looked set for fifth and his best result of the year, but caught by Spies just after half-distance and then fell into the hands of the group dice. Also suffered from dehydration again, just as he had in the previous two races at Sepang.

9 MARCO MELANDRI In practice it seemed he'd finally found the confidence in the bike he'd been chasing all year, but after just two laps the old problem was back: every time he let go of the brakes the front end wanted to tuck. Started running wide, went off track on lap six, then took a long time to get past de Puniet.

10 RANDY DE PUNIET Suffered from front-end troubles all weekend. Decided to race with the harder front tyre, compromising his usual enthusiastic corner entry. Decided to take no risks, but his eighth place in the championship was now under threat.

11 HECTOR BARBERA Suffered from the instability that blighted his Japanese race: the Ducati was fine on the brakes this time, but still troublesome coming out of corners. Decided, when he saw the guys in front pulling away, to use the race as a test session, experimenting with different lines and braking points.

12 MIKA KALLIO Made up a couple of places off the start but suffered from the heat and the reappearance of his shoulder

problems. At least he got to the flag for the third race in a row.

COLIN EDWARDS Looked to be continuing the Motegi momentum when a start-line problem with his front brake forced a change to his riding style, leading to an inevitable crash. His crew repaired the bike and he rejoined to salvage some points but, unfortunately, didn't complete enough laps to qualify as a finisher.

ALEIX ESPARGARO Took three laps to get his tyres up to temperature, attacked on lap six, making up two places, before crashing while flicking the bike from right to left in a slow change of direction.

Unfortunately a handlebar broke so could not rejoin the race.

LORIS CAPIROSSI Another horrible weekend. Crashed on his out-lap for Saturday morning free practice and hurt his right foot. Ignored the pain to qualify, only to have the bike stop on him for the second race running. The ubiquitous electrical fault got the blame.

CASEY STONER Crashed on the brakes at the last corner of the first lap, caught out by a cold front tyre. Had chosen the harder option and thought he was taking things as gently as possible in third place.

DANI PEDROSA Stayed at home in Barcelona, recuperating from the operation to plate the collarbone he'd broken at the previous weekend's Motegi race.

ISLAND LIFE

Casey Stoner claimed to be nervous before the race but you'd never have known it as the Ducati man made it three wins in four races

An Australian journalist at the Aragon GP asked Valentino Rossi what his target was at Phillip Island. The response was instant: 'Beat Casey.' He was referring to the fact that Stoner had won the three previous Australian GPs but no doubt also thinking that the Aussie's form made a fourth victory a distinct possibility – and that was before Ducati found the fix that helped Casey win two in a row. Then, just as everyone thought the cure was complete, he tipped off at Sepang. Stoner obviously came home with mixed feelings and the expectations of his home fans and the Australian media weighing a little heavier than usual on his shoulders. Even his 25th birthday celebrations on the Saturday couldn't quite dispel the doubts.

Casey needn't have worried. The weekend turned into a classic example of how the guy operates. He appeared to need no time on the bike to find a set-up with which he could work, doing fewer laps and shorter runs than anyone yet still being three-quarters of a second quicker than the rest in second free practice and two-thirds of a second quicker in qualifying. And all without a hint of front-end uncertainty. Before the race the opposition appeared to have already conceded victory. The cold conditions and gusting winds, often accompanied by driving rain, just didn't seem to affect Stoner. Any time he went out on track he lapped in the low 1m 31s bracket almost instantly and quickly got down to the 1m 30s. Most of the other riders' post-qualifying quotes contained advance warning of their post-race excuses in the form of phrases like 'Casey is so fast here' – and, sure enough, he was an astonishing 1.8s faster than anyone else in warm-up.

New champion Lorenzo was second to Stoner in most

Right The stresses and strains of Phillip Island were too much for Dani Pedrosa's freshly plated collarbone

Opposite Casey Stoner was untouchable and made it four home wins in a row the day after his 25th birthday

Below Ben Spies leads Hayden, Rossi and Simoncelli in the fight for third place early in the race

sessions and for one fleeting moment thought he might be in with a chance. That moment came on the grid when he looked to his left and saw that Stoner was on a brand-new tyre. Jorge's optimism evaporated after a couple of corners, with Casey finishing the first lap over one-and-a-half seconds ahead of him, and by the end of the second lap the Aussie's lead was over two seconds. It was astonishing even before taking into account the number of times this season that Casey and the Ducati have crashed because of problems with front-tyre feedback – or rather lack of it. Stoner's first eight flying laps were in the 1m 30s bracket, and he completed a total of 11 laps in that range; Lorenzo, on the other hand, didn't get down to those lap times until lap five and then only managed to run that pace five times.

Once Casey had bolted, with Jorge following him at a respectable distance, the race resolved itself into a showdown between Rossi and Nicky Hayden for third place, with another duel between Ben Spies and Marco Simoncelli for fifth, a fight that would also settle who was Rookie of the Year. No Repsol Hondas were involved. Dani Pedrosa was already on his way home after riding in practice and qualifying just two weeks after the accident which shattered his left collarbone. He had wanted to try and ride in Malaysia but Japanese HRC management had vetoed the idea. Not surprisingly, Dani found that hanging on to the RCV in gusting wind on one of the fastest tracks on the calendar was all too much. The wind had also been a big problem for Andrea Dovizioso in practice but, once again, he and his crew appeared to find an answer for race day. Andrea was up to fifth and on the tail of Simoncelli when he started running wide and could be seen wrenching at

'I WAS MORE NERVOUS THAN I NORMALLY AM. MAYBE I SHOULD BE LIKE THAT MORE OFTEN, BECAUSE I DIDN'T MAKE MISTAKES'
CASEY STONER

his handlebars. He had no option but to pull into the pits where the Honda was diagnosed with terminal steering-damper mounting problems.

Valentino Rossi also raced a lot better than he qualified on a track he loves. He took third off Hayden on lap seven with an outbraking move at MG Corner that involved a fair bit of hip and shoulder contact. Nicky retook him three laps from the flag at Honda Corner only to have Rossi make the same move on the

last lap. Afterwards Valentino looked as if he'd won the race: his record at this track and his reputation as the man no riders want wheel-to-wheel combat with in a last-lap fight are very important to him.

Spies ultimately got the better of Simoncelli, who had a great race and ran in third early on. The American got past coming out of the final corner – 'The first time I passed anyone in a straight line this year.' Marco's style is very hard on his rear tyre while Ben is as good

Right Lorenzo exacts a bit of revenge from a carefree Stoner on the rostrum

Opposite Third place came down to a last-lap fight between Rossi and Hayden

Below Simoncelli was again strong early in the race

as anybody on worn rubber. On-board footage from Spies's Yamaha graphically illustrated the difference; just as the viewer expected to watch the Honda shrink into the distance it filled the screen and Ben went past without bothering to use the slipstream.

Arguably Spies should have been in that fight for third, but he was pushed out at the first corner and then made a mistake all of his own at the same spot, which kept him out of the fight for the last rostrum place. He had the consolation of being confirmed as Rookie of the Year and also top satellite rider in the final standings.

THE GYRO CAM

TV viewers have been enjoying pictures from cameras on board MotoGP bikes since 2003, when a miniature camera mounted on the tail of Rossi's Honda showed us the back of Valentino's leathers. Nowadays, every bike in the field carries a camera that could be looking at anything from the rider's throttle hand to the track ahead. This season, on-board cameras took another step forward with the introduction of the 'gyro cam'. Again seat-mounted, the device maintains a constant horizon so the viewer has the full effect of leaning with the rider. For years, Dorna's TV department had been looking for a compact electronic module that could track the exact position of a bike on the track and measure its lean angle in real time.

It wasn't until Valencia in 2009 that the answer was found, thanks to UAV Navigation, a Spanish company specialising in flight-control systems. Using experience acquired in the Red Bull Air Race, UAV came up with a system adapted to the constraints of a MotoGP bike using two accelerometers, a triaxial gyroscope platform, GPS and an on-board data processor. The GPS provides real-time data on the location of the bike and the three gyro sensors calculate lean angle. A miniature electronic motor under the control of the on-board processor rotates the camera's lens to compensate for the lean angle. At home the viewer now sees the horizon staying where it should be and the bike sweeping across the screen as the rider goes from upright to nearly 60 degrees of lean angle, right and left.

So far this expensive, experimental technology has only been used on a single bike in any one race, but a proliferation of gyro cams is likely in 2011.

AUSTRALIAN GP
PHILLIP ISLAND

ROUND 16
October 17

RACE RESULTS

CIRCUIT LENGTH 2.760 miles
NO. OF LAPS 27
RACE DISTANCE 74.620 miles
WEATHER Dry, 15°C
TRACK TEMPERATURE 29°C
WINNER Casey Stoner
FASTEST LAP 1m 30.458s, 108.807mph, Casey Stoner
LAP RECORD 1m 30.059s, 110.482mph, Nicky Hayden, 2008

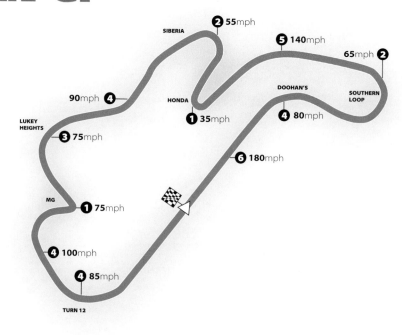

QUALIFYING

	Rider	Nationality	Team	Qualifying	Pole +	Gap
1	Stoner	AUS	Ducati Team	1m 30.107s		
2	Lorenzo	SPA	Yamaha	1m 30.775s	0.668s	0.668s
3	Spies	USA	Yamaha	1m 31.386s	1.279s	0.611s
4	Simoncelli	ITA	Honda	1m 31.402s	1.295s	0.016s
5	Edwards	USA	Monster Yamaha Tech 3	1m 31.415s	1.308s	0.013s
6	Hayden	USA	Ducati Team	1m 31.530s	1.423s	0.115s
7	De Puniet	FRA	LCR Honda MotoGP	1m 31.554s	1.447s	0.024s
8	Rossi	ITA	Fiat Yamaha Team	1m 31.627s	1.520s	0.073s
9	Dovizioso	ITA	Repsol Honda Team	1m 32.018s	1.911s	0.391s
10	Melandri	ITA	San Carlo Honda Gresini	1m 32.367s	2.260s	0.349s
11	Espargaro	SPA	Pramac Racing Team	1m 32.542s	2.435s	0.175s
12	Kallio	FIN	Pramac Racing Team	1m 32.816s	2.709s	0.274s
13	Aoyama	JPN	Interwetten Honda MotoGP	1m 33.190s	3.083s	0.374s
14	Bautista	SPA	Rizla Suzuki MotoGP	1m 33.224s	3.117s	0.034s
15	Pedrosa	SPA	Repsol Honda Team	1m 33.384s	3.277s	0.160s
16	Barbera	SPA	Paginas Amarillas Aspar	1m 33.390s	3.283s	0.006s
17	Capirossi	ITA	Rizla Suzuki MotoGP	1m 34.269s	4.162s	0.879s

FINISHERS

1 CASEY STONER Fourth win in a row at Phillip Island. Started from pole and led every lap despite admitting to feeling more pressure than usual thanks to the expectations of home fans. It's frightening to think what he might do here if someone ever pushed him hard.

2 JORGE LORENZO Happy with second place for once, conceding – like the other 'Aliens' – that this was Stoner's race. Pushed hard to about half-distance before realising that every time he closed the gap slightly, Casey took the time straight back. First MotoGP rostrum at Phillip Island.

3 VALENTINO ROSSI Set-up problems meant working hard again from a lowly eighth on the grid. Got up to third after eight laps but couldn't shake off Hayden: it took a tough last-lap pass at Honda Corner to settle the issue and secure Rossi's 13th podium finish in 14 races here. Lost third in the standings to Stoner.

4 NICKY HAYDEN His fifth fourth place of the year, and only conceded the final rostrum spot on the last lap after a tough fight with Rossi. A run-on in warm-up curtailed track time so took a while to get confidence in the bike. Involved in a fight for third with Simoncelli and Spies before pulling away to battle Valentino.

5 BEN SPIES Ensured Rookie of the Year and top satellite team rider status, but felt he should have been fighting for third. Pushed out at the first corner and later had a major moment there, both incidents costing him places. As usual, though, he was strong on used tyres and was able to overhaul Simoncelli.

6 MARCO SIMONCELLI Top Honda in both qualifying and the race. Ran in third early on but couldn't stay with Hayden and Rossi when they came past. Was then stalked by Spies, who waited until four laps from the flag to come past.

7 COLIN EDWARDS Equalled his best qualifying of the year but had problems with rear grip all through the race – he thought it was probably down to the extreme changes in conditions over the weekend.

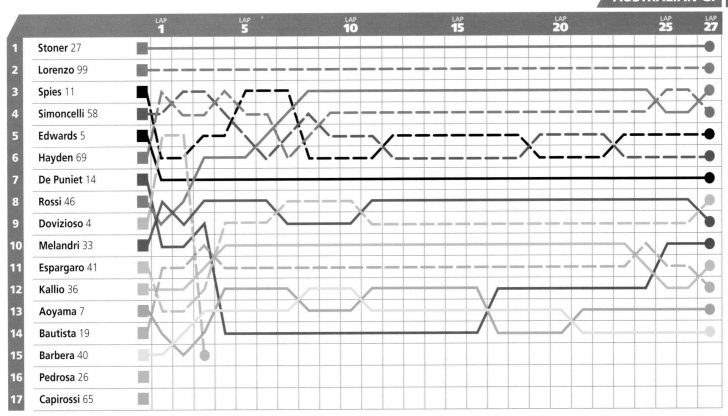

		LAP 1	LAP 5	LAP 10	LAP 15	LAP 20	LAP 25	LAP 27
1	Stoner 27							
2	Lorenzo 99							
3	Spies 11							
4	Simoncelli 58							
5	Edwards 5							
6	Hayden 69							
7	De Puniet 14							
8	Rossi 46							
9	Dovizioso 4							
10	Melandri 33							
11	Espargaro 41							
12	Kallio 36							
13	Aoyama 7							
14	Bautista 19							
15	Barbera 40							
16	Pedrosa 26							
17	Capirossi 65							

RACE

	Rider	Motorcycle	Race Time	Time +	Fastest Lap	Av Speed	B
1	**Stoner**	Ducati	41m 09.128s		1m 30.458s	108.807mph	S/H
2	Lorenzo	Yamaha	41m 17.726s	8.598s	1m 30.796s	108.429mph	S/H
3	Rossi	Yamaha	41m 27.125s	17.997s	1m 31.072s	108.019mph	S/H
4	Hayden	Ducati	41m 27.163s	18.035s	1m 31.059s	108.017mph	S/H
5	Spies	Yamaha	41m 31.339s	22.211s	1m 31.529s	107.837mph	S/H
6	Simoncelli	Honda	41m 34.145s	25.017s	1m 31.547s	107.715mph	S/H
7	Edwards	Yamaha	41m 44.296s	35.168s	1m 31.665s	107.279mph	S/H
8	Espargaro	Ducati	41m 55.322s	46.194s	1m 32.088s	106.808mph	S/H
9	Melandri	Honda	41m 55.422s	46.294s	1m 32.314s	106.804mph	S/H
10	De Puniet	Honda	42m 08.763s	59.635s	1m 32.217s	106.241mph	S/H
11	Kallio	Ducati	42m 08.792s	59.664s	1m 32.342s	106.240mph	S/H
12	Bautista	Suzuki	42m 08.860s	59.732s	1m 32.869s	106.237mph	S/H
13	Aoyama	Honda	42m 14.157s	1m 05.029s	1m 33.059s	106.015mph	S/H
14	Barbera	Ducati	42m 14.181s	1m 05.053s	1m 32.841s	106.013mph	S/H
	Dovizioso	Honda	4m 49.675s	24 laps	1m 31.716s	103.049mph	S/H

CHAMPIONSHIP

	Rider	Team	Points
1	Lorenzo	Fiat Yamaha Team	333
2	Pedrosa	Repsol Honda Team	228
3	Stoner	Ducati Team	205
4	Rossi	Fiat Yamaha Team	197
5	Dovizioso	Repsol Honda Team	179
6	Spies	Monster Yamaha Tech 3	163
7	Hayden N	Ducati Team	152
8	Simoncelli	San Carlo Honda Gresini	102
9	De Puniet	LCR Honda MotoGP	100
10	Melandri	San Carlo Honda Gresini	93
11	Edwards	Monster Yamaha Tech 3	90
12	Barbera	Paginas Amarillas Aspar	76
13	Bautista	Rizla Suzuki MotoGP	73
14	Espargaro	Pramac Racing Team	60
15	Aoyama	Interwetten Honda MotoGP	47
16	Kallio	Pramac Racing Team	43
17	Capirossi	Rizla Suzuki MotoGP	41
18	De Angelis	Interwetten Honda MotoGP	11
19	Hayden R	LCR Honda MotoGP	5
20	Akiyoshi	Interwetten Honda MotoGP	4
21	Yoshikawa	Fiat Yamaha Team	1

8 ALEIX ESPARGARO Equalled his best result of the year. Lost three positions off the start but came back strongly and spent much of the race brawling with Melandri.

9 MARCO MELANDRI It all looked better than usual for a while but the race turned into the usual story: no heat in the tyres and no confidence on the brakes. Passed by Espargaro between the final two corners.

10 RANDY DE PUNIET His race was spoiled by running on at Honda Corner while dicing with Melandri early on. That mistake put him to the back of the field on lap four, from where he rode really well to pass four riders before the flag.

11 MIKA KALLIO Tenth for most of the race despite some serious pain from his shoulder. Passed by de Puniet and Bautista in the closing stages but retook the Suzuki on the run to the flag. Mika will be replaced by Carlos Checa for the last two GPs of the year.

12 ALVARO BAUTISTA Another impressive ride, given the Suzuki's dislike of long corners and cold tracks. Only lost tenth on the run to the flag – thought the bike lost a bit of power and drive in the final 40m – and his pass on de Puniet on the last-lap run up to Lukey Heights was a candidate for move of the race.

13 HIROSHI AOYAMA Struggled all weekend and never got enough heat into his tyres on race day to have confidence in the bike.

14 HECTOR BARBERA Down on confidence after two crashes on Saturday, and his preference for setting the front end quite high meant the strong Phillip Island wind made his life even more difficult. Was happy to bring it home and to have solved the rear-grip problems of the previous two races.

NON-FINISHERS

ANDREA DOVIZIOSO Looked to be making up for disappointing qualifying with a good start and was up to fifth when he started to feel his steering stiffening up. When Dovi pulled in his crew found it was an unfixable problem with the steering-damper mounting, and he was forced to retire.

NON-STARTERS

DANI PEDROSA Rode in practice and qualified 15th but found the effort of controlling a MotoGP bike in gusting wind was too much – not surprisingly, just two weeks after having his collarbone plated.

LORIS CAPIROSSI Crashed in qualifying and tore a groin muscle. On top of his recently operated-on finger and damaged ankle this was enough for Loris to return to Europe on medical advice, in an effort to get fit for the last two races of the year.

BACK TO EARTH

It was the same result as a year ago – a runaway win for Lorenzo – and he reprised his spaceman act as well

When the weather intervenes at a GP it's easy to think, or hope, that the conditions will produce a surprise. The late October weather in the westernmost part of Europe was extreme. All three practice sessions were wet, to put it mildly, and conditions on Saturday afternoon were so dreadful that qualifying was abandoned and the grid taken from combined free-practice times. Warm-up was wet, too, so after the sun came out for the start of racing everyone went to the grid with precisely nothing in the way of relevant information on tyre choice or, more importantly, fuel mapping. Surely there'd be an upset? Well, no.

The race saw complete and total domination by the Fiat Yamahas to sew up Yamaha's third consecutive triple crown of rider, constructor and team championships. The gap at the flag between winner Jorge Lorenzo and third-placed Andrea Dovizioso was just under 26.5 seconds, an advantage of fractionally under a second a lap. A lot of observers wondered if it might have been a Yamaha one–two–three finish had Ben Spies survived the sighting lap, but he'd come off at Turn 4, the first left-hander, and given the ankle he'd hurt at Le Mans and Silverstone another painful tweak. The American saw Aoyama and Capirossi have big moments as well, but he was caught out by his cold tyre.

The other potential challengers looked to be the factory Ducati riders. Nicky Hayden led in the early stages, the first time he'd been at the front of a MotoGP race for a while, and it seemed that Casey Stoner's run of form was set to continue. He was up to third and closing on Lorenzo when he fell in the long, final corner. This wasn't a repeat of the front-end problems of the first two-thirds of the season, though; it was a repetition

of his error at the first race in Qatar. Casey ran a little wide, tried to use a fraction more steering input and, already at maximum lean, lost the front.

The only other man who might have given the Yamahas a race was Dani Pedrosa, but he was unsurprisingly handicapped by his still-healing collarbone. His top-ten finish was no mean achievement under the circumstances. Dovizioso had another stealthy race to third, aided by a stunning start, and he finished with cool thinking at the chicane. Simoncelli, who was a close fourth, slammed past his fellow Italian on the entry but couldn't carry the speed through the corner and Dovi went back past when the Gresini rider made a small mistake on the exit.

All of which happened well behind the two factory Yamahas. Rossi led after the skirmishing of the first few laps and, when the lead got up to nearly two seconds, it looked as if Valentino was going to reassert his authority. Then, on lap 12, the gap suddenly dropped to just over a second, and two laps later it was a mere quarter of a second. Jorge shadowed his team-mate before passing him on lap 17 and pulling away inexorably to a winning margin of over eight seconds. He then replayed his Apollo 11 tribute of last year with a slo-mo walk through the gravel trap in front of his team-mate to plant the Lorenzo's Land flag. And he didn't take the Neil Armstrong replica helmet off until he was standing on the rostrum.

Valentino did his best to put a positive spin on his weekend. He'd wanted a wet race not just because he'd been fast all weekend and fastest in warm-up but also because he'd finished a distant fourth here 12 months

'I KNEW I COULD WIN HERE AT MY FAVOURITE TRACK'
JORGE LORENZO

Above Hiro Aoyama demonstrates just how wet it was – the photographers ran for cover when it got really bad

Opposite Lorenzo stalks Rossi on the drying track

Right Nicky Hayden led, faded, then fought back

best lap of the race just after Jorge came past, but he soon realised that he wasn't going to be able to win and consciously backed off. Was the shoulder a problem? Definitely, but only in the closing stages. The outgoing champion did all the right things, congratulating Jorge on the slow-down lap and shaking hands with him on the rostrum, but he couldn't disguise his feelings. 'I didn't have the pace,' he said afterwards, with a shrug.

The one new factor was Marco Simoncelli, who was only kept off the rostrum by some clever and calculating riding by Dovizioso at the chicane on the final lap. Up until now Marco has undoubtedly been fast, but his aggressive style gives the tyre a hard time and his considerable extra weight compared to, say, Pedrosa doesn't help. This race looked like a breakthrough. Things are not easy for a rookie, because the restrictions on testing mean they are learning at the races, and Simoncelli took at least half the season to stop crashing once a day and to start really understanding a MotoGP bike.

There was also Randy de Puniet's return to form to admire. He had his best race since his comeback from injury, despite running on at the first corner at least three times. The Frenchman was definitely back to his spectacular self. An old favourite was back in the MotoGP paddock, too, with Carlos Checa replacing Mika Kallio at Pramac Ducati for the final two races of the year. He suffered the same arm-pump problems as Michel Fabrizio experienced when he took time out of the World Superbike team to ride a MotoGP Ducati in 2009.

But some things never change. Despite the rain and wind, despite the disruption, despite the loss of qualifying, the results had a familiar look. The fast guys are always the fast guys.

Above If anybody deserved a medal, it was the spectators

Opposite Andrea Dovizioso won the battle for third with Marco Simoncelli

Below Carlos Checa made a welcome return but was halted by arm pump

previously. The team needed some even more inspired set-up work than normal, given their lack of data, and some big changes were made to the bike compared to 2009. As usual, Jerry Burgess and the crew did improve matters, but it was not enough. Lorenzo and his crew chief, Ramon Forcada, didn't have that problem, however. They simply went with what had worked last time.

Rossi took a few risks from the start, on a track with a scattering of damp patches, while Lorenzo was more cautious. Valentino stuck with him and set his

RIDER SHUFFLE

Speculation about who would be where in MotoGP in 2011 started earlier than in any season in living memory. Casey Stoner was the first subject, mainly because of his old Ducati mentor Livio Suppo's move to HRC. Sure enough, Casey was officially confirmed as a Honda rider for the 2011 season as early as the second week of July. HRC also said that they hoped to retain their two existing Repsol team riders, leading to speculation about a three-man factory team.

Stoner's move left a vacancy at Ducati that reignited rumours about the possibility of Rossi moving to the Italian outfit. He was known to be unhappy with continuing to have Lorenzo as his team-mate and the speculation quickly became reality, with Rossi's deal announced in mid-August.

By this time HRC had a problem, because both Dani Pedrosa and Andrea Dovizioso had fulfilled the performance criteria in their contracts that guaranteed them factory rides for 2011. Dani duly re-signed at Aragon, leaving Dovi and his manager fuming at the suggestion that they might be in the Gresini team next year, albeit with full factory machinery.

At Yamaha it was announced that, as expected, Ben Spies would be moving up to the factory team and that Jorge Lorenzo would stay; no surprises there. The situation at Suzuki, though, was unclear – one bike or two? Unfortunately, it was likely to be one, with Alvaro Bautista the only man in blue.

There was also a question concerning the number of bikes the Pramac Ducati satellite team would field. When the Interwetten Honda squad folded, HRC's hand was forced into running a three-bike Repsol team and moving Aoyama to Gresini. Because of considerable political pressure to reward Toni Elias for his Moto2 championship, he'll be back in the top class. The original idea was that Elias would go to Pramac but because he had an unhappy year there in 2008 he decided to sign for LCR. De Puniet therefore moves to Pramac with Capirossi.

The good news is one new team for 2011, Cardion AB, with a sixth Ducati for young Czech rider Karel Abraham. The only other rookie will be Cal Crutchlow, who moves to Tech 3 from Yamaha's World Superbike team.

Whatever transpires, and however many bikes there are on the grid, it will be a fascinating season. There hasn't been such a major shake-up of the top riders for decades.

Above Yamaha's Superbike star Cal Crutchlow will be one of only two rookies in MotoGP 2011

BRIDGESTONE

TYRE OPTIONS
FRONT SOFT (**S**) / MEDIUM (**M**)
REAR MEDIUM (**M**) / HARD (**H**)

OFFICIAL TIMEKEEPER

PORTUGUESE GP
ESTORIL

ROUND **17**
October 31

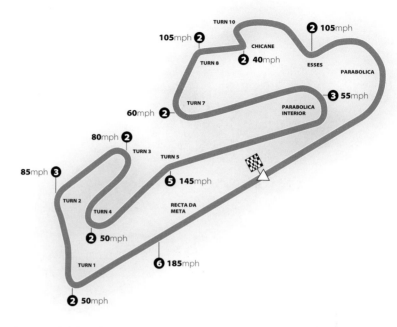

RACE RESULTS

CIRCUIT LENGTH 2.599 miles
NO. OF LAPS 28
RACE DISTANCE 72.772 miles
WEATHER Dry, 19°C
TRACK TEMPERATURE 26°C
WINNER Jorge Lorenzo
FASTEST LAP 1m 37.928s, 96.505mph, Jorge Lorenzo
LAP RECORD 1m 36.937s, 96.505mph, Dani Pedrosa

QUALIFYING DETERMINED BY COMBINED PRACTICE TIMES

	Rider	Nationality	Team	Qualifying	Pole +	Gap
1	**Lorenzo**	SPA	Fiat Yamaha Team	**1m 48.522s**		
2	Hayden	USA	Ducati Team	**1m 48.657s**	0.135s	0.135s
3	Rossi	ITA	Fiat Yamaha Team	**1m 48.883s**	0.361s	0.226s
4	Stoner	AUS	Ducati Team	**1m 49.061s**	0.539s	0.178s
5	Spies	USA	Monster Yamaha Tech 3	**1m 49.721s**	1.199s	0.660s
6	Melandri	ITA	San Carlo Honda Gresini	**1m 49.784s**	1.262s	0.063s
7	Dovizioso	ITA	Repsol Honda Team	**1m 50.007s**	1.485s	0.223s
8	De Puniet	FRA	LCR Honda MotoGP	**1m 50.043s**	1.521s	0.036s
9	Edwards	USA	Monster Yamaha Tech 3	**1m 50.313s**	1.791s	0.270s
10	Simoncelli	ITA	San Carlo Honda Gresini	**1m 50.500s**	1.978s	0.187s
11	Espargaro	SPA	Pramac Racing Team	**1m 50.787s**	2.265s	0.287s
12	Pedrosa	SPA	Repsol Honda Team	**1m 50.824s**	2.302s	0.037s
13	Capirossi	ITA	Rizla Suzuki MotoGP	**1m 51.518s**	2.996s	0.694s
14	Bautista	SPA	Rizla Suzuki MotoGP	**1m 52.734s**	4.212s	1.216s
15	Barbera	SPA	Paginas Amarillas Aspar	**1m 53.131s**	4.609s	0.397s
16	Aoyama	JPN	Interwetten Honda MotoGP	**1m 53.317s**	4.795s	0.186s
17	Checa	SPA	Pramac Racing Team	**1m 53.933s**	5.411s	0.616s

FINISHERS

1 JORGE LORENZO A little wary early on when the track was still damp in places but then overhauled Rossi and pulled away for his third win in three years here at Estoril. Crossed a two-second gap to Valentino, then won by over eight seconds, a commanding performance after a barren spell since Brno.

2 VALENTINO ROSSI Fast in the wet and much better than last year in the dry, but still not good enough to race Lorenzo. Realised he wouldn't be able to compete and backed off, but still managed to finish well clear of the chasing Hondas. Also suffered from his shoulder injury late in the race.

3 ANDREA DOVIZIOSO Started from the front of the third row but up to fourth at Turn 1 and in third by the end of the first lap. Involved in a race-long fight for the last rostrum spot, first with Stoner and Hayden, then with Simoncelli, and achieved it by keeping calm after Marco rushed past him at the chicane.

4 MARCO SIMONCELLI Best race of the year. From tenth on the grid he'd joined the leaders by lap five and was in the fight for third right up to the flag. Looked as if he'd worked out how to make his tyre last. Quicker than Dovi in the lap's second half, taking him at the chicane last time round, but a small mistake on the exit meant he just missed his first rostrum in MotoGP.

5 NICKY HAYDEN Led the race on lap two, the first time he'd done that for a while. Felt good with the bike until he had a couple of big moments on damp patches and dropped to sixth. Regained his confidence and came back to the fight for third, finishing less than half a second behind the two Italians.

6 RANDY DE PUNIET Back to his buccaneering best for the first time since his nasty accident in Germany. Would have been involved in the fight for third but for the lingering effects of his broken leg giving him problems braking and downshifting. Ran on several times at Turn 1, losing three seconds on the first occasion.

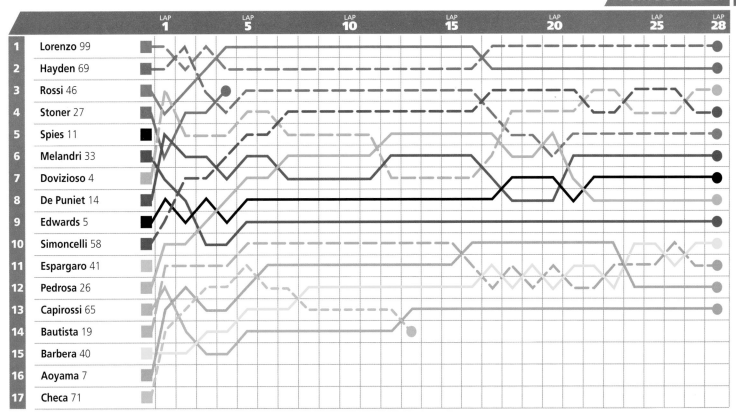

			LAP 1	LAP 5	LAP 10	LAP 15	LAP 20	LAP 25	LAP 28
1	Lorenzo 99								
2	Hayden 69								
3	Rossi 46								
4	Stoner 27								
5	Spies 11								
6	Melandri 33								
7	Dovizioso 4								
8	De Puniet 14								
9	Edwards 5								
10	Simoncelli 58								
11	Espargaro 41								
12	Pedrosa 26								
13	Capirossi 65								
14	Bautista 19								
15	Barbera 40								
16	Aoyama 7								
17	Checa 71								

RACE

	Rider	Motorcycle	Race Time	Time +	Fastest Lap	Av Speed	B
1	Lorenzo	Yamaha	46m 17.962s		1m 37.928s	94.294mph	M/M
2	Rossi	Yamaha	46m 26.591s	8.629s	1m 38.325s	94.002mph	M/M
3	Dovizioso	Honda	46m 44.437s	26.475s	1m 39.038s	93.404mph	M/M
4	Simoncelli	Honda	46m 44.496s	26.534s	1m 39.077s	93.402mph	M/M
5	Hayden	Ducati	46m 45.116s	27.154s	1m 38.871s	93.382mph	S/M
6	De Puniet	Honda	46m 46.259s	28.297s	1m 39.143s	93.344mph	M/M
7	Edwards	Yamaha	46m 48.071s	30.109s	1m 39.051s	93.283mph	M/M
8	Pedrosa	Honda	47m 02.909s	44.947s	1m 39.173s	92.793mph	M/M
9	Melandri	Honda	47m 31.611s	1m 13.649s	1m 40.827s	91.859mph	S/M
10	Barbera	Ducati	47m 35.683s	1m 17.721s	1m 40.828s	91.728mph	S/M
11	Bautista	Suzuki	47m 35.870s	1m 17.908s	1m 40.709s	91.722mph	S/M
12	Aoyama	Honda	47m 50.987s	1m 33.025s	1m 40.569s	91.239mph	S/M
13	Capirossi	Suzuki	47m 57.714s	1m 39.752s	1m 41.579s	91.026mph	S/M
	Checa	Ducati	22m 31.090s	15 laps	1m 41.889s	90.015mph	M/M
	Stoner	Ducati	6m 49.552s	24 laps	1m 39.012s	91.370mph	M/M

CHAMPIONSHIP

	Rider	Team	Points
1	Lorenzo	Fiat Yamaha Team	358
2	Pedrosa	Repsol Honda Team	236
3	Rossi	Fiat Yamaha Team	217
4	Stoner	Ducati Team	205
5	Dovizioso	Repsol Honda Team	195
6	Spies	Monster Yamaha Tech 3	163
7	Hayden N	Ducati Team	163
8	Simoncelli	San Carlo Honda Gresini	115
9	De Puniet	LCR Honda MotoGP	110
10	Melandri	San Carlo Honda Gresini	100
11	Edwards	Monster Yamaha Tech 3	99
12	Barbera	Paginas Amarillas Aspar	82
13	Bautista	Rizla Suzuki MotoGP	78
14	Espargaro	Pramac Racing Team	60
15	Aoyama	Interwetten Honda MotoGP	51
16	Capirossi	Rizla Suzuki MotoGP	44
17	Kallio	Pramac Racing Team	43
18	De Angelis	Interwetten Honda MotoGP	11
19	Hayden R	LCR Honda MotoGP	5
20	Akiyoshi	Interwetten Honda MotoGP	4
21	Yoshikawa	Fiat Yamaha Team	1

7 COLIN EDWARDS Started well and felt happy with the bike despite the total lack of dry testing. Shadowed the fight for third for the whole race but couldn't quite get on terms with the group. Made up time on the brakes but outpowered on the straights.

8 DANI PEDROSA Knew from the third lap that he wouldn't be able to maintain his pace: still handicapped by the collarbone he broke in Japan and unsurprisingly suffered in the closing stages. Did enough to keep his second place in the championship, though, with a healthy advantage over Rossi.

9 MARCO MELANDRI Another horrible day at the office. Marco maintained that no-one had done anything to help him all year; the team said they'd done everything possible. The nightmare continued.

10 HECTOR BARBERA Won the three-way battle for tenth despite crashing twice in practice. Lost time at the start but gained in confidence and enjoyed himself for the first time since Aragon.

11 ALVARO BAUTISTA A cold track is always a Suzuki rider's nightmare, and this time the problem was straight-line instability bad enough to make Alvaro close the throttle on the straight. Strong cross-winds were blamed, but other bikes didn't have the same difficulty. There wasn't much grip from his tyres either.

12 HIROSHI AOYAMA Very wary of the patchy track in the opening laps. Got quicker mid-race, caught and overtook the group, but then ran very wide and handed the positions back.

13 LORIS CAPIROSSI Suffered all the same chronic instability problems as his team-mate, but happy to finish a race for the first time since Indianapolis. Loris's catalogue of injuries didn't help matters.

NON-FINISHERS

CARLOS CHECA Back on a MotoGP bike for the first time in three years, replacing Mika Kallio in the Pramac Ducati team. Under the circumstances the lack of dry practice was a nightmare, but it was arm pump in the right forearm that ended Carlos's race early.

CASEY STONER Looked likely to be the only man able to give the Fiat Yamahas a race when he ran a little off line, lost the front and crashed in the final corner of lap five while lying third and closing on Lorenzo. This didn't look like a return of the Ducati's front-end problems, more a case of the rider being caught out.

ALEIX ESPARGARO Didn't make it round the first lap. Lost the rear when he was in ninth place, probably on a damp section of track, and was highsided.

NON-STARTERS

BEN SPIES Caught out by a cold tyre at Turn 4, the first left-hander, on the sighting lap. Did some more damage to the ankle he hurt at Le Mans and banged again at Silverstone. Early reports said it was a dislocation, but Ben said he had every intention of riding at the final race of the year and in the test that followed it.

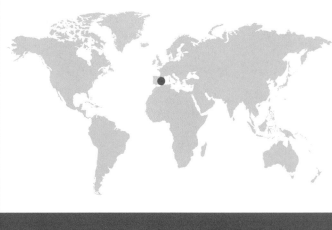

DIAMOND GEEZER

Jorge Lorenzo steals the show, in more than one way

The final race of the 2010 season brought the curtain down on several long-term relationships. Among them, of course, were Valentino Rossi's seven-year affair with his Yamaha M1 and Casey Stoner's four-year fling with Ducati, and there were numerous departures further down the grid. But despite the best attempts of those who were waving goodbye to loved ones, the show was stolen utterly and completely by Jorge Lorenzo.

For starters Jorge used a £10,000 crash helmet of dubious taste featuring several thousand Swarovski crystals picking out his 'por fuera' logo on top of a gold colour scheme. As if that wasn't enough, just before the riders emerged to go to the grid, an Air Europa Airbus flew low over the track with a giant picture of Jorge emblazoned on its fuselage. 'Beat that, boys' was the bling-encrusted message. And Jorge was pretty sharp on track as well.

It looked as if the comparatively restrained Casey Stoner would be near impossible to beat after he qualified on pole for the third year running. In 2008 he was never headed, last year he managed to crash on the warm-up lap, and this time everyone assumed he'd got it in the bag. What we didn't know was that a typically brave qualifying lap obscured the real problems and Casey was one of comparatively few to opt for the harder rear tyre for the race.

Dani Pedrosa said that he could see very early on that Casey was in trouble with his tyre choice. Dani got a close look much earlier than he could have expected; from eighth on the grid he made his usual bullet start but his progress up to the second corner was astonishing. Luckily, the TV director had

Above Stoner leads, Pedrosa attacks Hayden and Lorenzo drops back behind Simoncelli

Below Hayden's Ducati after Nicky's high-speed crash

Opposite Ben Spies ghosted through to fourth

'I USED TO BE KNOWN AS A CRAZY RIDER WHO CRASHED TOO MUCH'

JORGE LORENZO

a forward facing on-board camera to show us Dani weaving between bikes as got up to third behind the two factory Ducatis. Lorenzo, meanwhile, was getting boxed in at the second corner and shuffled back to fifth.

It promptly got worse for the champion-elect on the last corner of the second lap. Lorenzo tried to pass Simoncelli on the inside only to have the Italian lay across his front wheel. Jorge was pitched off the inside of his bike but somehow bounced back into the saddle and continued, shaking his head. He was now eighth. Nicky Hayden then put him up a place by crashing spectacularly at Turn 1 and Jorge began his march forward. Spies was immediately dispatched, and then it took three laps to get Dovizioso and three more to get Simoncelli.

Two laps later Dani Pedrosa's left arm started to go numb and he slipped back after a quite astonishing opening ten laps during which he set the fastest lap of the race. The collarbone injury was bad enough, but there was nerve and vascular damage as well which led not just to loss of power in the arm but numbness right down to his hand. Under the circumstances, his defence of his second place in the championship was more than brave; he described the race as one of his hardest and one of which he was most proud.

Someone else who thought he had a good race was Valentino Rossi. The Valencia track has never been particularly kind to him and after qualifying he looked in all sorts of trouble. Warm-up didn't indicate that Jerry Burgess had found an answer to his traction problems, but in the race Vale made rapid progress and

corner and Lorenzo was through and immediately able to pull out a significant lead. He was over four seconds ahead at the flag, putting the seal on a record-breaking season in which he racked up more points in a year than anyone had done before and finished in the top four in all 18 races – a unique feat.

Rossi cruised to an untroubled third place in front of Ben Spies, who made another late charge and went past all three factory Hondas in the last ten laps, taking Simoncelli and Pedrosa in one lap. Rossi was surprisingly happy with what he said was one of his best ever races at Valencia, especially considering the trouble he was in during qualifying. On the slow-down lap he stopped and kissed his M1 in a re-enactment of that first win in South Africa seven years previously. That was the first of 46 wins and four titles on a Yamaha, and if you'd have offered Valentino that tally back in 2004 he would 'have signed in blood'. Masao Furusawa, Yamaha's head of research, said the difference between 2004 and 2003, Yamaha's worst ever year, was the difference between heaven and hell. Valentino and his crew marked the parting of the ways with T-shirts emblazoned with 'Bye bye baby' – another reference to his love affair with the M1.

It was all good stuff and in any other year would have hogged the attention of the photographers and TV cameras, but not this time. Jorge Lorenzo's race upstaged even the Doctor. Jorge's crew also had special T-shirts: on theirs was written '3_ _' and the missing digits were filled in after the race with a marker pen to read '383', his record points haul for the season. An understated little reminder of what Jorge had done to the rest of them this year.

Above Loris Capirossi's final race with Suzuki ended in retirement

Below No team orders as the factory Hondas of Pedrosa, Simoncelli and Dovizioso fight over fifth place

Opposite The Doctor said goodbye to Yamaha with a rostrum finish

pushed past Simoncelli to take third on the sixth lap. When Pedrosa started to suffer, Rossi went second and briefly he even thought that he could pass Stoner and win. Then Valentino's own lack of fitness started to tell and Lorenzo came past on lap 12.

Stoner might have been in trouble with his tyres but he made life difficult for Jorge. Casey was braking late and going deep into corners in an attempt to defend his place but he eventually ran wide at the first

ALEX CRIVILLE

Spain's first senior class champion, Alex Criville, is an obvious man to ask about the unique achievement of Spanish riders in finishing first and second in all three classes this year. This is what he had to say.

'The success of Spanish riders in all classes this year of course gave me a lot of pleasure. I won on a 500, Jorge Lorenzo won on a MotoGP machine, but the championships are the same. No-one is ever given a world title. I had to work hard for mine, overcome injury and deal with very tough rivals. Jorge did the same. This year he has been astonishingly consistent, hardly ever off the front row or the rostrum. This is the mark of a real champion, and he has achieved this level in just three years in the top class.

'Jorge came to the top class via the traditional route of the small classes, 125 and 250. I did the same, but against rivals who came from a different background of dirt track and superbikes. But there is one other thing that links us, and that is Javier Ullate. He was one of my mechanics in the 1999 Repsol Honda team and it was he who held out the pit board at Rio to tell me I was World Champion. It gave me real pleasure to see Javier, now one of Jorge's crew at Fiat Yamaha, hold out the board for him at Sepang. And Ramon Forcada, who did such a good job as Jorge's crew chief, worked on my title-winning 125 with the great Antonio Cobas. These things are important and remind us that racing is not just about the rider but the whole team. It is because of people like this that Spanish racing is strong today.'

Above Alex Criville now works for Spanish TV as an expert summariser

VALENCIAN GP
CIRCUITO RICARDO TORMO

ROUND 18
November 7

RACE RESULTS

CIRCUIT LENGTH 2.488 miles
NO. OF LAPS 30
RACE DISTANCE 74.640 miles
WEATHER Dry, 22°C
TRACK TEMPERATURE 27°C
WINNER Jorge Lorenzo
FASTEST LAP 1m 32.914s, 94.927mph, Dani Pedrosa
LAP RECORD 1m 32.582s, 96.767mph, Casey Stoner, 2008

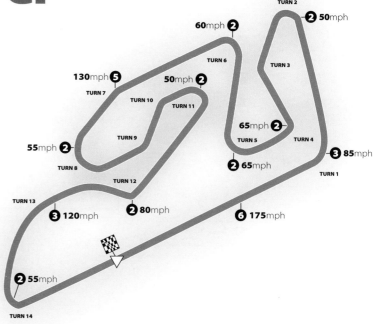

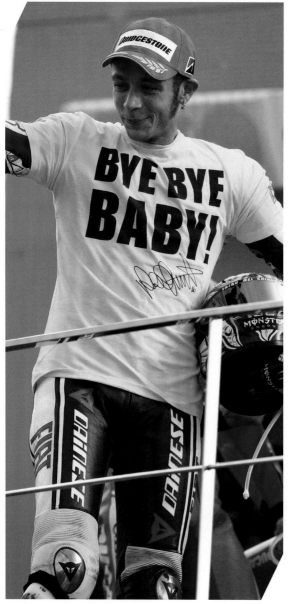

QUALIFYING

	Rider	Nationality	Team	Qualifying	Pole +	Gap
1	Stoner	AUS	Ducati Team	1m 31.799s		
2	Lorenzo	SPA	Fiat Yamaha Team	1m 32.130s	0.331s	0.331s
3	Simoncelli	ITA	San Carlo Honda Gresini	1m 32.244s	0.445s	0.114s
4	Rossi	ITA	Fiat Yamaha Team	1m 32.330s	0.531s	0.086s
5	Hayden	USA	Ducati Team	1m 32.422s	0.623s	0.092s
6	Spies	USA	Monster Yamaha Tech 3	1m 32.566s	0.767s	0.144s
7	Edwards	USA	Monster Yamaha Tech 3	1m 32.579s	0.780s	0.013s
8	Pedrosa	SPA	Repsol Honda Team	1m 32.603s	0.804s	0.024s
9	Dovizioso	ITA	Repsol Honda Team	1m 32.886s	1.087s	0.283s
10	Melandri	ITA	San Carlo Honda Gresini	1m 32.917s	1.118s	0.031s
11	De Puniet	FRA	LCR Honda MotoGP	1m 32.925s	1.126s	0.008s
12	Espargaro	SPA	Pramac Racing Team	1m 33.085s	1.286s	0.160s
13	Barbera	SPA	Paginas Amarillas Aspar	1m 33.170s	1.371s	0.085s
14	Capirossi	ITA	Rizla Suzuki MotoGP	1m 33.339s	1.540s	0.169s
15	Aoyama	JPN	Interwetten Honda MotoGP	1m 33.343s	1.544s	0.004s
16	Checa	SPA	Pramac Racing Team	1m 33.499s	1.700s	0.156s
17	Bautista	SPA	Rizla Suzuki MotoGP	1m 33.515s	1.716s	0.016s

FINISHERS

1 JORGE LORENZO Probably his best race of the year, and certainly his most eventful. Blocked in at the first corner, nearly on the floor after a coming together with Simoncelli at the end of the second lap that put him back to eighth, and then a brilliant ride up to Stoner. It took him a long time to find a way past, but when he did he pulled away. A champion's ride.

2 CASEY STONER Disguised problems with set-up and tyre choice with his usual blazing qualifying lap for pole. Went with the harder tyre option, which may have been a mistake, but did a great job on the brakes to make Lorenzo work hard for his winning pass. Happy to leave Ducati with a rostrum.

3 VALENTINO ROSSI Probably not the way he wanted to leave Yamaha, but it was the 'best race of my career at Valencia'. At one point Valentino thought he might be able to win, but it was his body rather than the bike that let him down. In the last laps his overall lack of fitness told. Five consecutive podiums is not a bad way to finish the year.

4 BEN SPIES Another vastly impressive race to secure sixth place in the championship table, as well as the honour of being top American. Seventh for most of the race but caught the ailing Pedrosa and then passed Dovizioso and Simoncelli in one lap before pulling away to a safe fourth.

5 ANDREA DOVIZIOSO Another good start to make up for tough qualifying on a track he's never gone well at in any class. Up to fourth early on but Dovi never really threatened the leaders. By the end of the race his tyres were far gone and he had no answer to Spies.

6 MARCO SIMONCELLI Enhanced his reputation as a tough guy with his willingness to put his body in the path of Lorenzo's front tyre. However, his decision to go with the harder rear tyre may have been an error. Marco couldn't match the times he'd done in practice and lost out to Dovizioso for the second weekend in a row.

7 DANI PEDROSA Given the state of his injury, this was a miraculous race. Dani

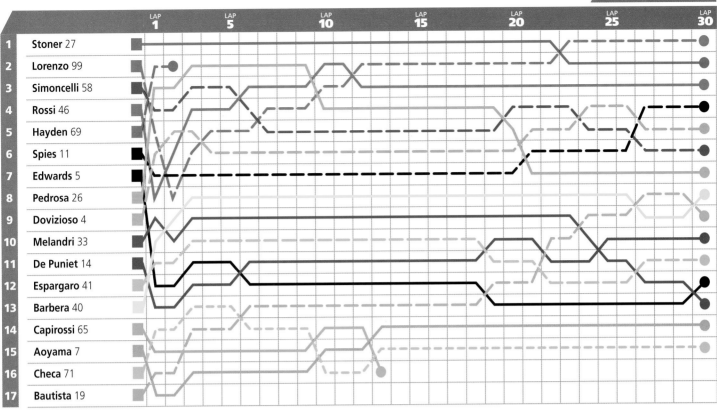

			LAP 1			LAP 5			LAP 10			LAP 15			LAP 20			LAP 25			LAP 30
1	Stoner 27
2	Lorenzo 99
3	Simoncelli 58
4	Rossi 46
5	Hayden 69
6	Spies 11
7	Edwards 5
8	Pedrosa 26
9	Dovizioso 4
10	Melandri 33
11	De Puniet 14
12	Espargaro 41
13	Barbera 40
14	Capirossi 65
15	Aoyama 7
16	Checa 71
17	Bautista 19

RACE

	Rider	Motorcycle	Race Time	Time +	Fastest Lap	Av Speed	
1	Lorenzo	Yamaha	46m 44.622s		1m 32.940s	95.834mph	M/M
2	Stoner	Ducati	46m 49.198s	4.576s	1m 33.018s	95.678mph	M/H
3	Rossi	Yamaha	46m 53.620s	8.998s	1m 32.970s	95.527mph	M/M
4	Spies	Yamaha	47m 02.265s	17.643s	1m 33.294s	95.235mph	M/M
5	Dovizioso	Honda	47m 03.782s	19.160s	1m 33.279s	95.184mph	M/H
6	Simoncelli	Honda	47m 05.296s	20.674s	1m 33.245s	95.133mph	M/H
7	Pedrosa	Honda	47m 11.419s	26.797s	1m 32.914s	94.927mph	M/M
8	Barbera	Ducati	47m 13.910s	29.288s	1m 33.735s	94.844mph	M/M
9	Bautista	Suzuki	47m 14.073s	29.451s	1m 33.675s	94.838mph	S/M
10	De Puniet	Honda	47m 14.482s	29.860s	1m 33.620s	94.825mph	M/H
11	Espargaro	Ducati	47m 16.383s	31.761s	1m 33.784s	94.761mph	M/M
12	Edwards	Yamaha	47m 18.226s	33.604s	1m 33.723s	94.700mph	M/M
13	Melandri	Honda	47m 21.244s	36.622s	1m 33.784s	94.599mph	M/H
14	Aoyama	Honda	47m 23.590s	38.968s	1m 34.087s	94.521mph	M/M
15	Checa	Ducati	47m 40.791s	56.169s	1m 34.163s	93.952mph	M/M
	Capirossi	Suzuki	20m 48.058s	17 laps	1m 34.231s	93.321mph	M/M
	Hayden	Ducati	3m 13.356s	28 laps	1m 33.546s	92.671mph	M/M

CHAMPIONSHIP

	Rider	Team	Points
1	Lorenzo	Fiat Yamaha Team	383
2	Pedrosa	Repsol Honda Team	245
3	Rossi	Fiat Yamaha Team	233
4	Stoner	Ducati Team	225
5	Dovizioso	Repsol Honda Team	206
6	Spies	Monster Yamaha Tech 3	176
7	Hayden N	Ducati Team	163
8	Simoncelli	San Carlo Honda Gresini	125
9	De Puniet	LCR Honda MotoGP	116
10	Melandri	San Carlo Honda Gresini	103
11	Edwards	Monster Yamaha Tech 3	103
12	Barbera	Paginas Amarillas Aspar	90
13	Bautista	Rizla Suzuki MotoGP	85
14	Espargaro	Pramac Racing Team	65
15	Aoyama	Interwetten Honda MotoGP	53
16	Capirossi	Rizla Suzuki MotoGP	44
17	Kallio	Pramac Racing Team	43
18	De Angelis	Interwetten Honda MotoGP	11
19	Hayden R	LCR Honda MotoGP	5
20	Akiyoshi	Interwetten Honda MotoGP	4
21	Checa	Pramac Racing Team	1
22	Yoshikawa	Fiat Yamaha Team	1

stayed with Stoner in the early stages before lack of strength and numbness in his left arm told. Along the way he set the fastest lap of the race and hung on to his second place in the championship. It was, he said, one of the hardest races of his life.

8 HECTOR BARBERA The confidence in the bike he rediscovered at Portugal transferred to Valencia and Hector won the now traditional midfield group fight, holding off Bautista on the last lap. Equalled his best result of the year but said this was his best race because he found his best set-up of the year and rode at 100 per cent from the start.

9 ALVARO BAUTISTA A remarkable ride from dead last on the grid. Alvaro

took a gamble on his settings on Sunday after a disastrous Friday and Saturday. His lap times should have seen him fighting for fifth but again it was qualifying that was the problem. His team manager declared it the ride of Alvaro's season. The man himself thought he should have been eighth!

10 RANDY DE PUNIET Couldn't use the corner speed he usually does, probably because of conservative engine-mapping and worrying too much about tyre life. Not the result Randy wanted to end his five-year association with the LCR team; he thought he could and should have been in the top six.

11 ALEIX ESPARGARO He would have wanted a better result to end his

first year as a full-time MotoGP rider. It looked good in warm-up and in the early stages of the race but he couldn't make progress when the tyres were worn.

12 COLIN EDWARDS Very encouraging practice and qualifying on the harder rear tyre, but went for the softer option on race day due to the cooler conditions. That resulted in a severe lack of grip under acceleration.

13 MARCO MELANDRI Another horrible day at the office, but this time it was the last one. As usual Marco didn't want to talk about the race, and as usual the team said they'd done all they could to help him. This was Marco's last GP of a 15-year career.

14 HIROSHI AOYAMA It was the usual story for Hiro – lacking in confidence at the start of the race but able to turn very good lap times once the tyres warmed up. This time, though, he also hit trouble at the end of the race and his lap times tailed off.

15 CARLOS CHECA Replaced Mika Kallio for the second time in the Pramac Ducati team and at least finished the race on this occasion. Never had the time to get any sort of feeling with the Desmosedici but was able to pass Aoyama and Capirossi in the opening stages.

NON-FINISHERS

LORIS CAPIROSSI Pulled in after 12 laps citing a sudden loss of power. The team couldn't spot anything immediately; a sad end to Loris's time with Suzuki.

NICKY HAYDEN Got into the first corner of the third lap a little too hot, bottomed out the fork and crashed at speed while second. Very angry with himself, especially as he'd been fastest in warm-up and thought he should have been fighting for the podium.

WORLD CHAMPIONSHIP CLASSIFICATION

MotoGP

	Rider	Nation	Motorcycle	QAT	SPA	FRA	ITA	GBR	NED	CAT	GER	USA	CZE	INP	RSM	ARA	JPN	MAL	AUS	POR	VAL	Points
1	Lorenzo	SPA	Yamaha	20	25	25	20	25	25	25	20	25	25	16	20	13	13	16	20	25	25	383
2	Pedrosa	SPA	Honda	9	20	11	25	8	20	20	25	–	20	25	25	20	–	–	–	8	9	245
3	Rossi	ITA	Yamaha	25	16	20	–	–	–	–	13	16	11	13	16	10	16	25	16	20	16	233
4	Stoner	AUS	Ducati	–	11	–	13	11	16	16	16	20	16	–	11	25	25	–	25	–	20	225
5	Dovizioso	ITA	Honda	16	10	16	16	20	11	2	11	13	–	11	13	–	20	20	–	16	11	206
6	Spies	USA	Yamaha	11	–	–	9	16	13	10	8	10	13	20	10	11	8	13	11	–	13	176
7	Hayden	USA	Ducati	13	13	13	–	13	9	8	9	11	10	10	–	16	4	10	13	11	–	163
8	Simoncelli	ITA	Honda	5	5	6	7	9	7	–	10	–	5	9	2	9	10	8	10	13	10	125
9	De Puniet	FRA	Honda	10	7	9	10	10	10	13	–	–	6	3	3	–	7	6	6	10	6	116
10	Melandri	ITA	Honda	3	8	10	11	–	–	7	6	8	8	–	6	7	5	7	7	7	3	103
11	Edwards	USA	Yamaha	8	4	4	3	7	8	5	–	9	9	–	9	4	11	–	9	9	4	103
12	Barbera	SPA	Ducati	4	3	8	4	5	4	6	7	–	7	6	7	5	3	5	2	6	8	90
13	Bautista	SPA	Suzuki	–	6	–	2	4	2	11	–	–	–	8	8	8	9	11	4	5	7	85
14	Espargaro	SPA	Ducati	–	1	7	8	6	6	–	–	–	4	7	5	6	2	–	8	–	5	65
15	Aoyama	JPN	Honda	6	2	5	5	–	–	–	–	–	4	4	3	6	9	3	4	2		53
16	Capirossi	ITA	Suzuki	7	–	–	6	–	3	9	5	6	–	5	–	–	–	–	–	3	–	44
17	Kallio	FIN	Ducati	–	9	3	–	3	5	4	–	7	–	–	–	2	1	4	5	–	–	43
18	De Angelis	RSM	Honda	–	–	–	–	–	–	–	4	4	3	–	–	–	–	–	–	–	–	11
19	Hayden RL	USA	Honda	–	–	–	–	–	–	–	–	5	–	–	–	–	–	–	–	–	–	5
20	Akioshi	JPN	Honda	–	–	–	–	–	1	3	–	–	–	–	–	–	–	–	–	–	–	4
21	Checa	SPA	Ducati	–	–	–	–	–	–	–	–	–	–	–	–	–	–	–	–	–	1	1
22	Yoshikawa	JPN	Yamaha	–	–	–	–	–	–	1	–	–	–	–	–	–	–	–	–	–	–	1

CONSTRUCTOR

	Motorcycle	QAT	SPA	FRA	ITA	GBR	NED	CAT	GER	USA	CZE	INP	RSM	ARA	JPN	MAL	AUS	POR	VAL	Points
1	Yamaha	25	25	25	20	25	25	25	20	25	25	20	20	13	16	25	20	25	25	404
2	Honda	16	20	16	25	20	20	20	25	13	20	25	25	20	20	20	10	16	11	342
3	Ducati	13	13	13	13	13	16	16	16	20	16	10	11	25	25	10	25	11	20	286
4	Suzuki	7	6	–	6	4	3	11	5	6	–	8	8	8	9	11	4	5	7	108

TEAM

	Motorcycle	QAT	SPA	FRA	ITA	GBR	NED	CAT	GER	USA	CZE	INP	RSM	ARA	JPN	MAL	AUS	POR	VAL	Points
1	Fiat Yamaha Team	45	41	45	20	25	25	26	33	41	36	29	36	23	29	41	36	45	41	617
2	Repsol Honda Team	25	30	27	41	28	31	22	36	13	20	36	38	20	20	20	–	24	20	451
3	Ducati Team	13	24	13	13	24	25	24	25	31	26	10	11	41	29	10	38	11	20	388
4	Monster Yamaha Tech 3	19	4	4	12	23	21	15	8	19	22	20	19	15	19	13	20	9	17	279
5	San Carlo Honda Gresini	8	13	16	18	9	7	7	16	8	13	9	8	16	15	15	17	20	13	228
6	Rizla Suzuki MotoGP	7	6	–	8	4	5	20	5	6	–	13	8	8	9	11	4	8	7	129
7	LCR Honda MotoGP	10	7	9	10	10	10	13	–	5	6	3	3	–	7	6	6	10	6	121
8	Pramac Racing Team	–	10	10	8	9	11	4	–	7	4	7	5	8	3	4	13	–	6	109
9	Paginas Amarillas Aspar	4	3	8	4	5	4	6	7	–	7	6	7	5	3	5	2	6	8	90
10	Interwetten Honda MotoGP	6	2	5	5	–	1	3	4	4	3	4	4	3	6	9	3	4	2	68

TECHNICAL REVIEW
NEIL SPALDING

Moto2 TECH

Would a street engine in a race chassis make for a good race series? With the advent of Moto2 it was time to find out

Motorcycle Grand Prix racing's new intermediate class arrived in 2010, replacing the 250s that had graced the championship since 1949. Moto2, as it is now called, is not designed to be a prototype or technical development class, or an arena for factories to display their technical superiority. It is meant, instead, to be an affordable rider-development class.

The birth was difficult. It took years to negotiate the 250s out of the paddock, and several different sets of rules allowing different engine types were drafted, but at the last moment it was decided that a control engine was what the class required. After a tendering process that saw no factories interested in providing motors, Honda stepped in 'to help the sport'. By early 2009 the basics were in place: Honda CBR600RR control engines in prototype chassis with a minimum weight of 135kg. At the beginning of March 2010 the engines finally arrived, and Moto2 was up and rolling.

Moto2 isn't a prototype class like MotoGP or the 125s – there are too many control components for that – but there are a lot of ways to build a bike, and a number of different manufacturers turned up with new chassis, so it rapidly became a question of who could get their chassis to work best in the fastest time. Obviously the rider matters too, but in a situation like this it's the teams who have the best people at all levels that tend to get to the top.

Chassis specification is open. Teams can do what they want as long as they stay within the FIM's specs for construction and use, and this covers everything from the design and shape of the footpegs through to the size and shape of the fairing. In short, these are full-on racing bikes with specially tuned Honda engines. So with control engines, ECUs, tyres, clutches and data-logging, in which areas can there be technical competition between teams?

Above Moriwaki chassis, as raced by Toni Elias, was very effective from the beginning of the series

Below Aspar's decision to run the ill-fated RSV Motor chassis for the initial tests and the first two races cost his team dear

AERODYNAMICS

If all the bikes have the same power and the same tyres, then speed on the straight will be down to three things: weight, ability to accelerate off the corner (let's call that 'set-up') and aerodynamics. Theoretically, the bikes that have the best aerodynamics will be the fastest. But brilliant aerodynamics don't count for much if the rider is bigger than the fairing, and a small frontal area doesn't help if the bike cannot get cooling air into, through and out of the radiator as a result. The fast bikes aren't always the smallest, but they are the 'cleanest', aerodynamically speaking.

COOLING

There were worries at the start of the year about heat management. Honda and their engine-servicing contractor, Geo Technology, made it quite clear that they wanted peak temperatures controlled to a safe level. In Supersport racing, where power outputs are higher, heat control has been a problem, but a little less power, and therefore wasted heat, clearly made things easier.

The FTR has tapered front engine mounts for the same reason. Some of the larger bikes cooled better because their radiators had bigger exhaust ducts to pass more air out. Honda didn't get the 80 degrees Celsius limit they wanted, but major overheating problems didn't occur.

FRAME DESIGN

Most of the bikes at the start of the year had aluminium beam frames, but two in particular were different. The Promo-Harris bike used a beam CNC machined from solid, with a lightweight hanger dropping down to the front engine mounting. The second was the short-lived RSV with its aluminium tube chassis; it always looked quite big, and was clearly based on the dimensions of a standard Honda CBR600RR frame. Efforts were made to improve frontal area, with Aspar's team grafting on a 250 Aprilia fairing for the first race, but it was gone by the third race.

ENGINES

Moto2 was clearly a child of the credit crunch. Final negotiations for its format took place as the world's stock markets tumbled, and it was clear that the engine budget was limited. The major factories didn't want to support a new series, and Dorna wanted to keep the costs as low as possible. Power costs money – if higher revs had been allowed, shorter service intervals would have been required, and more items would have needed replacement during those services. The regime that was settled upon, then, gave 'enough' power for the right sort of money.

Dorna and IRTA appointed Swiss-based Geo Technology to carry out the servicing of the engines. Honda provided CBR600RR motors and, under their supervision, Geo Technology carried out minimal modifications. The gearbox was swapped for the HRC kit gearbox, which is stronger than the standard item and has a higher first gear. The cams were replaced by 'Supersport style' items, and the head was ported. Initial promises of 'about 150bhp' changed to claims of 140bhp at the crank for the engines that finally turned up – which probably equates to 125bhp at the rear wheel, some way short of what was initially expected – but the 'lost' horsepower was compensated for with a particularly useable, torquey mid-range.

More than 100 engines were delivered by Honda as the basis for the series and each rider was issued with one. These were exchanged for new ones as they achieved a notional 1,500km – that is every three GPs – to minimise shipping costs and hassle. To safeguard the engines, IRTA have a monitoring team to review engine data on a daily basis and a system of fines and penalties is used to ensure that the engines are not abused.

Hidehito Ikebe of Geo Technology explains: 'The bike is reliable to 1,500km; at that time we change many things, most consumable components, most moving parts. Depending on the data we can also change the gearbox. If we are worried that there is some over-revving, we have to report this to IRTA; if the rider is intentionally over-revving there may be a penalty. We recommended that the bikes

do not go over 85 degrees but we knew this might be impossible to comply with; a lot depends on the radiator concept. My personal opinion is that we might be concerned if you were over 100 degrees. We use ENI [Agip] oil; it's good for the whole 1,500km.'

Should a team believe their engine to be under-powered, there is a system to allow them to request a replacement. Any team wanting to protest the power level of any of their engines has to put down a deposit of €20,000; a replacement engine is then issued and the old one is taken away and dyno tested. If it proves to be within spec the old engine is returned and the team lose their €20,000; if it is out of spec then the team keep the new engine and their €20,000 is returned.

There is a clear plan to stop engines being misused, the first line of defence being an ECU that stops the revs at 16,000, but that is far from all that is available. Data-logging from 2D is compulsory and, at the end of each

Above Swiss based Geo Technology S.A. won the contract to service the Honda CBR600RR control engines

Below The modified Honda engine mounted in a Suter chassis; note the reinforcing plate on the front engine mounts

Above Honda's Nakamoto with Mamoru Moriwaki

Below Results for the Kalex Moto2 bike weren't as good as it deserved

we do want to make sure that nothing gets abused.

'We are able to impose penalties on teams that misuse things but the system is very fluid; we are going to have to learn as we go along. The rulebook is difficult to write, because the only data Honda gave us were the operating temperatures at which the engine was designed to run: 65–85 degrees. All of this has to come with a bunch of common sense. If we see deliberate misuse we have the ability to impose a penalty – a fine, points, or whatever. The primary thing with those engines is to keep them reliable. There is a bit of leeway built in, but a line has to be drawn somewhere.

'The official power figure is 140bhp. I don't know what the drive train losses are. It isn't optimised for top-end power, it's optimised for reliability, but I was stunned to see how close all the power outputs were.'

TYRES

Tyres are Dunlop's responsibility. Dunlop was the clear leader in the free market of 250 GPs and the company was contracted to be the control-tyre supplier for Moto2. Each team has to buy 12 tyres per GP at a total cost of €40,000 for the full year; a further four are available per race, depending on the team's needs, but these have to be paid for on top of the basic allocation. At every GP each team receives seven rears and five fronts, with the allocation being split between a hard tyre (guaranteed to finish the race) and a softer version that trades tyre life for grip. This last option might be marginal in terms of finishing the race, but it exists to give those teams who have found a good balanced set-up an advantage in terms of grip as a reward. The maximum allocation per rider per GP is therefore 16 tyres made up of five rears of one spec and four of the other, while at the front it is four of one spec and three of the other.

According to some Dunlop engineers, 'We are following the rules IRTA have set, but the actual construction and compounding are down to us. We will decide, depending on our expectations of any given circuit. We have a lot of data on the circuits: some will require multi-compounds, places like Sachsenring and Phillip Island will get different compounds. The size of the tyres came out of a test programme held in the Spanish championship, that's what they wanted. There are two compounds. Both will definitely do race distance: one is good and durable and one is "take a gamble if you want to" and might look a bit tatty after a Grand Prix race distance. It's just like Honda, who deliberately detuned their engine for reliability.

'All these chassis are quite new, so there is a lot of set-up to do, weight distribution and all that, and there are a lot of different riding styles out there – ex-125 riders who are used to using full throttle at full lean, other guys who are used to four-strokes. It's going to take a little more time to see what development is needed. It's a steep learning curve. Similar versions of these tyres have been used in the German, Spanish, Italian and US championships. They are the N-Tec style used in the British championship a few years ago. We recommend a [certain] pressure. If you lower that pressure there is more grip on corner entry but more movement on corner exit. It will take some of them a while to get used to that.

'Every team gets the same tyres and specs. The tyre selection is done by IRTA, who come along with a barcode reader and select the tyres for each rider. We start with a big pile of tyres and they make the selection.'

day, an IRTA representative collects a USB stick of data for analysis. Geo Technology then scrutinises the data to make sure that the way in which the engine is being used is within Honda's expectations.

Mike Webb, the series scrutineer, is charged with making sure that the engines are treated properly. 'We data-log rpm, throttle position, all the temperature sensors (oil, water, air, etc), air/fuel ratio and gearbox output speed, so I have crankshaft speed and gearbox speed. Only channels that relate to engine functions are downloaded – we don't want to intrude on team suspension set-ups, but

THE BIKES

SUTER MMX

Over the last few years Eskil Suter has helped design chassis for the Kawasaki and Ilmor MotoGP projects. Now his signature 'paper dart' design has come out as the Suter MMX. With ten bikes regularly on the grid, Suter's race organisation received a lot of feedback and used it well. The first version utilised a Yamaha R6 engine, but the project had to be re-engineered for the Honda CBR600RR and its airbox when that became the 'control' engine for the class.

With a conventional twin-beam aluminium chassis and swingarm, the bike is notable for its small frontal area. The air intakes were originally a pair of holes in the lower edge of the front cowl. After experiments by teams showed that removing the support between the two inlets increased airbox pressure, a new front cowl was introduced midway through the year.

There were several other modifications through the year. The first was a modified swingarm to allow the rear of the bike to be run slightly shorter, in keeping with the weight-distribution preferences of the control Dunlops. The second was a stiffening of the front engine mounts and the rear-linkage support strut. At the same time, the area of the mainframe that supports the swingarm pivot was weakened. These modifications made the bike work better with the Dunlops, and also allowed it to be competitive on a greater variety of circuits.

FTR

Fabrication Techniques are a well-known fabricator of other people's designs: they made all the Red Bull Rookies frames and most of the KTM 125 parts too. They are also responsible for a lot of the modified fuel tanks and swingarms seen in the World Superbike paddock. With the company renamed FTR, the Moto2 bike was their first adventure in designing their own chassis.

The first version did a lot of testing over the winter before a second, more flexible version was introduced. Initially only one bike was entered as an FTR, but two other frames were used by glassfibre manufacturer Speed Up, who then used their own fairing design. These Speed Up bikes (particularly Iannone's) were fast. It was soon evident that the FTR had the right balance for the corners and the Speed Up version of the fairing was the best aerodynamically. This wasn't really a surprise as the bodywork had originally been developed for an official Aprilia entry into the class, before the firm's senior management closed down the project.

After some initial changes to accommodate the preference of the Dunlop rear tyres for a lot of load, the frame continued unchanged for the year. The FTR entries changed their fairing design, however, with new, more 'filled-in' side panels to improve their top speed and efficiency.

MORIWAKI

Mamoru Moriwaki has been around for years. Part of the Suzuka city tuning establishment, his first international effort was the Graeme Crosby Kawasaki back in the late-1970s. Since then his bikes have been regulars at the Suzuka Eight Hour race, and he also led the only team to make a wild-card entry in MotoGP with

their own machine. What Moriwaki built for the CBR600RR was very different from the steel tube frame he built for his 990: an aluminium twin-spar and swingarm with the reinforcing all underslung, just like current MotoGP thinking. This last detail helped get the rigidity of the swingarm correct, but it also helped that the exhaust pipe exited on the left-hand side of the bike.

Moriwaki had five bikes out in Moto2 races on a regular basis (and sometimes more), with the main effort via the Gresini team. Luthi also ran one for Daniel Epp's Interwetten team and the Nieto family ran them in Holiday Gym colours.

The mainframe remained unchanged for the year, although it's rumoured that up to six previous versions of it existed before racing started. New fairings were tried twice, with championship winner Elias using a version with a revised air intake for the second half of the season. A development version was used at the Aragon test but was unfortunately destroyed in a crash. The main issue appeared to be cracking of the crossbeam that supported the lower linkage mounting; new welds were obvious whenever the bike was being stripped and cleaned.

Above An early-season Suter; later versions had shortened swingarms and reinforcing plates on the outside of the front engine hangers

Below Elias tested a new cowl on his Moriwaki at Catalunya and decided to adopt it

Bottom Alex Debon's FTR was little changed over the course of the year

TSR/MOTOBI

Two 'MotoBi' bikes were entered but these were, in fact, made by TSR and badged MotoBi for sponsorship purposes. A conventional, if somewhat tall, twin-beam frame, the TSR has a good pedigree, the company having won 250 GP races in the past. The most obvious modifications during the year were to the fairing around the front edge to prevent lift. Aerodynamically the bike wasn't bad, frequently showing near the top of the top-speed print-outs.

KALEX

German car racing specialists Kalex's Moto2 bike was only the third motorcycle the company had ever built. The very well-finished machine was campaigned solely by the Sito Pons squad. Made from CNC-machined aluminium spars, the Kalex was on the large side but the size allowed a free breathing radiator and a fairing that provided full coverage for the rider. The problem with only having one customer team was that Kalex didn't have the technical feedback that clearly helped the Suter outfit.

TECH 3

Below Tech 3 added strengtheners to the engine mounts at Catalunya

Bottom The Burning Blood chassis shown at both start and finish of the year: note added flexibility

Tech 3's effort had good mechanics, good riders, good skills and attitude, but it never seemed to gel. The linkage design was quite unusual, mimicking Yamaha's current design – possibly to be expected, given Tech 3's close links to that factory. The trouble was that as set-ups evolved, and it was discovered that Dunlop's N-Tec tyres had a distinct preference towards more load on the rear, the position of the Tech 3 linkage stopped them

shortening the back of the bike as much as they would have liked.

Just like the Suter, the front engine mounts needed some reinforcement, and at Catalunya a late-night welding session saw large reinforcing plates added to the outside of the front engine spars. It made a difference, and they won that race, but for the rest of the year results were patchy at best.

PROMO-HARRIS

The Harris frame had a quite unique construction. Two main beams were CNC-machined out of solid, but rather than having the usual second skin welded on these were left 'open'. At the front the headstock was supported by a series of aluminium tubes, and the front engine supports were bolted on to machinings.

In a more experienced team, with more experienced riders, there might have been time to find the right set-up and carry out further development. However, 2011 will be interesting, with an opportunity to build a complete new bike based on this year's experience.

BIMOTA

The bespoke Italian bike specialist, known more these days for its Ducati-engined road bikes, were latecomers to the Moto2 scene, only taking part in the third of the three pre-season tests. Using their trademark steel tube front frame combined with aluminium swingarm supports, the bike took a while to make its mark. Changes were made to the fairing at Mugello, for better aerodynamics, after which came their best performance of the year, at the Assen round.

THE REST
AND THERE WERE A LOT OF THEM!

RSV Motor *A tubular aluminium concoction. The two teams using it changed chassis suppliers after just two races.*

Force GP10 *One bike destroyed in a fire at Catalunya. Team and constructor fell out shortly afterwards.*

Burning Blood *Another Japanese specialist company with GP pedigree supplied the Blusens team. Some good mid-pack performances, and they also built a spectacular twin-swingarm wild-card bike for Motegi.*

Caretta Technology *A classic Italian industrial collaboration using a hand-built aluminium beam frame made by ultra-light aircraft manufacturer ICP and run out of specialist metal cutting firm Caretta Technology.*

MZ-RE Honda *The old MZ concern rose from the ashes of another insolvency, this time with ex-GP rider Martin Wimmer at its head. After starting with a standard CBR600RR frame fitted with Ohlins suspension and a modified swingarm, MZ converted the bike in stages to a steel tube version of the CBR600RR. Seven different frames passed through the team over the course of the year, and none really seemed to suit rider Anthony West anywhere near as well as the original street set-up.*

ADV *Italian marketing company ADV commissioned their own chassis for the WTR team.*

CLASS WARFARE

Moto2 was the biggest change in Grand Prix regulations ever. Could the new production-based class really replace the pure-bred 250s?

Every motorcycle racing enthusiast agreed: the old 250cc two-strokes were the purest, most focused racing machines out there. They demanded total understanding of all aspects of set-up and utter precision on the track. For the purists they were exactly what a racing bike should be, designed for the track alone, with no compromises imposed by the demands of the street or marketing departments.

Trouble was, the class had become unviable. Only Aprilia made a competitive bike and even then a team had to get hold of one of the handful of works machines to stand a chance of success. Without one of the half-dozen top-spec bikes, what could a team sell to a sponsor? Grids shrunk, the gap between the haves and have-nots widened, and well-established privateer teams left the paddock. What was to be done?

The answer was total revolution and a departure from what many saw as a basic principle of Grand Prix racing. For the first time, a GP class was to have a control engine. The new Moto2 class would use a lightly modified 600cc Honda street-bike engine. Tyres, electronics and fuel would also be controlled, but teams could do what they wanted with the chassis. Building a GP racer around a street engine is nothing new, as anyone who remembers the H1R Kawasaki of the early 1970s will know; even the TZ Yamahas started life with road-bike crankcases. However, the use of a solus engine supplier was without precedent but deemed necessary to get the class up and running.

If affordability was the objective of the new regulations, they were a success. Forty riders were accepted for the championship and most races attracted wild cards. MotoGP exiles Toni Elias and Alex de Angelis were the pre-season favourites, partly because of their experience with four-strokes. The great unknown was how the guys moving up

Above Shoya Tomizawa celebrates under the Qatar lights after winning the first ever Moto2 GP

Upper right Kenny Noyes leads the pack at Jerez

Lower right Karel Abraham sits it out at Le Mans as Alex Baldolini takes avoiding action

from the 125s and 250s would cope. There were 19 GP winners and four world champions on the grid for the first race in Qatar, yet the race was won convincingly by a teenager whose best previous result was tenth on a 250. Smiling Shoya Tomizawa (CIP-Technomag Suter) became an instant star and backed up his form with more rostrums and pole positions. His death at Misano was a tragic reminder of how dangerous the sport can be.

Tomizawa had no four-stroke experience but adapted with minimal testing. Some top-class two-stroke racers never did – and it wasn't just the racers who had to adapt. Moriwaki became a supplier rather than running their own team; FTR, previously a fabricator of other people's designs, fielded their own bike; and names like

Harris and Bimota returned to the GP paddock. Teams that had never run four-strokes, such as Aspar's Mapfre outfit and Tech 3, found themselves on a steep learning curve. No surprise, then, that it took a long time for the pattern of the season to emerge.

Toni Elias (Gresini Moriwaki), eventually a very convincing champion, started the season injured but really took command after the summer break. Thomas Luthi (Interwetten Moriwaki) flattered to deceive and Andrea Iannone (Speed Up FTR) emerged as a genuine talent. The Italian set more fastest laps than anyone and, given a clear track, was nigh-on unbeatable. Two ride-through penalties, however, prevented him being a championship contender. Alex de Angelis finally found his

1 – QATARI GP

An all-new world championship was always going to cause some surprises, so it wasn't too remarkable that a 19-year-old with a best previous GP result of tenth place won the inaugural Moto2 GP.

Shoya Tomizawa (CIP Suter) ran away with this historic race, easily beating former 250 GP winner Alex Debon (Ajo FTR), who just got the better of Jules Cluzel (Forward Suter).

Tomizawa's winning margin of 4.6 seconds was by far the biggest of the night (Rossi won MotoGP by one second, Terol the 125 race by 2.4 seconds). But there was some close competition down the field and some spills and thrills, with a two-bike pile-up after just two corners – and it was no great surprise that Alex de Angelis (Scot) made history as the first man to crash out of a Moto2 race. But pity poor Stefan Bradl (Kiefer Suter) who was taken out by the wayward San Marinese rider.

Tomizawa took the lead on lap six and slowly but surely began to sneak away from the pack until he was well out of striking distance. Takahashi crashed out, leaving Cluzel, Debon and Elias scrapping over second place. Elias then dropped further back, coming under some pressure from GP returnee Roberto Rolfo (Italtrans Suter).

Mattia Pasini (JIR Motobi) won a four-way battle for sixth with Thomas Luthi (Interwetten Moriwaki), Simone Corsi (JIR Motobi) and Gabor Talmacsi (Speed Up FTR).

Tomizawa only just managed to avoid tears on the podium. Afterwards the former All-Japan 125 and 250 contender said: 'This is like a dream... My team focus very hard... It's very, very incredible that I can be here winning...'

2 – SPANISH GP

If the first Moto2 race wasn't the multi-rider brawl that many had expected, the second certainly served up plenty of action. The race was restarted after a lap two pile-up caused when Qatar winner Shoya Tomizawa collided with Simone Corsi while battling for the lead. Engine oil from Tomizawa's fallen bike brought down eight more riders in a matter of seconds, bringing out the red flags.

The restart was more of the same: it was more of a wrestling match than a motorcycle race, the first eight finishers covered by just 2.5 seconds. It was no surprise, then, that famed fighter Toni Elias came out on top after a hectic skirmish with Tomizawa and Thomas Luthi.

Elias was a heroic winner, the Spaniard still suffering from a nasty left-hand injury sustained during pre-season testing and hurting some more after falling victim to the lap-two oil slick. But when team boss Fausto Gresini – who demoted Elias from MotoGP for 2010 – tried to congratulate him in pit lane, Elias ignored the Italian.

Elias and Tomizawa dominated the first few laps, before American Kenny Noyes played a starring role, muscling into the lead with some daring passes. But Noyes – another oil-slick crasher – had used up his front tyre early and by now was down on speed against his smaller, lighter rivals.

As Noyes faded slightly, Yuki Takahashi and Luthi came to the fore, fighting back and forth with Tomizawa and Elias. Luthi led into the final lap, Elias dived past at turn two, then got sideways, only just staying ahead of Tomizawa. The local hero beat the Qatar winner by 0.190 seconds, Luthi a further 0.26 seconds back.

3 – FRENCH GP

Toni Elias won an incident-packed Moto2 race to move into the lead of the championship. Two weeks after winning a battle royal at Jerez, the Gresini Moriwaki rider had a mostly untroubled run to victory, chased all the way by 125 champion Julian Simon (Aspar Suter) who never quite got close enough to mount an attack.

But behind the leaders, carnage reigned. There were 13 crashes during the 26 laps, most of them occurring in a chaotic three-lap period soon after the start. Several of the incidents were scary indeed. Local star Jules Cluzel took the lead from Elias at the end of lap six, then moments later fell at the super-quick turn one. He was still lying in the gravel when another faller came flying past at speed, just feet away. Alex de Angelis also fell at turn one, his bike veering back on to the track and T-boning Xavier Simeon.

As the dust settled, Elias began to take control. He was only a few tenths ahead of Simon, but whenever the youngster piled on the pressure, Elias responded. During the final laps Elias dug deeper and managed to stretch the gap, denying Simon (riding his first race with a Suter frame) a chance to attack.

Simone Corsi (JIR Motobi) won a race-long duel for third place with Andrea Iannone (Fimmco FTR). Iannone's team-mate and former 125 world champion Gabor Talmacsi held on to fifth place, with three riders right behind him in the final laps: Sergio Gadea (Pons Kalex), Ratthapark Wilairot (Bimota) and Fonsi Nieto (Moriwaki). Stefan Bradl (Kiefer Suter) won a similarly hectic five-man contest for ninth place.

4 – ITALIAN GP

Andrea Iannone (Speed UP FTR) did what you aren't supposed to be able to do – he split from the pack, sometimes at the rate of more than a second per lap, to build an advantage of more than seven seconds at three-quarters distance. Not one of the other 40 riders even got close enough to use his draft. Had he fitted a Fireblade inside his British-made FTR chassis?

'At Le Mans we were already beginning to understand things, to find a good direction on set-up, but I still didn't think this could happen here at Mugello,' said the 20-year-old Italian.

Behind Iannone, it was Moto2 business as usual, with two packs of half riders fighting for the rest of the points. Sergio Gadea (Pons Kalex) won a frantic five-man battle for second place, making up two positions on the final lap to take his first Moto2 podium. He just edged out Simone Corsi (JIR Moto2), taking a second consecutive third place, Thomas Luthi (Interwetten Moriwaki), Toni Elias (Gresini Moriwaki) and Shoya Tomizawa (Technomag-CIP Suter). The five riders crossed the finish line covered by just 1.1 seconds, having swapped positions throughout the 21-lap race.

Iannone's team-mate Gabor Talmacsi had also been in the contest for second place until he lost touch with the group to finish a lonely seventh, some way ahead of a six-man battle for eighth won by Yuki Takahashi (Tech 3 Racing, Tech 3).

Left Reformed bad boy Andrea Iannone eyeballs Toni Elias and Thomas Luthi

Bottom left Karel Abraham proved he isn't scared of much, including Toni Elias

Below Jules Cluzel, one of nine different winners during the season, celebrates his victory at Silverstone

5 – BRITISH GP

This was another Moto2 classic, Frenchman Jules Cluzel (Forward Suter) winning his first GP after a four-way battle with Thomas Luthi (Interwetten Moriwaki), Julian Simon (Mapfre Suter) and Scott Redding (Marc VDS Suter). The four riders were covered by less than two tenths of a second. Cluzel had crashed out of the previous two Moto2 GPs.

Luthi was the star of the race, working his way into the lead from 17th on the first lap. But he nearly fell halfway through the final lap, allowing Cluzel to retake the lead. 'When I was in front on the last lap I didn't know if the others were close enough to use my slipstream, so I pushed too hard and had a big moment,' said Luthi.

Cluzel's team-mate Claudio Corti had also been in the fight for victory until he crashed on the penultimate lap. The second-group contest was won by Alex Debon (Ajo FTR) who crossed the line a fraction ahead of Shoya Tomizawa (Technomag Suter), Mike di Meglio (Mapfre Suter) and Xavier Simeon (Holiday Gym Moriwaki).

6 – DUTCH TT

At Assen Andrea Iannone (Fimmco FTR) pulled off his magic Moto2 disappearing trick for the second time in three races. The Italian is so far the only Moto2 rider who has been able to lead from the first lap to the flag and going away.

Pole-sitter Iannone grabbed the lead from Ratthapark Wilairot (Thai Honda Bimota) at the end of the first lap and had extended his advantage to nine seconds halfway through the 24 laps. This kind of performance isn't supposed to be possible in a class with control engines, tyres and ECUs.

'This is even better than my win at Mugello,' said Iannone, who slowed in the final yards to win by 4.5 seconds.

The action behind the leader was much busier, with Wilairot battling for his first GP podium finish with points leader Toni Elias (Gresini Moriwaki) and Thomas Luthi (Interwetten Moriwaki). In the end Elias got clear of the battle, leaving Luthi to win a frantic last-lap contest for third with his Thai rival.

Qatar winner Shoya Tomizawa (Technomag Suter) recovered from a big practice tumble to beat Julian Simon (Aspar Suter) for fifth. Silverstone winner Jules Cluzel won a three-way scrap for seventh.

7 – CATALAN GP

Former 250 GP winner Yuki Takahashi (Tech 3) scored a comfortable debut Moto2 victory after runaway leader Andrea Iannone (Fimmco FTR) was hit with a ride-through penalty for overtaking under the yellow flags displayed following a first-corner pile-up.

This dramatic race got underway in chaotic circumstances with a multiple pile-up at the first corner and it ended with a terrifying crash in the run to the finish line when Carmelo Morales (Pons Kalex) tagged the rear of seventh-placed Kenny Noyes (J&J PromoHarris). The first crash was caused by Alex Debon (Ajo FTR) colliding with Mike di Meglio (Aspar Suter) on the inside kerb of turn one.

Iannone had been fast enough to score his third runaway win in four races, but the Mugello and Assen winner had overtaken Takahashi going into turn one on the second lap. After confusing instructions from race direction, Iannone was only given his penalty after half-distance. He rejoined in 17th and finished an unlucky 13th.

Takahashi inherited the lead, already safely ahead of Thomas Luthi (Interwetten Moriwaki) and Julian Simon (Aspar Suter), who battled long and hard for what turned out to be second place, not third place.

Karel Abraham (Cardion AB FTR) beat points leader Toni Elias (Gresini Moriwaki) and Simone Corsi (JIR Motobi) for a career-best fourth place.

Spanish-based American Kenny Noyes scored his first world points with a brilliant charge from 28th on lap one to seventh at the end.

8 – GERMAN GP

Toni Elias (Gresini Moriwaki) bounced back from a difficult few races to win the Moto2 race ahead of pole-sitter Andrea Iannone (Fimmco Speed Up). It was the Spaniard's first win since Le Mans. He attributed the turnaround to crucial set-up work done during post-Catalan GP tests at Aragon, and in qualifying and morning warm-up at the Sachsenring.

Elias had to work extra hard, coming through from a first-turn collision that had left him 11th at the end of the first lap. By two-thirds distance Elias had fought his way into second place. From there he hunted down Iannone, who was looking likely to score his third win in five races. Once Elias was ahead, Iannone had little answer for his rival who seemed to have more grip to play with.

The final place on the podium went to Roberto Rolfo (Italtrans Suter), who fought a thrilling duel with former 250 rival and fellow 250 winner Fonsi Nieto (Holiday Gym Moriwaki).

Right Julian Simon leads Toni Elias at Indianapolis

Below The minute's silence for Shoya Tomizawa at Aragon; the whole paddock mourned

Opposite Toni Elias celebrates his title in Sepang

form at the end of season, with his third team of the year, while men like Mike di Meglio and Raffaele de Rosa scarcely troubled the scorers. In between those extremes there were one-hit wonders like Jules Cluzel (Forward Racing Suter), who won at Silverstone, and Kenny Noyes (Jack & Jones Promo-Harris), who took pole at Le Mans. British fans were delighted to see Scott Redding, the youngest man in the field, overcome his early problems and become a serious player. Redding and Iannone were the two riders who did their reputations and market value most good.

The one thing everyone was agreed on, purists and philistines alike, was that Moto2 provided great entertainment. There were worries about too many bikes on track, but with the quality of teams applying for 2011 it's going to be difficult for IRTA to thin them out. Long term, the real question is whether Moto2 will do what the 250s demonstrably did and provide the next generation of MotoGP riders.

Toni Elias articulated the problem, querying whether the bikes were too easy to ride. His view was that another 10 or 15 horsepower would really sort out the men from the boys. As for the purists' principled objection to the single engine supplier, that will be resolved at the end of the current three-year contract when Moto2 will become open to all production 600cc engines.

There is no doubt that Elias is right in that quite a few aspects of Moto2 have been very conservative, such as the level of engine tuning – and even FTR couldn't persuade a team to buy their steering-stem-less frame. That shouldn't surprise anybody in the first year of a new formula. Did anyone expect Honda to build engines that were going to blow up? Or any team to gamble with an unproven radical design? But with Moto2's entertainment value now proven, regulations can allow the class to edge back towards what the traditionalists would regard as 'real' Grand Prix racing.

9 – CZECH REPUBLIC GP

Toni Elias (Gresini Moriwaki) scored a determined win at Brno to extend his points lead. The Spaniard started relatively slowly and but then began to hunt down leader Andrea Iannone (Fimmco FTR). Iannone ended up third behind Yuki Takahashi (Tech 3) who came through strongly in the final stages of the race.

Pole position man Shoya Tomizawa (Technomag Suter) led the first few laps but the Japanese couldn't maintain his pace and got shuttled all the way back to tenth at the flag. During the early laps Elias also found himself going backwards. But then he gathered himself for his challenge and moved steadily through the pack. By the time he took second place at half-distance, Iannone already had a one-second lead, but Elias steadily chipped away, just as he had at the German GP. Toni took the lead on lap 13, but Iannone fought back as Roberto Rolfo (Italtrans Suter) also joined the battle.

Elias stole a small advantage while Rolfo got the better of Iannone, only to suffer an engine blow-up. After that it was Elias all the way, Iannone dropping back into the clutches of Takahashi, whose bike clearly worked better on worn tyres.

'At the beginning the problem was me,' said Elias. 'I knew I had the rhythm to do 2m 4s lap times all race, so maybe I was too relaxed. In the first laps I lost several places and it looked like I had no answer to my rivals. When Iannone passed me I found some motivation.'

Silverstone winner Jules Cluzel (Forward Suter) won a tight four-way battle for fourth place.

10 – INDIANAPOLIS GP

Rarely has a racer looked so ill as Elias did at Indy, but a bout of flu didn't stop the Spaniard from claiming his third win in a row. And if his sickness hadn't been enough, Elias and his fellow riders had to deal with two starts, after the race was red-flagged following two big pile-ups at the second corner.

At least the restart was shortened – to keep MotoGP on schedule – but nonetheless the 17 laps were a real ordeal for Elias, who wasn't given an easy ride by Simon. The reigning 125 champ cut ahead of Elias at one point, but he couldn't make the break. Elias retook the lead with five laps to go, bravely riding around the outside of Simon into the high-speed turn one.

'I had very little energy today, so I reserved what I had to push during the last five laps,' said an exhausted Elias. 'That is how I won.'

Redding had his best weekend yet in 2010, claiming his first Moto2 front-row start and then scoring his first podium in the class. But he was hardly in a state to enjoy the champagne ceremony – the Briton suffered so badly in the heat that he claimed he was hallucinating during the final few laps, when he came under pressure from Iannone. The Italian rode a heroic race, coming through from 26th on the grid, the legacy of a qualifying crash that left him nursing a cracked wrist bone.

The nine or so victims of the first-lap carnage included Tomizawa, who hurt a hand and was unable to make the restart. Roger Lee Hayden – riding a Moriwaki entered by former 500 world champion Kevin Schwantz – was also involved in the pile-up. He finished the restart in 17th spot.

11 – SAN MARINO GP

Toni Elias's Indy illness didn't stop him winning his fourth Moto2 race in dominant style, but his success isn't what the 11th round of the 2010 Moto2 series will be remembered for.

The tragedy happened on the 12th lap between turns 11 and 12, the fast rights at the end of Misano's short back straight. Elias (Gresini Honda) was already firmly in the lead, chased hard by Simone Corsi (JIR Motobi) and then Julian Simon (Aspar Suter), Shoya Tomizawa (Technomag Suter), Alex de Angelis (JIR Motobi) and Scott Redding (Marc VDS Suter), the four of them just inches apart.

When Tomizawa crashed at 140mph, he was hit by the two riders behind him. He didn't stand a chance.

Elias and Simon carried on unawares, the leader running short of energy in the closing stages, allowing Simon to slightly close the gap. Thomas Luthi (Interwetten Moriwaki) completed the podium, coming all the way through from 14th on lap one.

Andrea Iannone (Speed Up FTR) had a luckless day which lost him second place overall in the championship to Simon – he got a ride-through for jumping the start but fought back into the points, only for his bike to stop.

12 – ARAGON GP

Andrea Iannone may not have won the inaugural Moto2 world title, but he's undoubtedly the fastest rider of the lot when things go his way. The Italian FTR rider ran away with the Aragon race, just as he had at Mugello and Assen.

At one stage of the race he was taking more than half a second per lap out of his pursuers, which suggests that his team had fixed the tyre-wear issues that had troubled him at some earlier races. He crossed the finish line 6.2 seconds ahead of Julian Simon (Aspar Suter), who just edged out Iannone's team-mate Gabor Talmacsi for the runner-up spot. Iannone rode the victory lap waving a special flag commemorating the memory of Shoya Tomizawa.

'It's been a great day, but in no way easy or simple,' said Iannone. 'After my injury in practice at Indianapolis I suffered a lot in the race at Indy and again at Misano, so it was great to feel strong again this weekend. I stayed on top in every practice and today's win repays the team for all the hard work the team has done in fixing problems.'

Championship leader Toni Elias made a heroic charge through the pack from his third-row start, a legacy of a tumble during qualifying. The Spaniard, who had won the previous four races, ended the first lap in 14th and fought his way through to fourth, just eight-tenths behind Talmacsi.

Scott Redding (Marc VDS Suter) came in eighth – due to front grip issues – after qualifying on the front row. His speed throughout the weekend suggested he wasn't badly scarred by his involvement in the Tomizawa accident.

13 – JAPANESE GP

Toni Elias took one more step towards an historic success in the first Moto2 world championship with an error-free ride to victory, just ahead of compatriot Julian Simon (Aspar Suter). Just like Stoner in the MotoGP race, Elias didn't put a wheel wrong. Unlike Stoner, he was under full pressure throughout the race, Simon never more than a few tenths behind. This was Elias's seventh win from the first 13 Moto2 races.

Before the race Fausto Gresini told the runaway series leader that he didn't need to win, but Elias wanted to win, so he could dedicate his race to Misano victim Shoya Tomizawa.

Elias grabbed the lead from Simon at the third corner and Simon got back in front only once during the 23 laps and then only very briefly, holding first place for just two corners on lap three. Elias never gave him another chance and finally crossed the line three-tenths ahead.

'We didn't expect to win because although my pace in practice was fast, it wasn't as fast as Julian's,' said Elias. 'But anyway the win is perfect – one more step to the championship and I won in Japan, the home of Moriwaki and the home of Tomizawa. I dedicate this to him.'

The two Spaniards left the rest of the pack behind, the battle for third going to the wire – Czech rider Karel Abraham (AB Cardion FTR) out-braking Alex de Angelis (JIR Motobi) just three corners from the flag, the pair colliding as they headed into the final esses. It was Abraham's first GP podium, which may go some way to silencing doubters who say he doesn't deserve his 2011 Ducati MotoGP deal.

14 – MALAYSIAN GP

Roby Rolfo completed a six and a half year round trip at Sepang, scoring his first GP win since May 2004. The Italian returned to GPs this season after four years in the wilderness in WSB.

Third in July's German GP, Rolfo qualified fifth at Sepang and had to work hard to get to the front. Toni Elias (Gresini Moriwaki) and Tom Luthi (Interwetten Moriwaki) disputed the early lead, then Andrea Iannone (Speed Up FTR) got ahead on lap five, chased by Luthi, Elias and pole-sitter Julian Simon (Aspar Suter), the only man with a mathematical chance of beating Elias to the crown. Three laps later both Luthi and Simon crashed, handing the title to Elias.

For once, Iannone wasn't able to make the break and he quickly came under pressure from Alex de Angelis (JIR TSR) and Rolfo. These last two were the fastest men on track and they were soon out on their own. De Angelis briefly took the lead on the penultimate lap but Rolfo crossed the line 0.040 seconds in front.

'It's been a long time,' said Rolfo. 'Moto2 is quite complicated because if everything isn't 100 per cent, you can easily find yourself at the back.'

The duel for third place also went down to the wire. Elias was anxious to celebrate his title on the podium, but he didn't quite have it in him to beat Iannone.

'Finally we reached our target,' said Elias. 'To win this championship we had to lose two – a 125 (in 2001) and a 250 (in 2003). All that experience made me stronger and gave me what I needed to win this championship.'

15 – AUSTRALIAN GP

One month after they were both involved in the huge Shoya Tomizawa accident at Misano, Alex de Angelis (Marc VDS Suter) finished one–two at Phillip Island.

Quite apart from that tragic day, de Angelis had had a horrible 2010. In June his Scot Moto2 team went broke, leaving him without a ride. After three races on the sidelines he filled in for injured MotoGP rider Hiroshi Aoyama, but when the Japanese returned he was once again without a ride until the JIR team stepped in.

'Today is a good day,' said de Angelis. 'It helps me re-evaluate a season that has been very difficult and in this happy moment I want to remember also Tomizawa.' Before going on the podium, de Angelis and Redding agreed they wouldn't spray champagne, in honour of Tomizawa (although the under-age Redding isn't allowed the alcohol anyway).

De Angelis's second GP win (four years after his first, in the 250 class) came the hard way. He had to close down early leaders Redding and Andrea Iannone (Speed Up FTR) and once he got in front with nine laps to go he had to keep working to shake off his rivals. In the end, he had more speed and left Redding to deal with Iannone.

'I really enjoyed the race,' said Redding. 'But I was so pumped I can't really remember what happened, so I was stood on the podium thinking "what's going on here then?".'

Julian Simon (Aspar Suter) got the better of Stefan Bradl (Kiefer Suter) for fourth, while Simon's team-mate Mike di Meglio scored by far his best Moto2 result in sixth.

16 – PORTUGUESE GP

This was another thrilling, topsy-turvy race, complicated by a track that was still damp in places. The race was won by first-time Moto2 winner Stefan Bradl (Kiefer Suter) who beat Alex Baldolini (Caretta I.C.P.) by seven hundredths of a second.

Baldolini got past Bradl, a former 125 GP winner and son of Helmut Bradl (who won five 250 GPs for Honda in 1991), with two laps to go, but the German had better pace and eventually Baldolini settled for a first-ever podium.

'The track was still damp in places, so I was careful in those areas and I pushed hard everywhere else,' Bradl explained. 'The first part of this season was difficult because it took me time to get used to the four-stroke riding style.'

The nine-man battle for the final podium place featured plenty of rough and tumble. Phillip Island winner Alex de Angelis (JIR Motobi) won the fight, outpacing Scott Redding (Marc VDS Suter) and impressive Moto2 first-timer Kenan Sofuoglu (Technomag-CIP Suter) in the run to the chequered flag. Both de Angelis and Redding had charged through the pack after completing the first lap 12th and 21st.

Sofuoglu ('Super Glu' to his fans) was the early star, bravely building a seven-second advantage in the first 11 laps. But he struggled with a loose left handlebar, the legacy of a crash during morning warm-up. That problem dropped the Turkish rider back into the clutches of de Angelis and Redding.

Andrea Iannone's spectacular charge from the ninth row ended when he crashed his Fimmco FTR out of fourth place with seven laps to go. Champ Toni Elias also fell.

Above Kenan Sofuoglu leads at Estoril with Yonny Hernandez and Gabor Talmacsi in close attendance

Top right Youngest man in the field Scott Redding thrilled the fans and scared the old guys

17 – VALENCIAN GP

Karel Abraham (Cardion FTR) won his first GP victory, coming out on top of a chaotic last-lap that saw leader Andrea Iannone (Speed Up FTR) robbed of the win and an out-of-control Toni Elias (Gresini Moriwaki) in the gravel.

Andrea Iannone led from the start, building what looked like a winning lead until he started to run short of rear grip. The man on the move was Julian Simon (Aspar Suter), who charged through from ninth on lap one to challenge for the lead in the closing stages. Iannone and Simon swapped the lead back and forth while Elias and Abraham were right behind them, looking for an opening.

Recently crowned champ Elias, who returns to MotoGP in 2011, wanted to go out with a bang, but this wasn't the kind of bang he had in mind. On the final lap he tried a manic move on Simon, ran in too hot and tagged the rear of Iannone's bike. Elias ran off the track and crashed while Iannone was forced wide, allowing Abraham to take the lead for the first time.

'I was a little lucky,' said Abraham, the first Czech to win a GP victory in the intermediate class. 'Toni made a big mistake, but that's racing – sometimes I get lucky, sometimes someone else gets lucky.'

Despite the last-lap collision, Iannone held on to second place, with Simon crossing the line third. Less than six tenths of a second covered the three podium finishers. Thomas Luthi (Interwetten Moriwaki) finished fourth, less than two-tenths behind Simon. Scott Redding (Marc VDS Suter) was fifth, a further three seconds back.

Estoril winner Stefan Bradl (Kiefer Suter) and Kenan Sofuoglu (Technomag-CIP Suter) had also been in the leading pack earlier in the race, but both crashed out, without injury.

CHAMPIONSHIP STANDINGS

	Rider	Nat	Team	Motorcycle	Points
1	Toni Elias	SPA	Gresini Racing Moto2	Moriwaki	271
2	Julian Simon	SPA	Mapfre Aspar Team	Suter	201
3	Andrea Iannone	ITA	Fimmco Speed Up	Speed Up	199
4	Thomas Luthi	SWI	Interwetten Moriwaki Moto2	Moriwaki	156
5	Simone Corsi	ITA	JIR Moto2	Motobi	138
6	Gabor Talmacsi	HUN	Fimmco Speed up	Speed Up	109
7	Jules Cluzel	FRA	Forward Racing	Suter	106
8	Scott Redding	GBR	Marc VDS Racing Team	Suter	102
9	Stefan Bradl	GER	Viessmann Kiefer Racing	Suter	97
10	Karel Abraham	CZE	Cardion AB Motoracing	FTR	96
11	Alex de Angelis	RSM	JIR Moto2	Motobi	95
12	Yuki Takahashi	JPN	Tech 3 Racing	Tech 3	86
13	Shoya Tomizawa	JPN	Technomag-CIP	Suter	82
14	Roberto Rolfo	ITA	Italtrans S.T.R.	Suter	75
15	Dominique Aegerter	SWI	Technomag-CIP	Suter	74
16	Alex Debon	SPA	Aerosport de Castello – Ajo	FTR	73
17	Sergio Gadea	SPA	Tenerife 40 Pons	Pons Kalex	67
18	Fonsi Nieto	SPA	Holiday Gym G22	Moriwaki	45
19	Alex Baldolini	ITA	Caretta Technology Race Dept	I.C.P.	38
20	Mike di Meglio	FRA	Mapfre Aspar Team	Suter	34
21	Yonny Hernandez	COL	Blusens-STX	BQR-Moto2	32
22	Ratthapark Wilairot	THA	Thai Honda PTT Singha SAG	Bimota	30
23	Anthony West	AUS	MZ Racing Team	MZ-RE Honda	26
24	Kenny Noyes	USA	Jack & Jones by A. Banderas	Promoharris	22
25	Claudio Corti	ITA	Forward Racing	Suter	20
26	Hector Faubel	SPA	Marc VDS Racing Team	Suter	18
27	Raffaele de Rosa	ITA	Tech 3 Racing	Tech 3	15
28	Mattia Pasini	ITA	JIR Moto2	Motobi	12
29	Kenan Sofuoglu	TUR	Technomag-CIP	Suter	11
30	Xavier Simeon	BEL	Holiday Gym G22	Moriwaki	10
31	Damian Cudlin	AUS	Tenerife 40 Pons	Pons Kalex	9
32	Jason di Salvo	USA	GP Tech	FTR	7
33	Axel Pons	SPA	Tenerife 40 Pons	Pons Kalex	7
34	Lukas Pesek	CZE	Matteoni Racing	Moriwaki	5
35	Michael Ranseder	AUT	Vector Kiefer Racing	Suter	4
36	Michele Pirro	ITA	Gresini Racing Moto2	Moriwaki	2
37	Vladimir Ivanov	UKR	Gresini Racing Moto2	Moriwaki	2
38	Arne Tode	GER	Racing Team Germany	Suter	2
39	Robertino Pietri	VEN	Italtrans S.T.R.	Suter	1
40	Yusuke Teshima	JPN	FCC TSR	Motobi	1

With more than 20 years of experience, this French brand has become one of the leaders within the helmet world. Funded and driven by former professional racers, SHARK, with the passion of racing still evident, designs helmets with the goal to ensure the highest level of performance and safety. The spirit of SHARK is to always push the technical boundaries and research new exciting innovations to allow each and everyone of us to enjoy the boundless pleasure and freedom of riding in safety.

NEW KID ON THE BLOCK

From an all-Spanish fight for the 125cc title Marc Marquez emerged as not just the champion but a new star on the world stage

Spain ruled all three classes in 2010, but none more than the 125s. It was rare for a rider of any other nationality to get on the front row or the rostrum as Marc Marquez (Red Bull Ajo Derbi), Nico Terol (Aspar Aprilia) and Pol Espargaro (Tuenti Derbi) fought it out. The only non-Spanish winner all year was Terol's team-mate Bradley Smith (GB) and he had to wait for the last race of the year to get his victory.

If the three Spaniards didn't block out the front row and rostrum, then their team-mates did – Smith, Efren Vazquez (SPA, Tuenti Derbi) and Sandro Cortese (GER, Mitsubishi Ajo Derbi). Unless you had one of the Aspar Aprilias or the factory Derbis you didn't stand a chance of seeing the front row regularly, never mind the rostrum. This echo of the problems that killed off the 250 class resulted in the MSMA deciding on the technical regulations for Moto3, which will replace the 125s in 2012. The new bikes will be 250cc singles with a cylinder bore of no more than 81mm and with a rev limit, control ECU and data logging to keep costs down. The first examples are already out there – motocross engines in Honda 125 chassis.

However, despite the growing gap between the haves and the have nots, the 2010 125 championship produced a new star in the shape of 17-year-old Marquez. He dealt with the experience and persistence of Terol and the sheer speed of Espargaro with growing confidence. He didn't just get neater, smoother and faster with every race, he did it with every lap. Before the start of this season Marc hadn't won a race and he got a severe attack of nerves when he qualified on pole for the first time. It took him four races to win for the first time but he promptly made it five in a row; not

a bad way to open your account. Some bad lack and a first-corner crash at Aragon put him back to third in the championship but Marquez then put in another four wins in a row. The last of that sequence, Portugal, was one of the most astonishing races you could hope to see. Just to rub it in, Marc failed to qualify for the front row only twice and set the fastest lap seven times. He now looks the complete package and will be in Moto2 for 2011.

Away from the three Spaniards, Bradley Smith was clearly the best of the rest despite having outgrown a 125, while Japanese veteran Tommy Koyama was the fastest man on previous-generation Aprilia technology. The lack of Italians in a class they used to dominate is quite amazing: the top Italian, Simone Grotzkyj, finished 19th in the championship. However, it was encouraging to a see the Italian Federation field their own team as wild

Above Pol Espargaro celebrates with a silly hat and a TV interview

Above right Nico Terol on top of the Indianapolis rostrum

Right Tommy Koyama got on the rostrum at his team's home race in Germany

Opposite Marc Marquez sets off from the Assen pitlane

1 – QATARI GP

The 125s – the sole-surviving two-stroke class – provided a thrilling start to 2010, with a gang of seven riders involved in a race-long skirmish. Nicolas Terol (Aspar Aprilia) won the battle to top an all-Spanish podium. The top seven finishers were covered by just 3.7 seconds.

Terol rode a perfect race, keeping his powder dry in the early and mid-stages, hitting the front for the first time with four laps to go. He immediately made the break to beat runner-up and first-time podium finisher Efren Vazquez (Tuenti Derbi) by 2.4 seconds.

'The race was a bit crazy,' said 21-year-old Terol. 'So I stayed calm and then went for it at the end.'

Pole sitter Marc Marquez (Red Bull Derbi) was third, two hundredths further back and followed in quick succession by Pol Espargaro (Tuenti Derbi), Sandro Cortese (Avant Derbi), Randy Krummenacher (Molenaar Aprilia) and Esteve Rabat (Blusens Aprilia).

2 – SPANISH GP

Pol Espargaro (Derbi) won an all-Spanish contest for 125 glory, comfortably beating Nicolas Terol (Aspar Aprilia) during the final few laps. In the early stages there were four or five men in the leading group, Espargaro and Terol gradually breaking clear along with Efren Vazquez (Derbi), who crashed out with three laps to go, leaving his two compatriots out front.

Terol had been just ahead for several laps when Vazquez went out, but the crash encouraged Espargaro to get out front. He made his winning move on the following lap and quickly built a safe lead, crossing the line 1.8 seconds ahead.

Esteve Rabat (Blusens Aprilia) was third, 13 seconds further back. Pole sitter Marc Marquez (Red Bull Derbi) fell on the first lap, dislocating a shoulder after his exhaust pipe fell off and got under his rear wheel.

3 – FRENCH GP

This was another all-Spanish affair, Pol Espargaro (Tuenti Derbi) beating compatriot Nicolas Terol (Aspar Aprilia) after a race-long duel. Espargaro's victory was his second win of the year and Spain's 13th consecutive 125 win, and it brought him to within two points of championship leader Terol.

Terol led the first two-thirds of the race, shadowed all the way by Espargaro, while Bradley Smith (Aspar Aprilia), Efren Vazquez (Tuenti Derbi), Marc Marquez (Red Bull Derbi) and Esteve Rabat (Blusens Aprilia) disputed third place.

Espargaro finally moved into first place on lap 16, the lead changing several more times as the pair ducked and dived on the draft and on the brakes. Espargaro was the stronger of the two and hung on to win by 0.9 seconds.

Smith held third place all the way until halfway through the final lap when Marquez got ahead. Smith counter-attacked three corners from the flag, the pair making contact, which allowed Vazquez to beat Smith into the final two corners, relegating the Briton to fifth.

4 – ITALIAN GP

Marc Marquez (Red Bull Derbi) scored his first GP win, and he did it in style, coming out on top of a brutal four-way battle with Nicolas Terol (Aspar Aprilia), Pol Espargaro (Tuenti Derbi) and Bradley Smith (Aspar Aprilia).

Widely tipped as a star of the future, 17-year-old Marquez failed to win a race in his first two GP seasons, often crashing out when victory seemed assured after a dazzling performance in practice. This time he qualified sixth and came from behind to catch early leaders Terol and Espargaro. The four-way contest was a real thriller, with positions changing constantly as they drafted down GP racing's longest straight and took liberties through Mugello's high-speed turns.

Marquez gained the lead for the first time on lap 20 but had to fight back and forth every inch of the way to defeat points leader Terol by just 0.039 seconds. The top four crossed the line separated by less than two tenths.

'I am very, very, very happy, especially because this is one of the toughest tracks,' said Marquez.

5 – BRITISH GP

Marc Marquez had ridden more than 30 GPs when he won his first victory at Mugello. Two weeks later at Silverstone he took his second victory after a vicious last-lap encounter with Pol Espargaro (Tuenti Derbi). The pair made contact at least once, then with three corners to go Espargaro seemed to crash. Somehow he managed to regain control but he ran off the track, leaving the way clear for Marquez. Espargaro finished second which was enough to move him into the points lead.

Bradley Smith (Aspar Aprilia) got his first podium of the year with third place after an entertaining duel with team-mate Nicolas Terol, whose fourth place lost him the series lead to Espargaro.

6 – DUTCH TT

Marc Marquez continued his amazing run at Assen, achieving an unbeaten sequence of three victories on the bounce.

But Marquez had a little help from wild card Dutchman Jerry van den Bunt, who nearly took out rival Nicolas Terol (Aspar Aprilia) a few laps from the finish. Until then Terol had been shadowing the leader throughout, perhaps waiting until the final stages to make his move. Van den Bunt didn't give way while being lapped, tangling with Terol and then crashing out. Terol stayed on but had lost too much time to come back at Marquez.

'My plan was to get to the last lap and see what happened,' said Terol. 'But the time I lost with the backmarker was crucial.'

After a poor start Pol Espargaro (Tuenti Derbi) took a lonely third – this was an unusually strung-out 125 race – unable to get close to the pace of the leading pair.

7 – CATALAN GP

At Catalunya the history books were rewritten – twice – by Marc Marquez. On Saturday the 17-year-old became the youngest rider in GP history to score a pole position hat-trick and on race day he became the youngest to win four consecutive GP victories. To underline the significance of those two achievements, the man who had held those records was Valentino Rossi.

Marquez led from the first corner to the flag, effortlessly easing a gap over a busy three-way contest for second place between points leader Nicolas Terol (Aspar Aprilia), team-mate Bradley Smith and Pol Espargaro (Tuenti Derbi).

'Winning my home race is like a dream,' said Marquez, who completed an incredible weekend by taking over the world championship points lead from Terol, who fell on the final lap. 'This is incredible – four wins in a row – but I need to keep my feet on the ground because who knows what will happen at the next races.'

Smith was winning the battle for second when Terol slid off four corners from the flag while involved in a last-lap struggle with Espargaro.

8 – GERMAN GP

Marc Marquez extended his astonishing run of success in Germany, winning his fifth successive GP, only six weeks after his first victory.

But it didn't come easy for the world championship leader. The race started on a track that was damp in places, and Marquez circulated down in sixth as he got a feel for the conditions. Once he moved to the front, though, he got stuck in a savage duel for the win with title rival Pol Espargaro.

Espargaro, who had led the series until Marquez hit his winning streak, was desperate to stop the rot, but overdid it on the penultimate lap, highsiding after touching the damp Astroturf on the exit of turn 13. Marquez missed him by inches, going on to win, beating the other podium finishers Tomoyoshi Koyama (Aprilia) and Sandro Cortese (Ajo Derbi) by 17 seconds.

9 – CZECH REPUBLIC GP

Nicolas Terol (Aspar Aprilia) made a perfect return from the back injury he sustained at Catalunya, winning the damp 125 race by 20 seconds. The Spaniard, who led the early stages of the championship, chose rain tyres on the drying track and disappeared, often putting two or three seconds a lap over his rivals, even though they also ran rain tyres. Pol Espargaro (Tuenti Derbi) won a three-way battle for second with Esteve Rabat (Blusens Aprilia) and Derbi team-mate Efren Vazquez, who slid off while trying to repass Rabat on the penultimate lap.

World championship leader Marc Marquez (Red Bull Derbi) had his points advantage squeezed when he finished seventh, just two days after dislocating his left shoulder. The Spanish teenager had won the previous five races and still led the title chase by 14 points.

Jasper Iwema (CBC Aprilia) finished a career-best eighth after changing to slicks after the sighting lap and starting from the pits after the main pack.

10 – INDIANAPOLIS GP

Nicolas Terol's second consecutive win changed everything in the championship – it moved him past Espargaro into second place and to within just four points of Marquez. But Terol only won because Marquez slid out of the lead at one-third distance.

While Terol thanked his lucky stars and rode to a pressure-free victory, Marquez picked up his battered Derbi, regained the track in 14th place and set about a mighty comeback which included passing three riders on the final lap to finish a remarkable fifth.

Smith was looking good for what would have been his third podium of the year, but he too was caught out by Indy's treacherously bumpy and slippery surface. Instead of another podium, the Briton suffered his first crash of the year. So the final two spots on the rostrum went to Cortese and Espargaro.

cards with a view to entering the championship full-time in 2011. Then there was the sight of another Italian name, Lambretta, on the grid. Some slick livery adorned the Engines Engineering project, basically a Honda with an Aprilia cylinder grafted on, but the bike didn't impress. The team's replacement rider for the final five rounds did

impress: Danny Kent came up from the Red Bull Rookies Cup to qualify the bike higher than it had managed all season and was even third fastest in a wet session at Phillip Island. He should be a full-time GP rider in 2011.

Of the top men, only Terol will be on a 125 again for 2011. Marquez, Espargaro and Smith are moving

11 – SAN MARINO GP

Points leader Marc Marquez retook the advantage in his 125 title battle with Nicolas Terol. The teenage Red Bull Derbi rider got the better of his older rival, who had won the previous two races.

The pair dominated this race, Marquez trying but failing to make the break midway through. Terol got back in front with eight laps to go, but Marquez was only keeping his best until last. With four laps remaining he passed Terol and quickly built a gap.

Marc's sixth win of the year more than doubled his championship lead, to nine points. It also extended Spain's winning streak in 125s to 21 victories in a row. Terol finished well clear of a four-man battle for third, won by Efren Vazquez, Pol Espargaro's team-mate in the Tuenti Derbi team. Pol himself had his worst race of the year so far and could only manage sixth.

12 – ARAGON GP

Pol Espargaro (Tuenti Derbi) won a thrilling showdown with Nicolas Terol (Aspar Aprilia) but the real winner of the day was Nicolas Terol, who retook the championship lead after pole-sitter Marc Marquez (Red Bull Derbi) got wiped out at the first corner by an errant Randy Krummenacher.

With Marquez out, Espargaro and Terol played a game of cat and mouse, each letting the other through to do the hard work. In the final stages Terol tried to make the break but couldn't shake off his fellow Spaniard, who retook the lead at the last corner to win by five hundredths of a second. It was his first win since Le Mans in May. Terol's team-mate Bradley Smith finished third.

13 – JAPANESE GP

Two weeks after his Aragon disaster had lost him the points lead, Marc Marquez (Red Bull Derbi) bounced back with another masterful win at Motegi. The teenager played cat and mouse with title rival Nicolas Terol (Aspar Aprilia) before inching away from his fellow Spaniard to win by more than two seconds. After his Aragon no-score, Marquez's seventh win of the year put him just six points behind Terol with four races remaining.

Terol's team-mate Bradley Smith was third for the second race in a row. Aragon winner Pol Espargaro came down to earth with a bump in Japan, running almost a second off Marquez's pace to cross the finish line ten seconds behind Smith and almost 18 seconds behind the winner.

14 – MALAYSIAN GP

Marc Marquez (Red Bull Derbi) retook the 125 world championship lead with a storming victory at Sepang – a win that underlined why he deserved the 2010 125 crown more than title rivals Pol Espargaro (Tuenti Derbi) and Nicolas Terol (Aspar Aprilia).

Once again Marquez was the class act. Second behind Terol for the first few laps, he took the lead on lap five but couldn't get away. At one point he slipped to fourth behind Terol, Espargaro and Terol's team-mate Bradley Smith. So he bided his time, then pulled the pin just after half distance, quickly building a buffer over his pursuers.

Espargaro chased Marquez hard, but to no avail, though his efforts did pull him clear of Terol. Smith was beaten for fourth place by Espargaro's team-mate Efren Vazquez.

15 – AUSTRALIAN GP

By Phillip Island, the 125 world title was the only crown left to be decided, but Marc Marquez (Red Bull Derbi) looked very much like a champion as he raced to his third victory in as many Sundays. The teenager led every lap to stretch his series lead over third-place finisher Nicolas Terol (Aspar Aprilia) to 12 points and his advantage over runner-up Pol Espargaro (Tuenti Derbi) to 17 points with two races remaining.

Like Stoner, Marquez was in another class, breaking away from the pack and steadily increasing his lead over his title challengers. Espargaro and Terol swapped places a couple of times, Terol coming through from a slow start to move into second at one-third distance. But he struggled more than most in the windy conditions, losing the front time and again, before relinquishing his position to Espargaro.

Their team-mates, Efren Vazquez and Bradley Smith, had a similarly charged duel for fourth place, dead-heating across the line. Vazquez was declared fourth by race direction.

Above and right Bradley Smith was the only non-Spanish rider to win a 125 race – at the final round of the year in Valencia

Opposite Marc Marquez celebrates one of his ten victories

to Moto2. The very last season of 125cc World Championship racing will have its work cut out to improve on this one. It will also be difficult to find another champion like Marquez. In fact if the championship ran for another ten years it is doubtful that it would produce another rider like Marc Marquez.

16 – PORTUGUESE GP

Marc Marquez certainly didn't make life easy for himself in the penultimate 125 race, which was stopped and restarted due to rain. The youngster slid off on the sighting lap for the restart and had to ride his battered bike back to the pits where his mechanics worked feverishly to fix the damage. Too late to take his place on the front row of the grid, he had to start from the back row.

Marquez's start was astonishing, taking him to fifth at the first corner, but he nearly overcooked it at least once on the first lap of the shortened nine-lap race. Once he had calmed down he hunted down title rival Nicolas Terol, who was riding with team-mate Bradley Smith. But whatever the Aspar Aprilia pair did they had no answer to Marquez, who grabbed the lead for the first time with one lap remaining. Terol counter-attacked twice, only to run wide, giving Marquez his tenth win of 2010, by just 0.15 seconds.

17 – VALENCIAN GP

Marc Marquez wrapped up the last-remaining world title at Valencia, coming home a safe and sensible fourth, while title rival Nicolas Terol (Aspar Aprilia) battled for second place with Pol Espargaro (Tuenti Derbi) behind race winner Bradley Smith (Aspar Aprilia).

Marquez went into the race 17 points in front of Terol, so the title was very much his to lose. After qualifying on pole he got out-dragged to the first corner by Smith and Terol, his hopes of running away out front immediately dashed. Instead it was Smith who made the break, chased by his team-mate and Marquez. In other words, Marquez was sitting pretty.

But when Espargaro caught the pair, things became a little more complicated. Marquez found himself in a sandwich and wisely decided that this was the worst place for him to be, so he waved Espargaro through and spent the remaining laps alone in fourth.

'This is unbelievable, like a dream,' said Marquez. 'Being world champion was my dream when I started on bikes, and now it's a reality. I'm so happy and I'm going to enjoy this moment.'

Smith crossed the line 2.7 seconds in front, ending a record-breaking run of 26 Spanish race winners in 125. Espargaro won the contest for second.

CHAMPIONSHIP STANDINGS

	Rider	Nat	Team	Motorcycle	Points
1	Marc Marquez	SPA	Red Bull Ajo Motorsport	Derbi	310
2	Nicolas Terol	SPA	Bancaja Aspar Team	Aprilia	296
3	Pol Espargaro	SPA	Tuenti Racing	Derbi	281
4	Bradley Smith	GBR	Bancaja Aspar Team	Aprilia	223
5	Efren Vazquez	SPA	Tuenti Racing	Derbi	152
6	Esteve Rabat	SPA	Blusens-STX	Aprilia	147
7	Sandro Cortese	GER	Avant Mitsubishi Ajo	Derbi	143
8	Tomoyoshi Koyama	JPN	Racing Team Germany	Aprilia	127
9	Randy Krummenacher	SWI	Stipa-Molenaar Racing GP	Aprilia	113
10	Danny Webb	GBR	Andalucia Cajasol	Aprilia	93
11	Johann Zarco	FRA	WTR San Marino Team	Aprilia	77
12	Luis Salom	SPA	Stipa-Molenaar Racing GP	Aprilia	72
13	Alberto Moncayo	SPA	Andalucia Cajasol	Aprilia	70
14	Jonas Folger	GER	Ongetta Team	Aprilia	69
15	Adrian Martin	SPA	Aeroport de Castello – Ajo	Aprilia	35
16	Jasper Iwema	NED	CBC Corse	Aprilia	34
17	Jakub Kornfeil	CZE	Racing Team Germany	Aprilia	28
18	Marcel Schrotter	GER	Interwetten Honda 125	Honda	27
19	Simone Grotzkyj	ITA	Fontana Racing	Aprilia	26
20	Alexis Masbou	FRA	Ongetta Team	Aprilia	20
21	Sturla Fagerhaug	NOR	AirAsia - Sepang Int. Circuit	Aprilia	12
22	Daniel Kartheininger	GER	Freudenberg Racing Team	KTM	6
23	Lorenzo Salvadori	ITA	Matteoni Racing	Aprilia	5
24	Zulfahmi Khairuddin	MAL	AirAsia - Sepang Int. Circuit	Aprilia	4
25	Isaac Viñales	SPA	CBC Corse	Aprilia	3
26	Alessandro Tonucci	ITA	Junior GP Racing Team FMI	Aprilia	3
27	Luigi Morciano	ITA	Junior GP Racing Team FMI	Aprilia	2
28	Louis Rossi	FRA	CBC Corse	Aprilia	2

RED BULL ROOKIES

PETER CLIFFORD

Above American Jake Gagne leads his championship rival, Briton Danny Kent, at Brno

The final race of the fourth Red Bull MotoGP Rookies Cup was a classic, but then there wasn't a single race in the ten-event season that wasn't superbly exciting. The championship was finally decided over 17 laps at Misano, and although 16-year-old Briton Danny Kent dominated the weekend and won, Californian Jake Gagne shadowed him across the line to take the Red Bull Rookies Cup by six points.

Going into the tenth and final race of the season in Italy, Gagne held an 11-point advantage over Kent. Jake turned 17 a week before the final round; his British rival was younger by just three months. Kent knew that simply winning the race wasn't enough to take the title, so after setting off from pole and securing the lead he repeatedly slowed the race down, allowing more riders to join the fight at the front in the hope that they could push Gagne down into fourth, which wouldn't have been good enough for the title. Gagne was just as skilled, though, and despite having to fight off a hoard of other rookies all intent on race glory, he placed himself perfectly over the final laps to tail Kent across the line, leaving third place in both race and Cup to the 16-year-old Japanese rider, Daijiro Hiura.

Stepping down from the podium with his FIM Cup medal, Gagne spoke of what the Rookies Cup meant to him. 'Just about all my road racing experience has been in the Rookies Cup,' explained the ex-motocrosser. 'I started

with the Rookies Cup in the US three years ago, and then with these two years in the Rookies Cup in Europe I have learnt so much, not just the great GP tracks I've ridden on, but so much about riding from the great coaches, Gustl (Auinger), Kevin (Schwantz) and Raul (Jara) and talking to the media, just everything to help me with my career.'

Gagne and Kent had found their way to that classic final race showdown via different routes. Kent started the year in great style, winning the first race on Saturday in Jerez and taking second in the Sunday clash in the double header, thus announcing himself as Cup favourite. By comparison, Gagne's opening races were disappointing. A fifth and a sixth in Spain were followed by an eighth in the single race at Mugello, while Kent picked up a fourth in the Italian battle, just losing out in the elbowing match out of the last corner to Hiura, Mathew Scholtz and Brad Binder.

Hiura had started the year as one of the riders 'most likely to', having claimed his first victory back in 2008, early in his first Rookie season. It seemed quite a wait for his second win, but the Italian victory did promote him to the Cup lead, having already taken a second and a third in Spain. The Japanese youngster's season began to fall apart at the next round, in Holland. He was fifth in the first race at Assen but his bike stopped in the second. Assen was even more of a disaster for Mathew Scholtz. He failed to

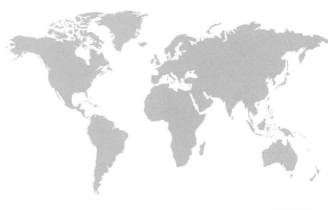

AMERICA'S CUP

make it to the start after colliding with a slower rider in practice and wrenching the big toe almost completely off his right foot. An operation saved it, but he was out for the rest of the season. It was a sad exit for one of the best Rookies.

A weekend to forget for some at Assen gave Gagne his first victory when he took command of the 12-man battle for the lead at the crucial moment in the first race, to cross the line ahead of first-time podium men Kevin Calia and Alessio Cappella. The second race in Holland was a seven-man fight for the win. Although Kent crossed the line first he had passed under a yellow flag and the stewards later relegated him to second behind Daniel Ruiz, with Harry Stafford third. The win propelled 18-year-old Spaniard Ruiz to a one-point lead over Kent in the standings. It was his second victory of the season. He was starting to look like a Cup favourite alongside Kent, as both seemed able to rack up the points consistently.

That form was knocked sideways in the two races at the Sachsenring. Gagne scored a stunning double and was chased home in both German races by Brad Binder. Hiura ran off in race one and only scored a single point. Ruiz crashed out of race two on the first lap, and while Kent was third in race one he also crashed in race two and only picked up four points for 12th after remounting.

As his rival's consistency evaporated Gagne seized the

Cup lead. His slow start to the year had been due to a crash at the pre-season test that wrenched his ankle and left him starting the year ill at ease on the machine. He just couldn't match the podium pace in the opening races, and felt the situation was aggravated by racing a 600 at home in the US between Rookies events, so he stopped doing that and focused exclusively on the Cup.

Once in the groove it was clear that Gagne was the man to beat. Leaving Germany with the Cup lead and three races remaining he had a 14-point lead over Kent, with Ruiz third another ten points adrift, but four clear of Hiura in fourth. Gagne's charge faltered slightly at Brno when he crashed in practice, and while he wasn't injured he went into race one with an imperfectly set-up bike. He could do no better than eighth while Kent was third and Hiura second in a race dominated by 15-year-old Italian Kevin Calia. Gagne turned that around with a brilliant race two win, stealing the lead from Kent going into the final S-bends and leaving the Briton to fend off fellow-countryman Stafford for the remaining rostrum places.

With three wins from four races Gagne clearly had the momentum heading for that final race in Misano, but Kent's last-race daring and tactics belied his age and experience. Both Gagne and Kent head for the 125 Grand Prix class next season with every chance of making an impact in the World Championship.

Above Jake Gagne celebrates winning the championship at the Grand Prix of San Marino

RIDERS FOR HEALTH
BARRY COLEMAN

Xxxxxxxxxx

SNAKES ON A BIKE

You know how it is with cobras. Sometimes they just can't resist showing off. That's how it was on the first day of Violet's real work as a motorcyclist. Violet, who lives in the distant Eastern Province of Zambia, was well trained. She could ride in all the various sorts of conditions to be found out there in the bush and she could do her daily maintenance checks. She was safety-conscious, and that first morning she did her routine thoroughly, zipped and buttoned up her riding suit and tightened her helmet strap carefully. She was ready.

The cobra, meanwhile, a couple of kilometres down the road, was just going about its own daily business, trying to sniff out a sleepy rat or something of the sort that would provide a pleasant lunch and an afternoon snooze under a rock. It must have seemed like a little piece of hell to the cobra when it looked up and saw a huge, red, roaring, slithering monster coming straight at it. No rat this. So up our cobra reared, as high as a snake can rear, spitting and hoping that the old, tried-and-tested huge scary routine would have whatever this intruder was thinking twice and veering off into the bush.

Which, more or less, is what happened: Violet saw the cobra rear just a little too late to correct for a snake attack and she threw the Yamaha into a thorn bush. She was really annoyed. After all, she said later, even if it had bitten me it would never have got its teeth through my suit.

So that was day one and Violet hasn't fallen off since, snakes or no snakes. She has never failed to do her job. What she does is collect blood samples from distant health centres and take those samples to laboratories for testing. She's a Riders for Health sample courier.

What they are looking for out there is AIDS. Until their sample is taken and tested, no patient can be put on treatment. With this being the case, and with HIV/AIDS being a problem of quite unimaginable scale in Africa, you would think that someone involved in the world's billion-dollar attempt to control it would have at least wondered how blood would get from the veins of people living deep in rural Africa into test tubes and into the testing machines. But no-one ever did. They came up with good pharmaceuticals and strategies. And they forgot about the tiny but essential bit that Violet now does for them, dust-storms and floods, snakes and all… just forgot

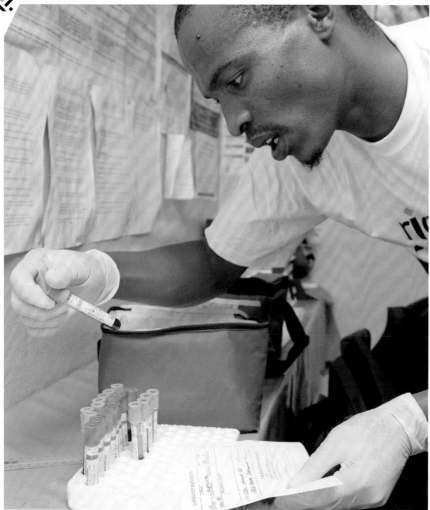

about it. So people were dying for absolutely no reason.

And that, of course, is where you come in. You and your very own humanitarian organisation, Riders for Health.

For the first time, there is now a fully functioning sample courier system for testing for HIV and other diseases on the African continent. Before Riders for Health and the sport of motorcycle racing put this system in place, there was no system.

It happened first in Lesotho. We've been working there for so long that Randy Mamola and Kevin Schwantz visited the programme when they were both still racing and were still (even) young(er) men. Randy did a return visit there last year to celebrate his 50th birthday – and to celebrate with many others the impact that Riders for Health (and thus the sport of motorcycle racing) has had on the health of that nation.

We had already started work on the general mobilisation of health workers on a fleet of bikes (Honda CTX200s) donated by the Elton John AIDS Foundation. Now he's a game old bird is Elton and you don't need me to tell you that he has an awful lot of energy and that he is serious about AIDS. Nevertheless, it came as something of a double-taking surprise to Andrea and me to be standing in a makeshift shelter in the grounds of a very basic clinic in rural Lesotho watching Elton John singing with the Minister of Health (though she does have a nice voice) and dancing with the delighted women of Lesotho. A positively hallucinogenic experience.

It was a couple of weeks later when we were cornered by the doctor in charge of laboratory testing (who also happened to be the Prime Minister's daughter, but we didn't know that at the time) and a young woman from Bill Clinton's Foundation who wanted to know if we could do anything about getting blood samples to labs and getting the results back. Where we come from, 240 horsepower is normal so nine isn't much of a problem. The answer was 'yes'. Bill's serious about AIDS too.

In Lesotho, before Riders and Bill Clinton and Elton John helped to start the sample transport programme, it took up to three months to get a result if you got one at all. Now you will get one in less than a week, max, and you can thus be prescribed anti-retroviral drugs and not die.

And all over Africa, ministries of health are now following suit. Everyone is talking about the sample courier system. Everyone wants it.

It's your sport. Your Riders for Health. You did it. And only you.

Clockwise from top left A sample courier at work in Lesotho; sample transportation on the roads of Zambia; delivery to the laboratory in Zambia; women patiently wait for their tests at the clinic

MOTHER-TO-CHILD TRANSMISSION

Without prompt diagnosis, there is a high risk that women who are HIV positive will pass the infection on to their babies, either during pregnancy or at birth. There are now over two million children living with HIV/AIDS in the world, almost all of them in sub-Saharan Africa.

This is why Riders for Health's sample couriers are so crucial. By carrying patients' blood samples rapidly from clinics to laboratories so that they can be tested and the results sent back in a week, Riders is ensuring that mothers-to-be are aware of their status and, if need be, can start their treatment.

After spending 20 years mobilising health-care workers in Africa, Riders knew how we could contribute to the reduction in mother-to-child transmission of HIV and so we set up a system of couriers with reliable motorcycles who could travel around rural health clinics collecting samples and returning a week later with the results.

In the 2009 *MotoGP Season Review* we wrote about two new programmes we were launching in Zambia and Lesotho. The sample courier programmes have now been running for over a year, and we have already seen that not only have our teams of couriers improved the speed of testing, but more people than ever are visiting health clinics, improving access to health care. As supporters of Riders for Health we thought we would share two of these stories with you.

'This is something big which I am part of'

Violet Ng'ambi was one of our first sample couriers in the Chadiza District in the Eastern Province of Zambia. Violet is part of a team of five professional sample couriers mobilised by Riders to support the diagnosis of HIV/AIDS, TB and other diseases in her district. Before being chosen to be a motorcycle rider and trained by Riders, Violet had never even ridden a bicycle. 'When you are not used to riding a motorcycle, that's when you find it difficult,' said Violet. 'I had to be courageous. I didn't want to embarrass myself!'

Riders' programme director in Zambia, Lloyd Chipere, was responsible for selecting the new sample couriers. In his words: 'We look for someone with the desire to serve the community at heart. A sample courier is someone disciplined and self-confident and above all willing to ride. They must be determined, focused and vigilant. But they also need to be a good rider. Without motorcycles they won't be able to do their job so the bike is the pillar and cornerstone of their work.'

Violet has already made a huge impact with the clinics she supports, and she is looking forward to helping even more people in future. 'This is a really good experience,' she says. 'People are counting on me and this is something big which I am part of.'

'They know that the motorcycle will be here every week'

In Lesotho one of the amazing things that clinics have seen as a result of the sample transport programme is an increase in the number of people coming to the clinics to access health care.

Thato Mokhele, the Nursing Sister at Thaba-Bosiu Health Centre, explains: 'We have a huge increase of patients coming to the clinic for services, because at first patients were reluctant to come and seek services because they knew that if ever some blood tests needed to be done they would be referred to the laboratory. Now they confidently know that the motorcycle will be here every week to collect blood and return their results.'

This pattern also seems to be improving equity of access to health care. 'In the past patients would have to fund themselves to transport their samples to the laboratory, and it was not easy because some were not able to afford that due to poverty,' explains Khanya Mamakhoathi, Nurse Assistant at Semonkong Health Centre. 'Now our attendance is drastically increasing because there is a stable sample transport.'

Just one motorcycle can:
- Reduce waiting time for test results from **one month** to **one week.**
- Facilitate an increase in patient tests by **73 per cent.**
- Allow an outreach health-care worker to visit **five** times more people than they could on foot.
- Increase the number of villages a health-care worker can see in a week from **three** to **20.**
- Increase the number of health education visits from **one** a week to **three** a week.
- Provide access to health care to **10,000** men, women and children in rural communities.

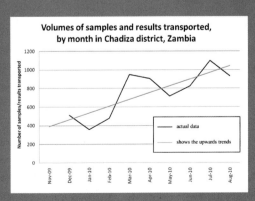

Volumes of samples and results transported, by month in Chadiza district, Zambia

— actual data
— shows the upwards trends